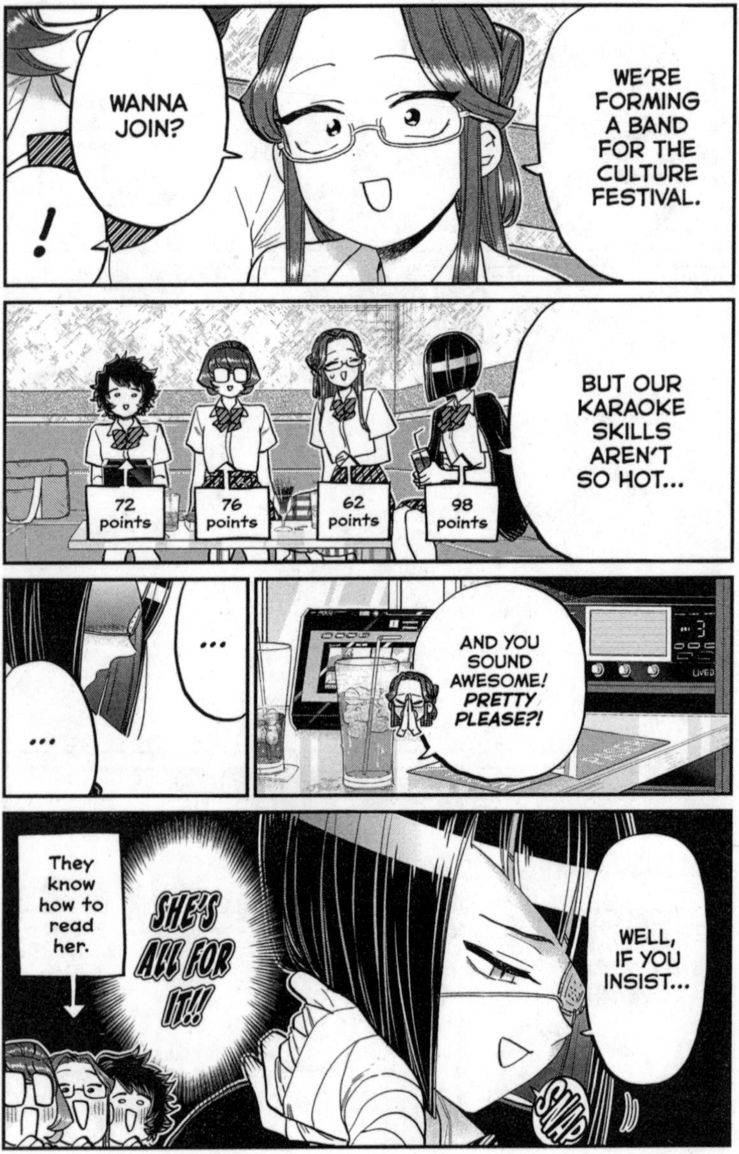
WE'RE FORMING A BAND FOR THE CULTURE FESTIVAL.
WANNA JOIN?
!
BUT OUR KARAOKE SKILLS AREN'T SO HOT...
98 points
62 points
76 points
72 points
AND YOU SOUND AWESOME! PRETTY PLEASE?!
...
...
WELL, IF YOU INSIST...
SHE'S ALL FOR IT!!
They know how to read her.

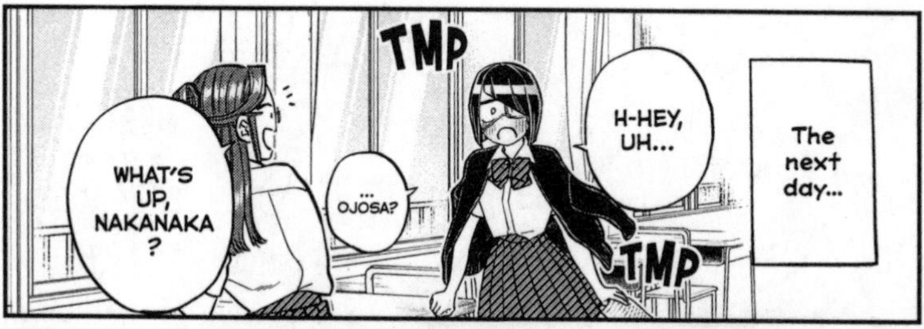
The next day...
H-HEY, UH...
TMP
TMP
...OJOSA?
WHAT'S UP, NAKANAKA?

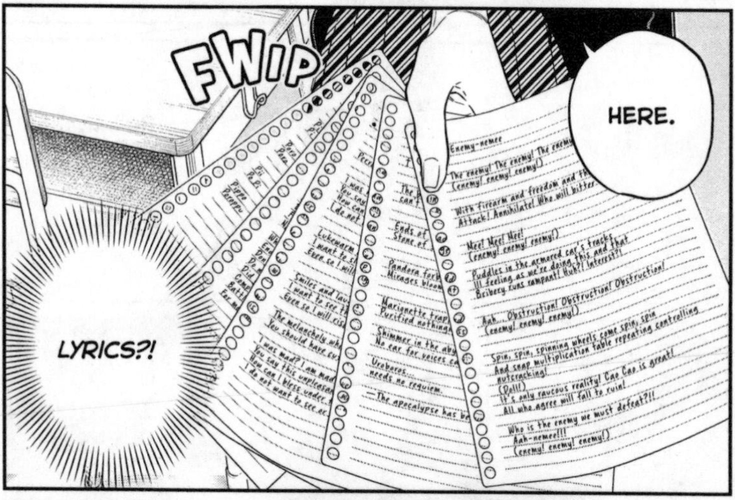
HERE.
FWIP
Enemy-nemee
The enemy! The enemy! The enemy
(enemy! enemy! enemy!)
With firearm and freedom and th
Attack! Annihilate! Who will bitter
Mee! Mee! Mee!
(enemy! enemy! enemy!)
Puddles in the armored car's tracks
Ill feeling as we're doing this and that
Bribery runs rampant! Huh?! Interest?!
Aah. Obstruction! Obstruction! Obstruction!
(enemy! enemy! enemy!)
Spin, spin, spinning wheels come spin, spin
And snap multiplication table repeating controlling
nutcracking!
(Doll!)
It's only raucous reality! Cao Cao is great!
All who agree will fall to ruin!
Who is the enemy we must defeat?!!
Aah-nemee!!!
(enemy! enemy! enemy!)
LYRICS?!

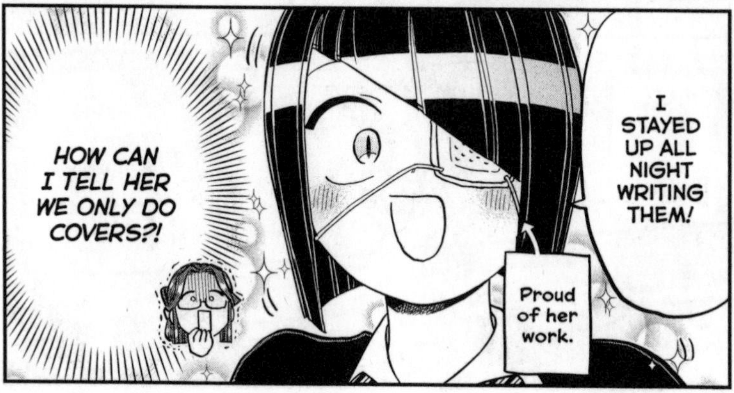
I STAYED UP ALL NIGHT WRITING THEM!
Proud of her work.
HOW CAN I TELL HER WE ONLY DO COVERS?!

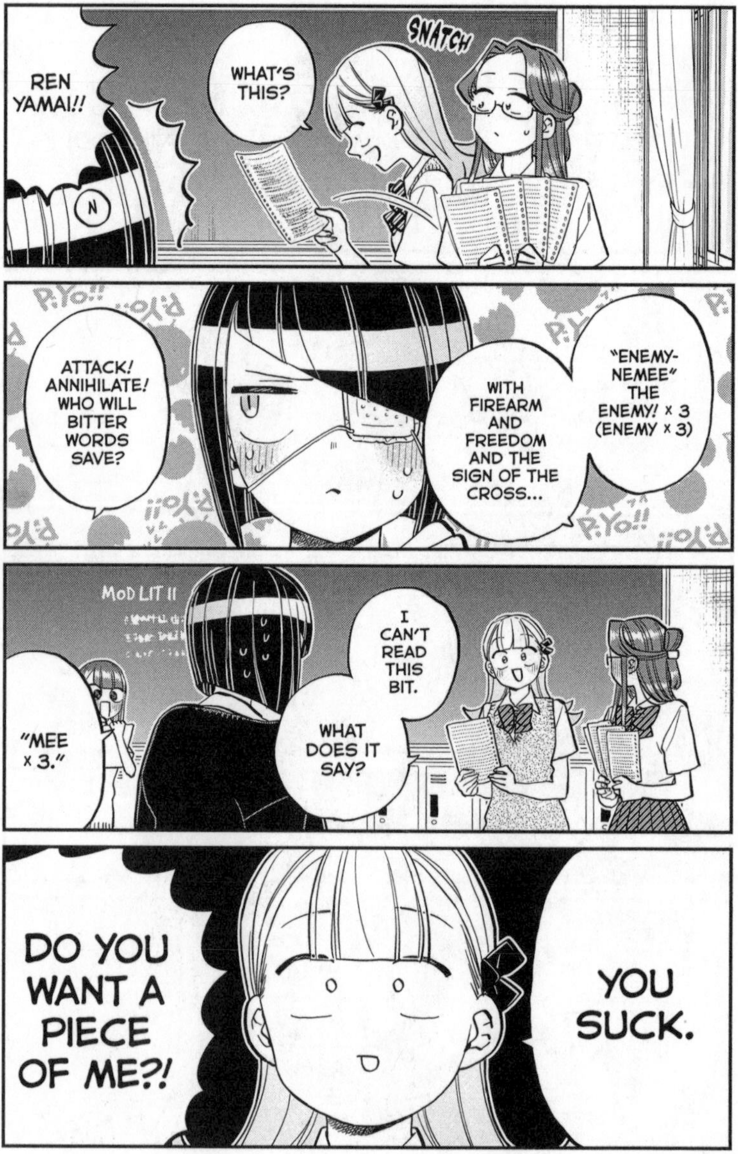
SNATCH
WHAT'S THIS?
REN YAMAI!!
"ENEMY-NEMEE" THE ENEMY! × 3 (ENEMY × 3)
WITH FIREARM AND FREEDOM AND THE SIGN OF THE CROSS...
ATTACK! ANNIHILATE! WHO WILL BITTER WORDS SAVE?
P.Yo!!
I CAN'T READ THIS BIT.
WHAT DOES IT SAY?
MOD LIT II
"MEE × 3."
YOU SUCK.
DO YOU WANT A PIECE OF ME?!

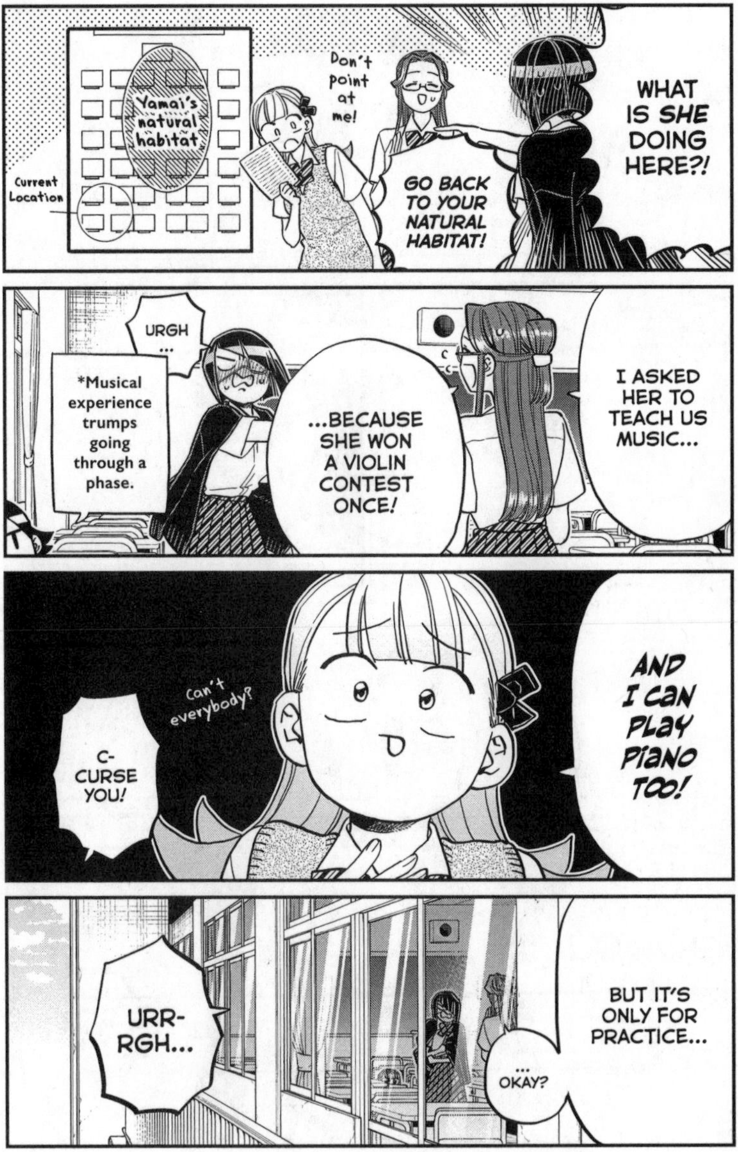
WHAT IS SHE DOING HERE?!
GO BACK TO YOUR NATURAL HABITAT!
Don't point at me!
Yamai's natural habitat
Current Location
I ASKED HER TO TEACH US MUSIC...
...BECAUSE SHE WON A VIOLIN CONTEST ONCE!
URGH...
*Musical experience trumps going through a phase.
AND I CAN PLAY PIANO TOO!
Can't everybody?
C-CURSE YOU!
BUT IT'S ONLY FOR PRACTICE...
...OKAY?
URR-RGH...

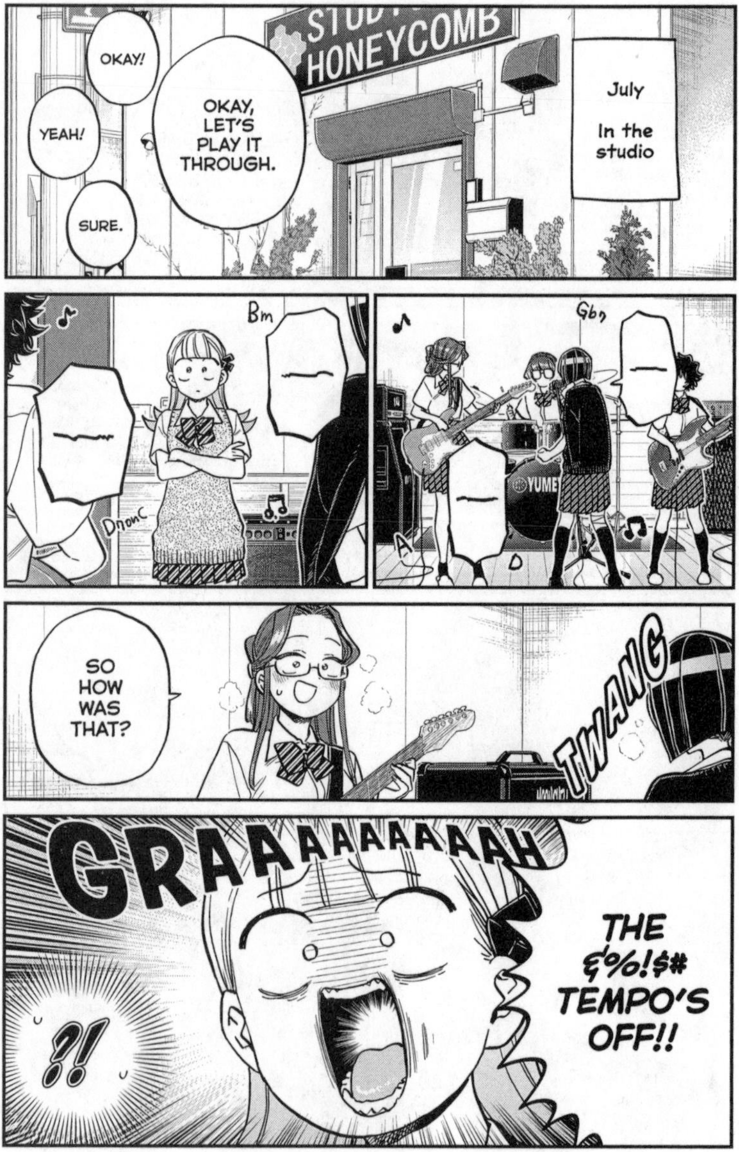
HONEYCOMB
July
In the studio
OKAY, LET'S PLAY IT THROUGH.
OKAY!
YEAH!
SURE.
Gb
A
D
Bm
TWANG
SO HOW WAS THAT?
GRAAAAAAAAAH
THE &%!$# TEMPO'S OFF!!
?!

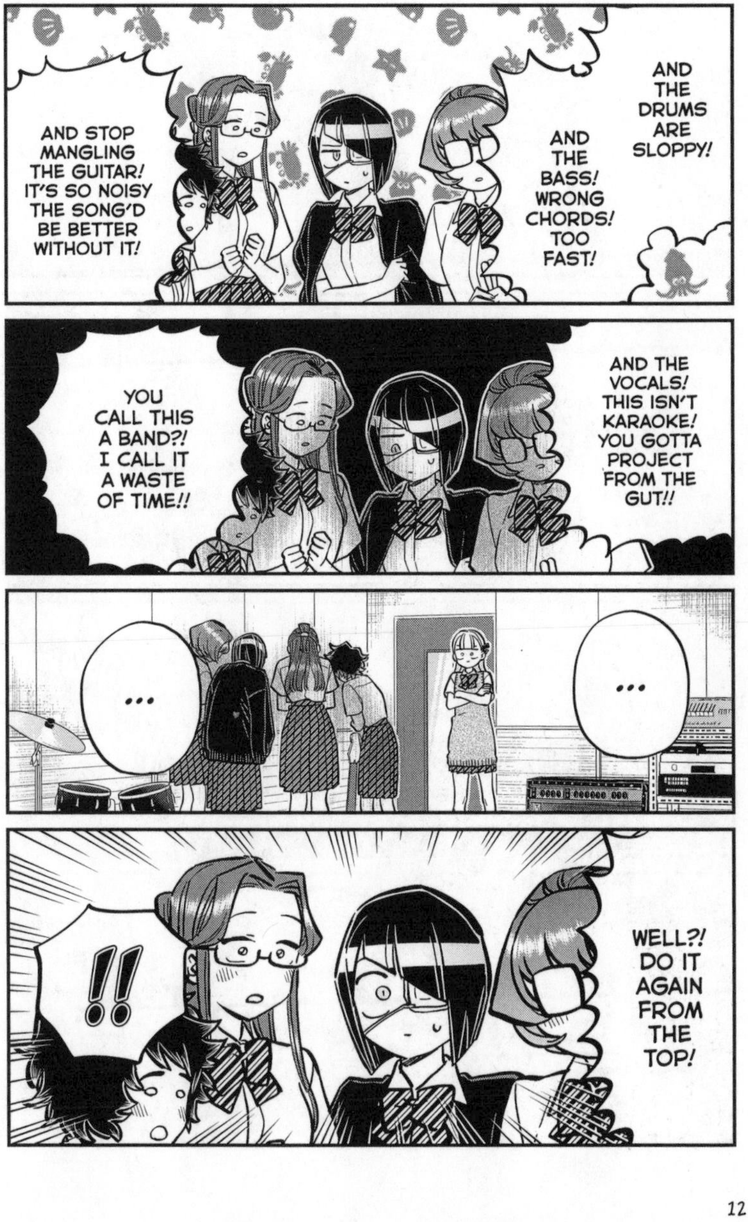
AND THE DRUMS ARE SLOPPY!
AND THE BASS! WRONG CHORDS! TOO FAST!
AND STOP MANGLING THE GUITAR! IT'S SO NOISY THE SONG'D BE BETTER WITHOUT IT!
AND THE VOCALS! THIS ISN'T KARAOKE! YOU GOTTA PROJECT FROM THE GUT!!
YOU CALL THIS A BAND?! I CALL IT A WASTE OF TIME!!
...
...
WELL?! DO IT AGAIN FROM THE TOP!
!!

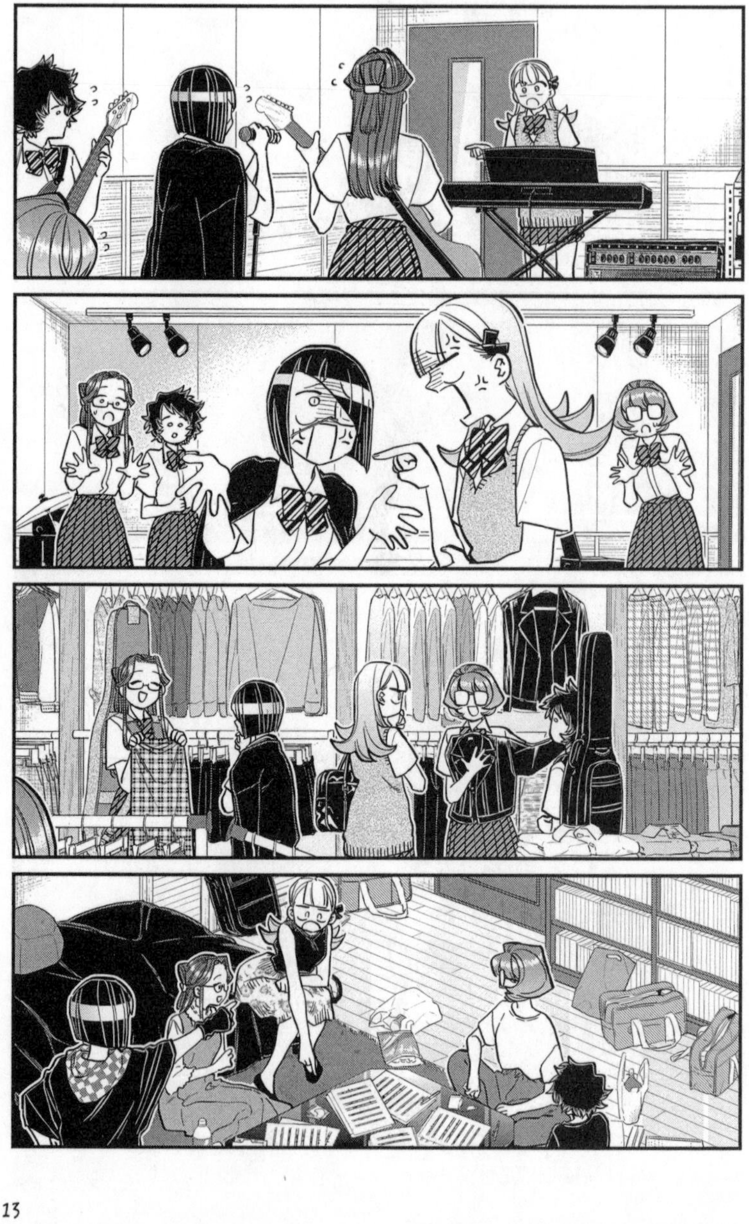

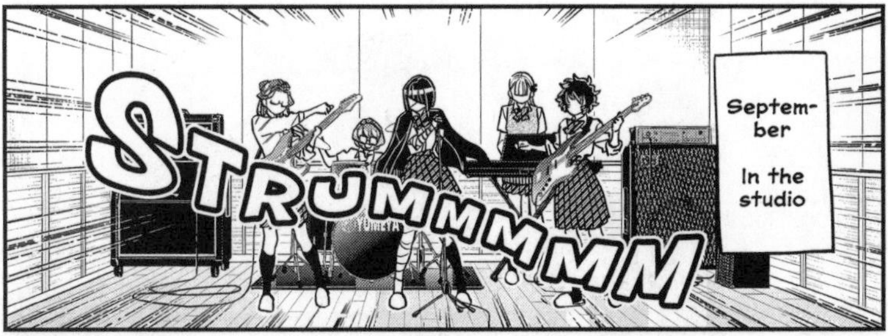
September
In the studio
STRUMMMMMM

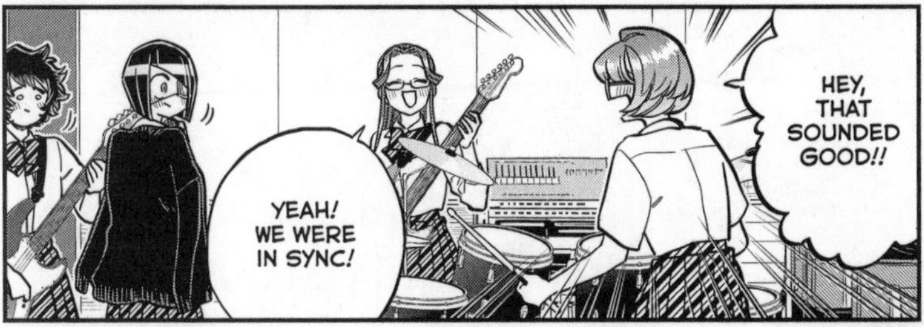
HEY, THAT SOUNDED GOOD!!
YEAH! WE WERE IN SYNC!

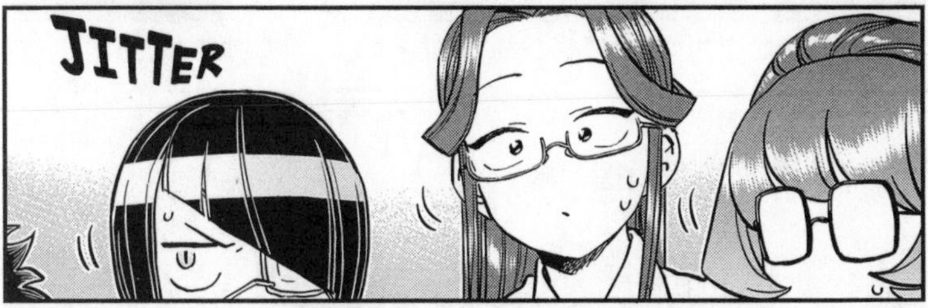
JITTER

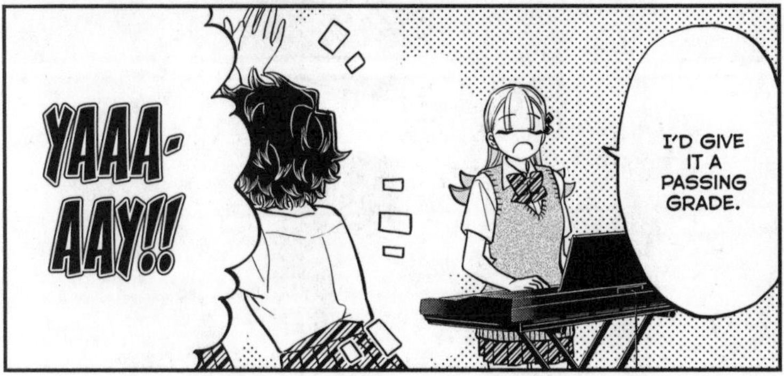
I'D GIVE IT A PASSING GRADE.
YAAA-AAY!!

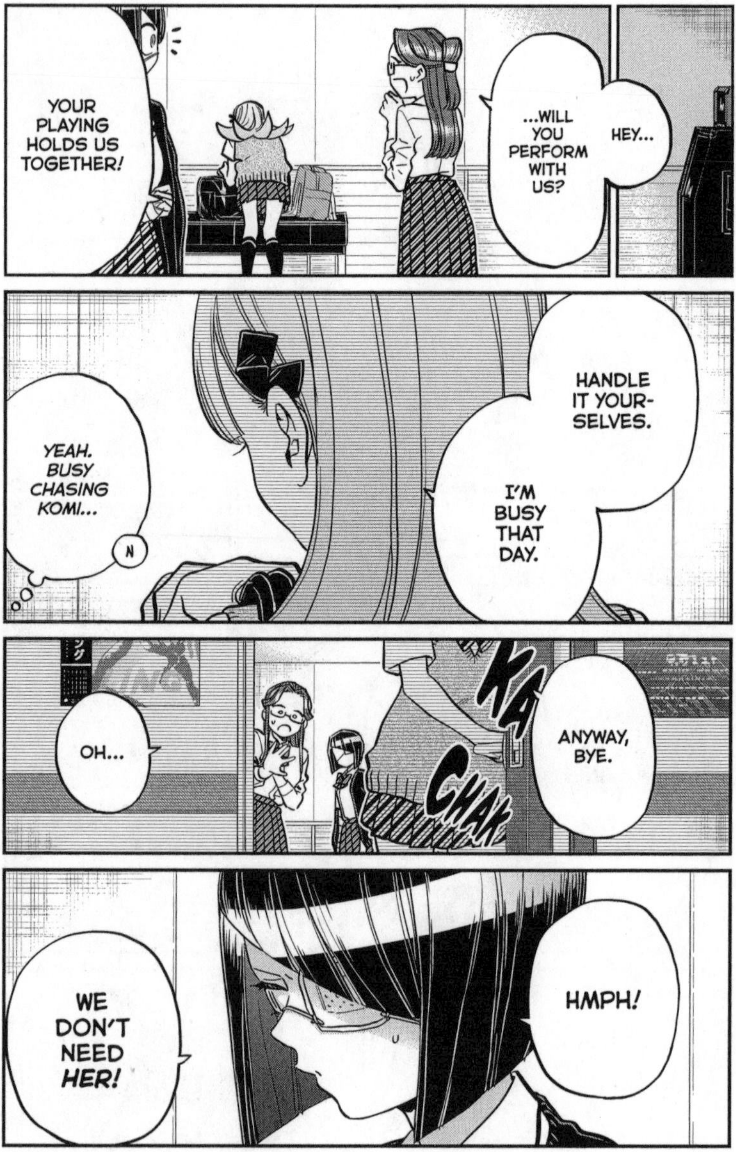
HEY...
...WILL YOU PERFORM WITH US?
YOUR PLAYING HOLDS US TOGETHER!
HANDLE IT YOURSELVES.
I'M BUSY THAT DAY.
YEAH. BUSY CHASING KOMI...
N
KA CHAK
ANYWAY, BYE.
OH...
HMPH!
WE DON'T NEED HER!

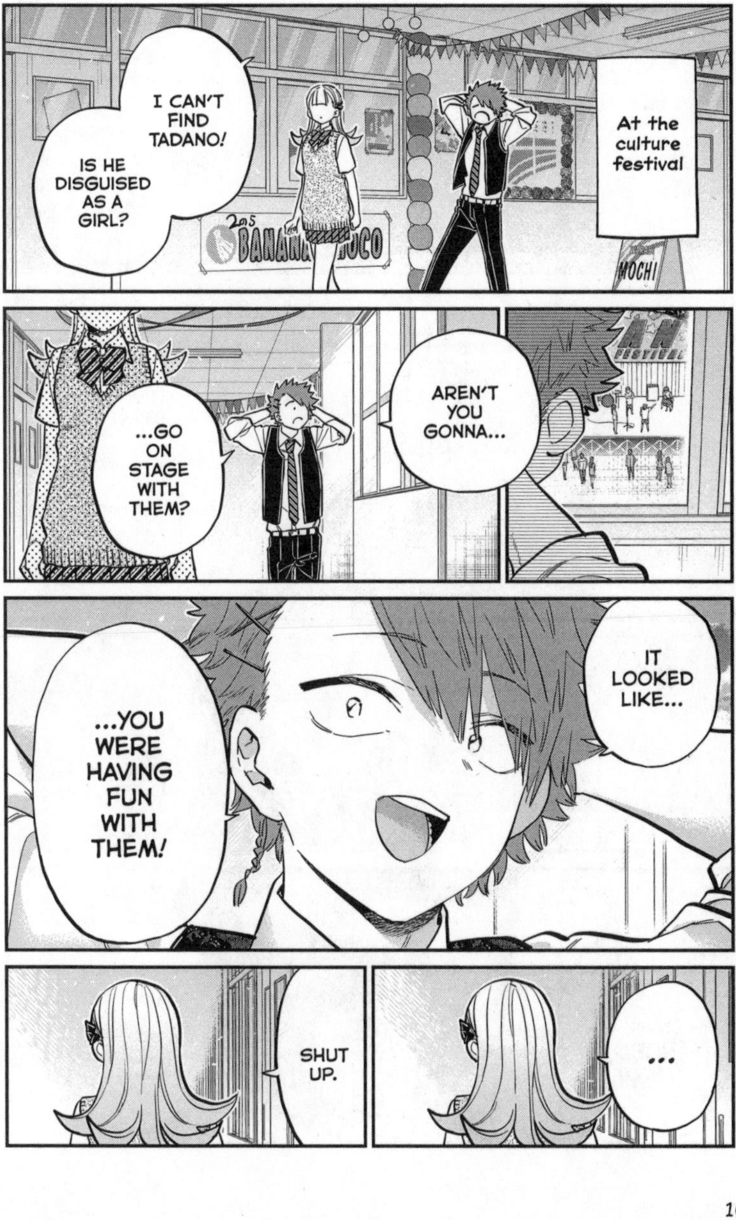
At the culture festival
I CAN'T FIND TADANO!
IS HE DISGUISED AS A GIRL?
MOCHI
AREN'T YOU GONNA...
...GO ON STAGE WITH THEM?
IT LOOKED LIKE...
...YOU WERE HAVING FUN WITH THEM!
...
SHUT UP.

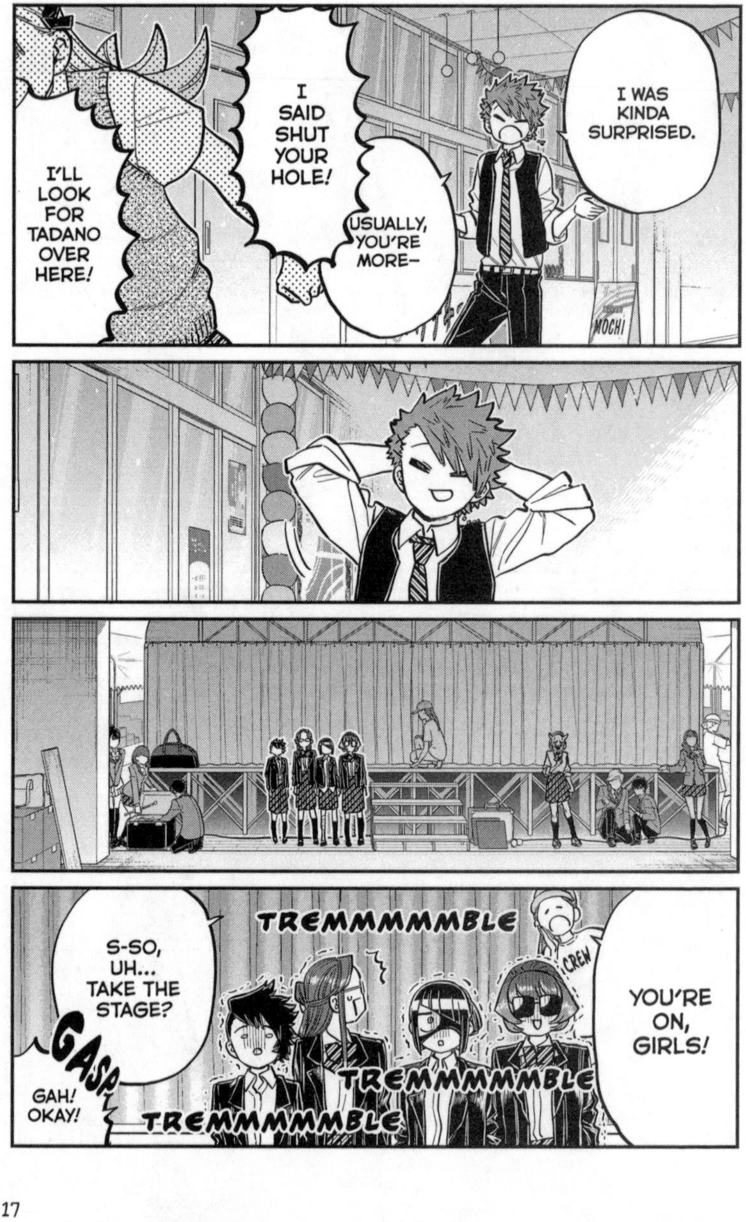
I WAS KINDA SURPRISED.
USUALLY, YOU'RE MORE–
I SAID SHUT YOUR HOLE!
I'LL LOOK FOR TADANO OVER HERE!
MOCHI
YOU'RE ON, GIRLS!
CREW
TREMMMMMMBLE
S-SO, UH... TAKE THE STAGE?
TREMMMMMMBLE
GASP
GAH! OKAY!
TREMMMMMMBLE

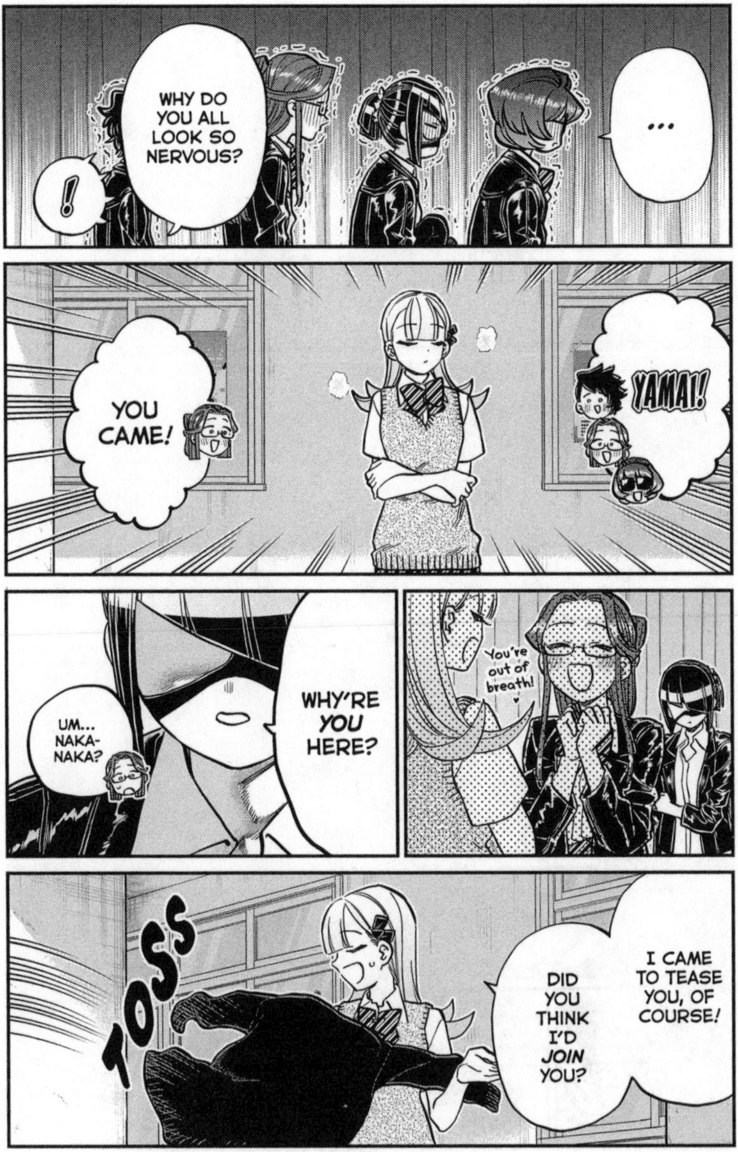
...
WHY DO YOU ALL LOOK SO NERVOUS?
!
YAMAI!
YOU CAME!
You're out of breath! ♥
WHY'RE *YOU* HERE?
UM... NAKA-NAKA?
I CAME TO TEASE YOU, OF COURSE!
DID YOU THINK I'D *JOIN* YOU?
TOSS

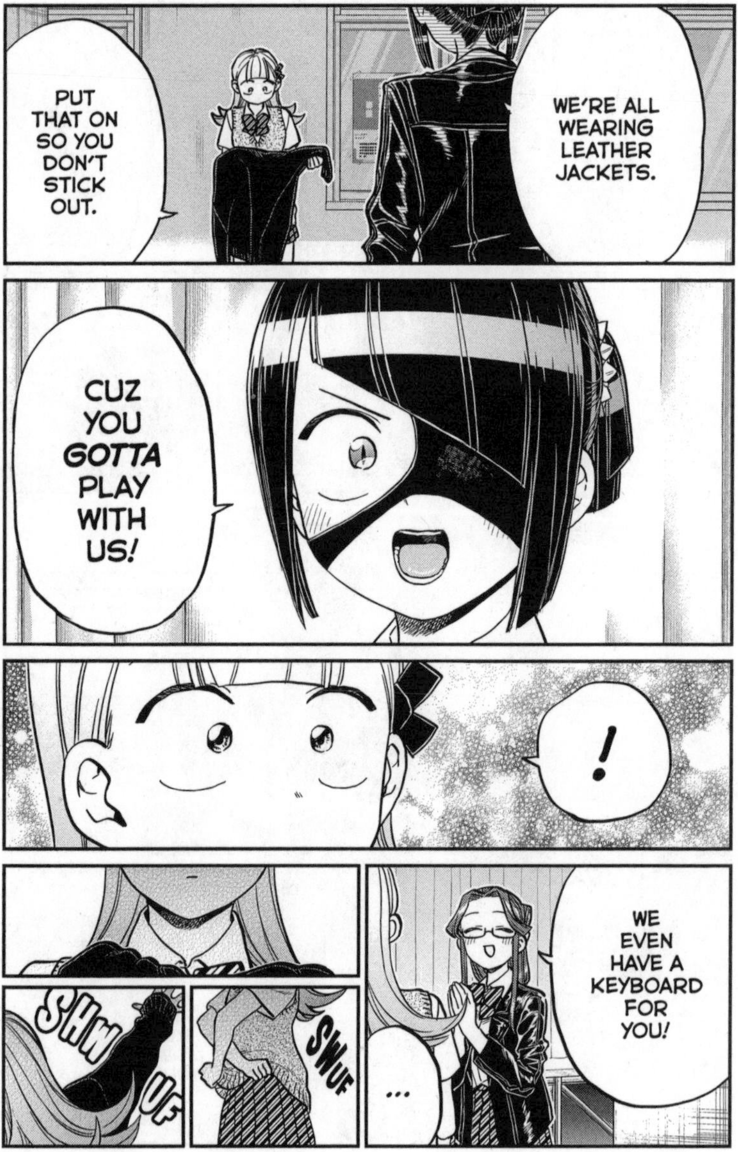
WE'RE ALL WEARING LEATHER JACKETS.
PUT THAT ON SO YOU DON'T STICK OUT.
CUZ YOU *GOTTA* PLAY WITH US!
!
WE EVEN HAVE A KEYBOARD FOR YOU!
...
SWUF
SHWUF

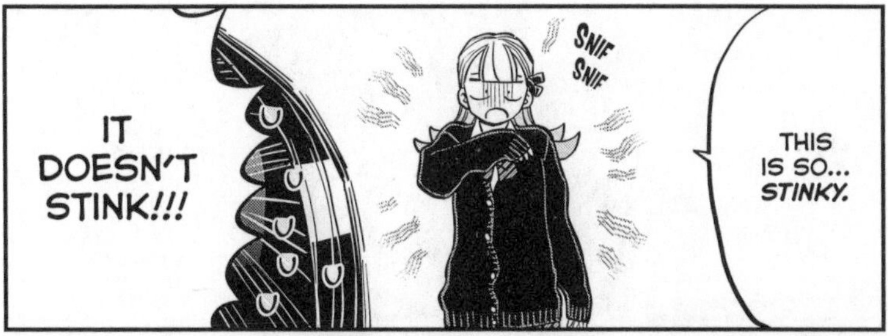
THIS IS SO... STINKY.
SNIF SNIF
IT DOESN'T STINK!!!
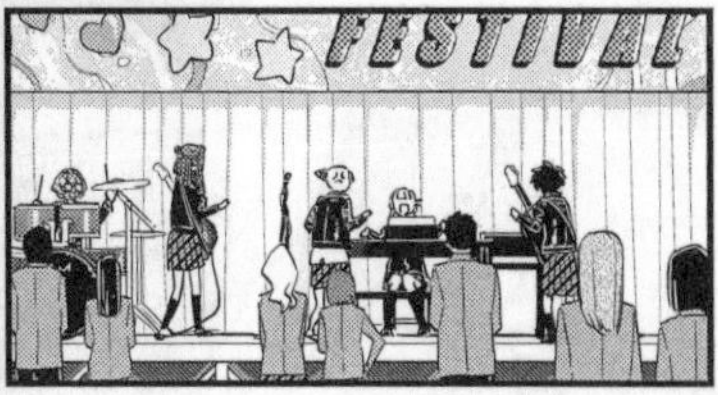
FESTIVAL
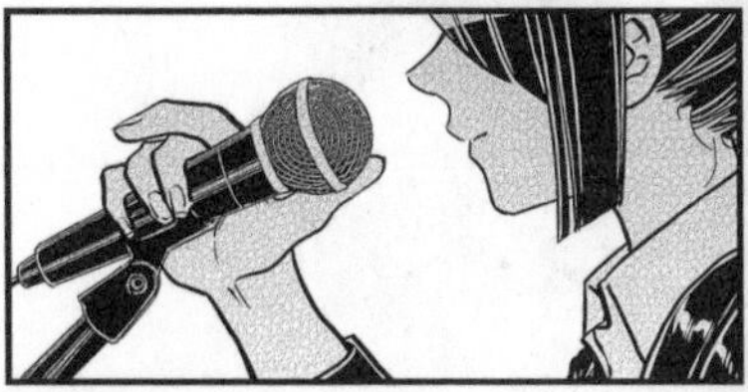
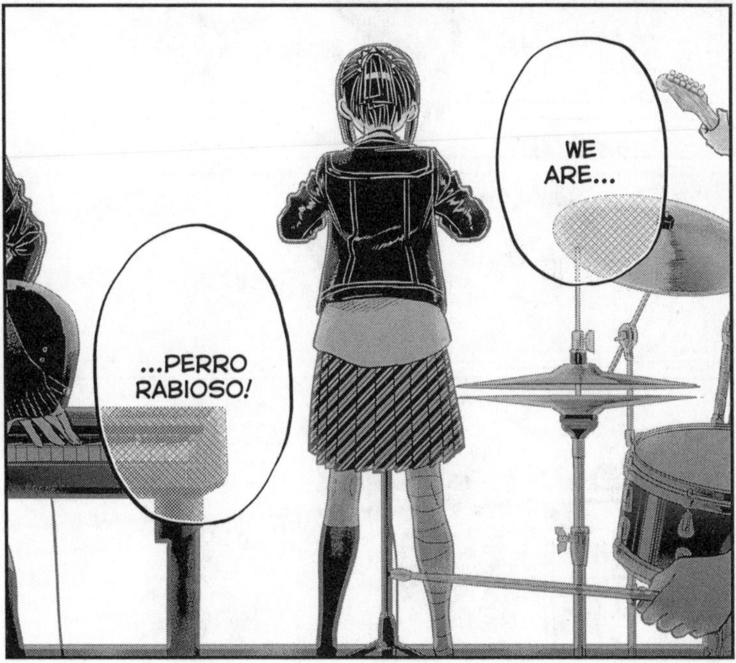
WE ARE...
...PERRO RABIOSO!

Communication 235 — The End

Komi Can't Communicate

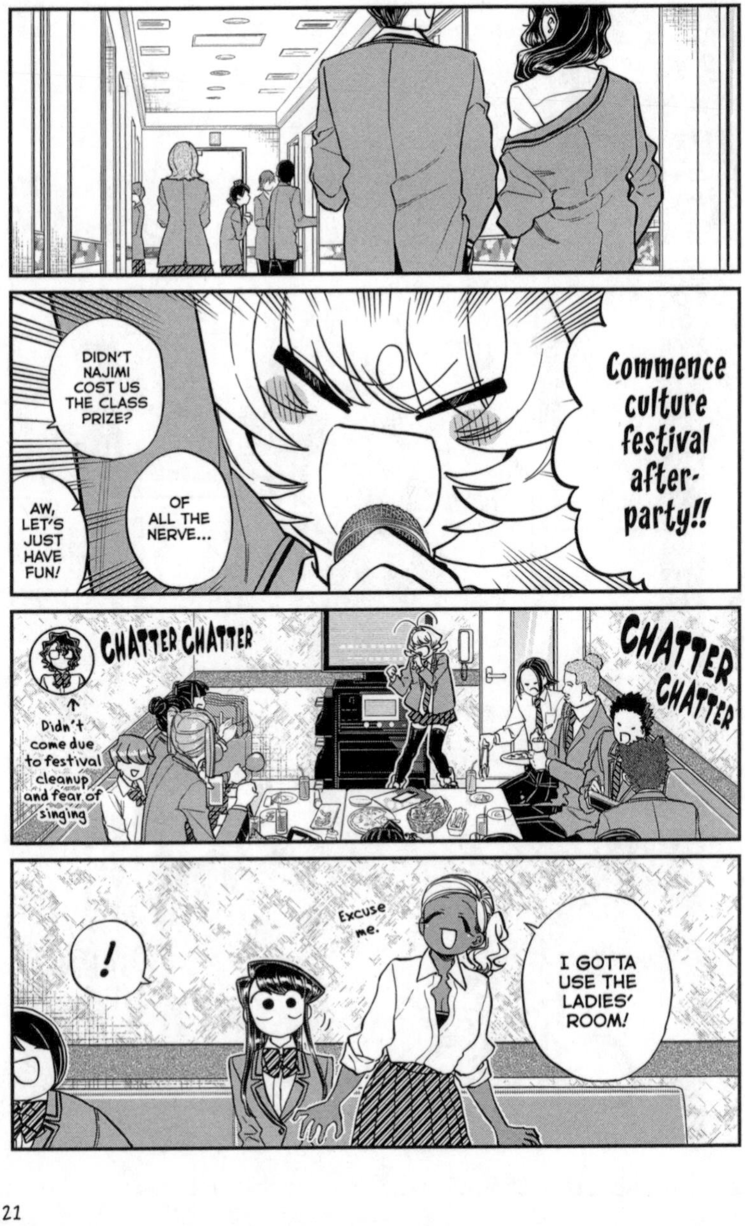
Commence culture festival after-party!!
DIDN'T NAJIMI COST US THE CLASS PRIZE?
OF ALL THE NERVE...
AW, LET'S JUST HAVE FUN!
CHATTER CHATTER
CHATTER CHATTER
Didn't come due to festival cleanup and fear of singing
I GOTTA USE THE LADIES' ROOM!
Excuse me.
!

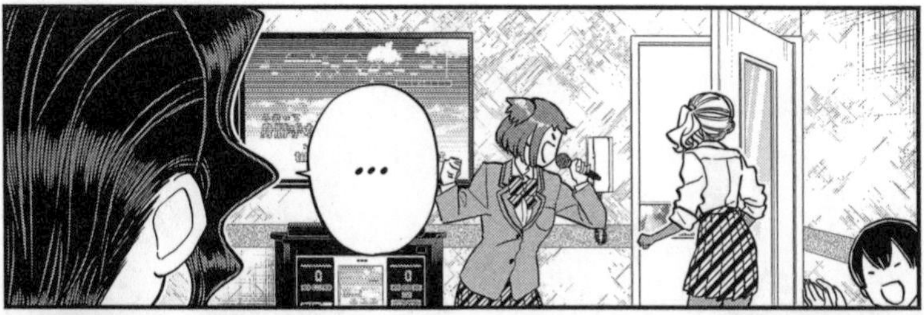
...

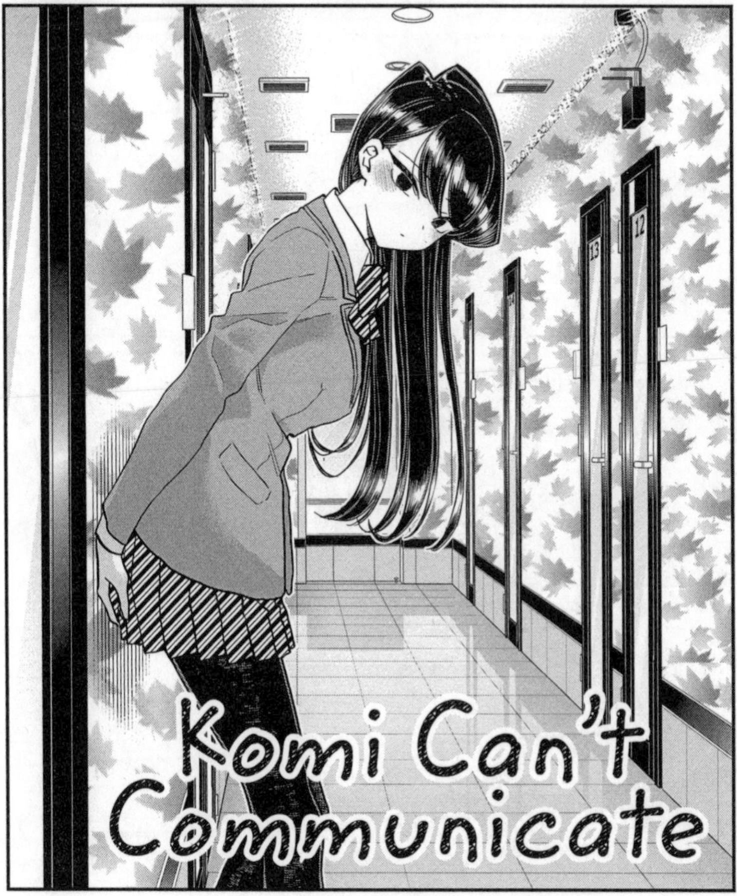
Komi Can't Communicate

Communication 236: Outside the After-Party

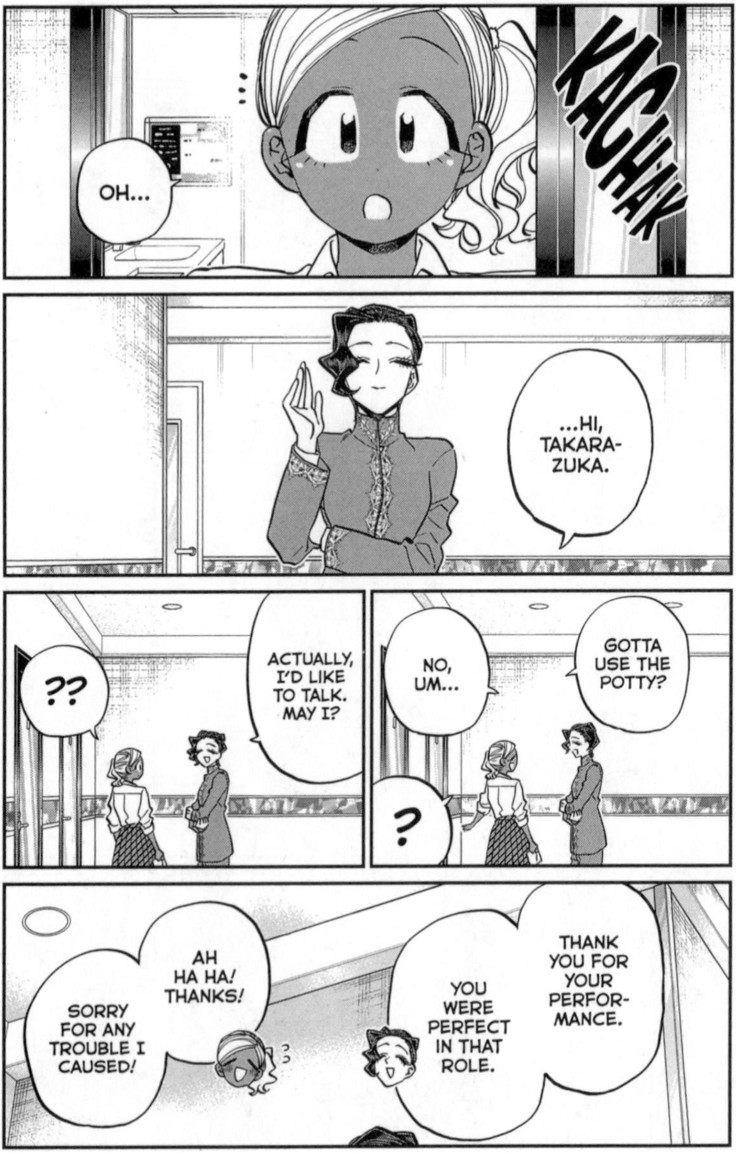
KACHAK
...
OH...
...HI, TAKARAZUKA.
GOTTA USE THE POTTY?
NO, UM...
?
ACTUALLY, I'D LIKE TO TALK. MAY I?
??
THANK YOU FOR YOUR PERFORMANCE.
YOU WERE PERFECT IN THAT ROLE.
AH HA HA! THANKS!
SORRY FOR ANY TROUBLE I CAUSED!

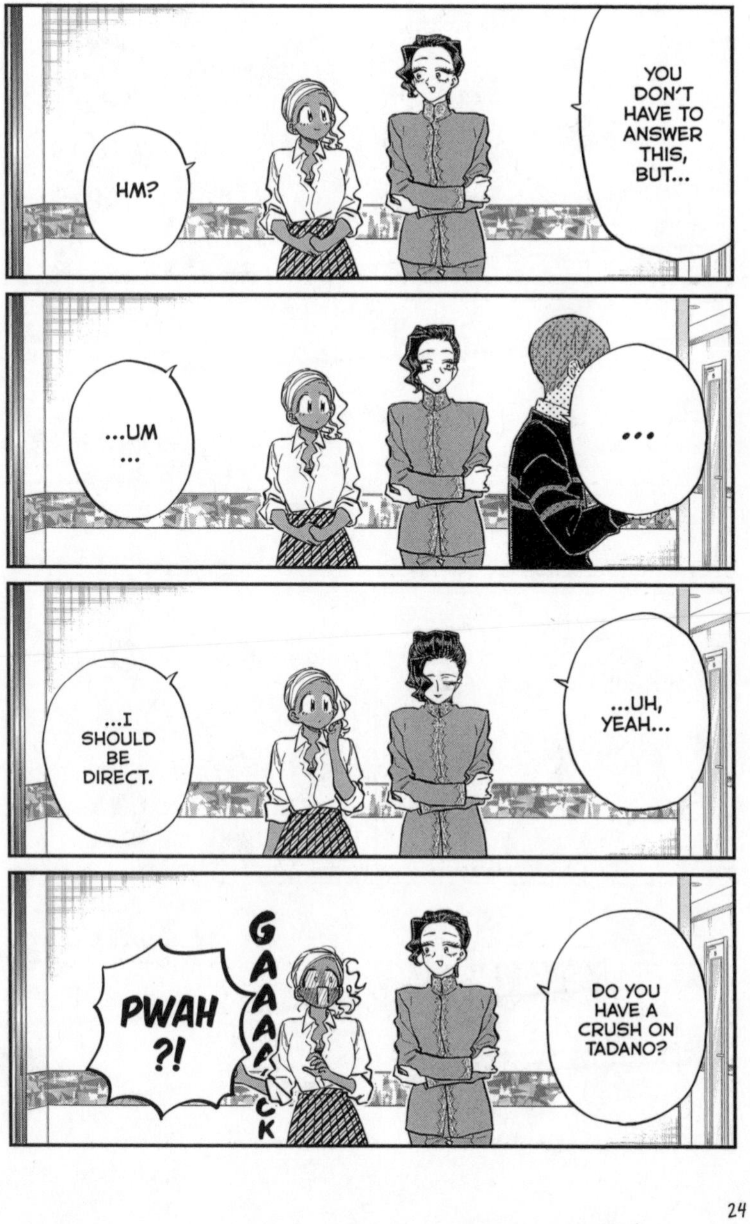
YOU DON'T HAVE TO ANSWER THIS, BUT...
HM?
...
...UM ...
...UH, YEAH...
...I SHOULD BE DIRECT.
DO YOU HAVE A CRUSH ON TADANO?
GAAAACK
PWAH ?!

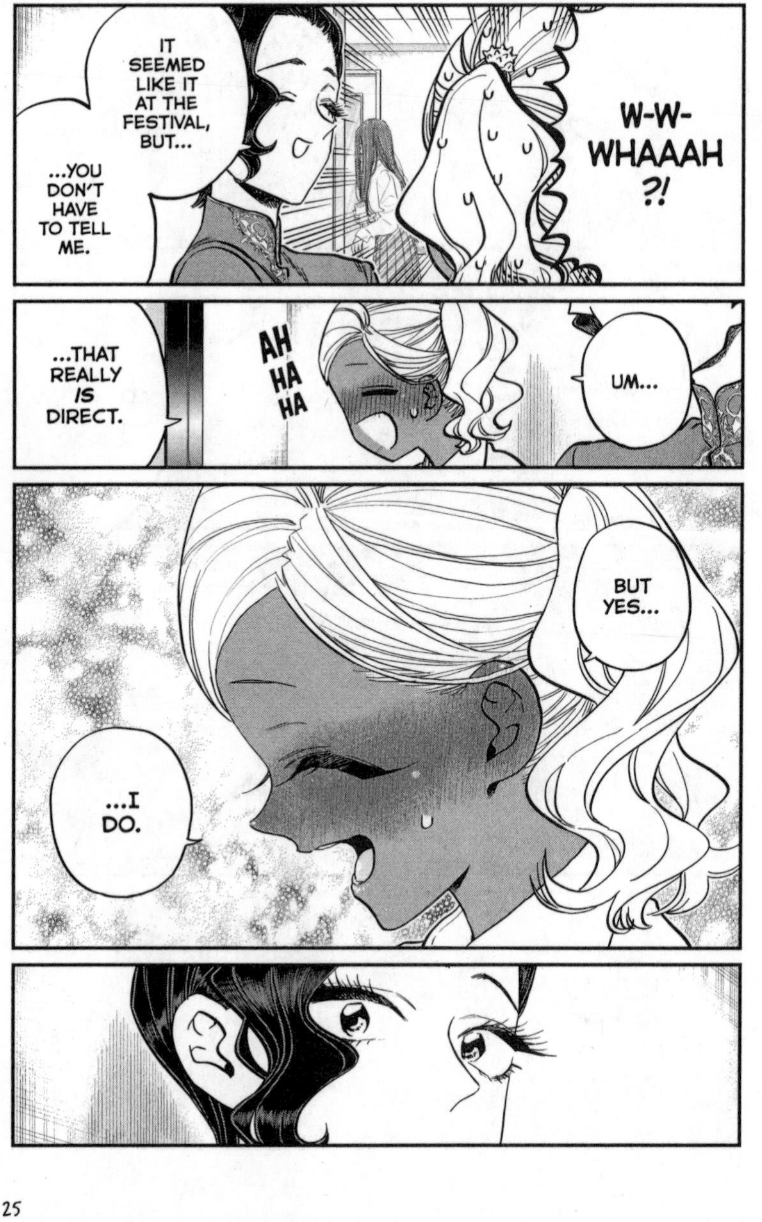
W-W-WHAAAH?!
IT SEEMED LIKE IT AT THE FESTIVAL, BUT...
...YOU DON'T HAVE TO TELL ME.
UM...
AH HA HA
...THAT REALLY *IS* DIRECT.
BUT YES...
...I DO.

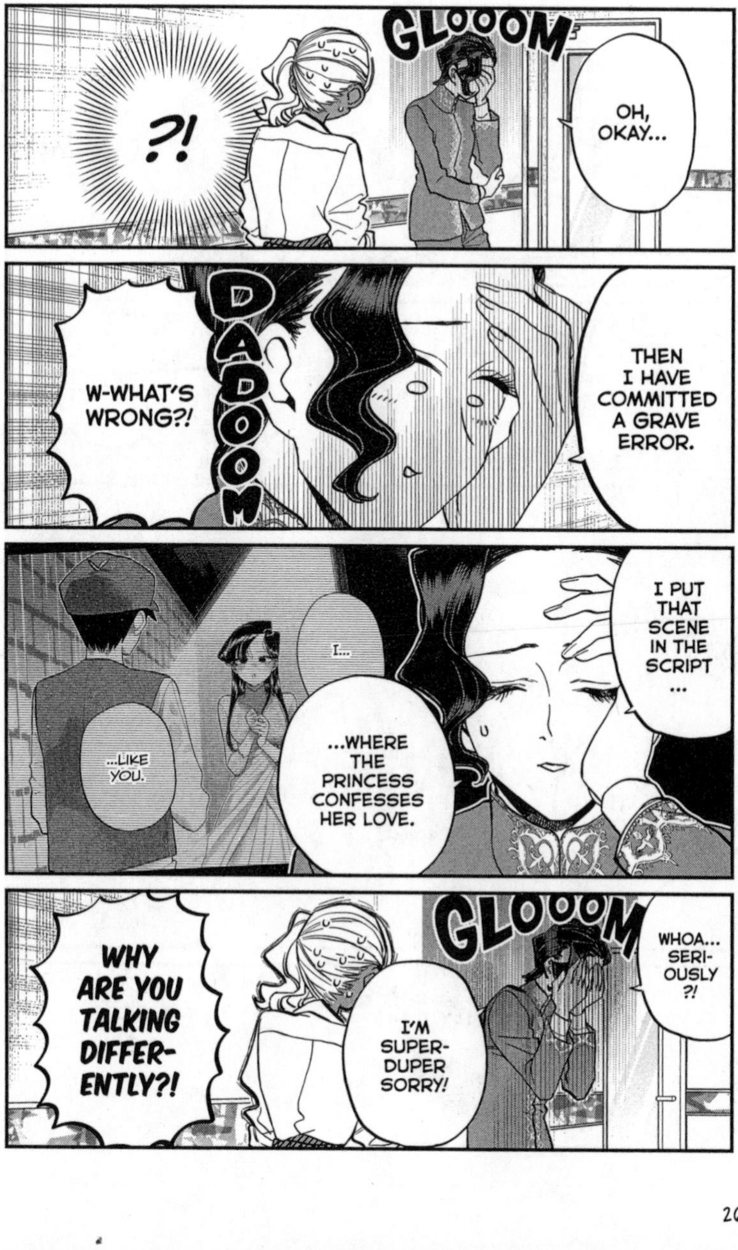
OH, OKAY...
GLOOOM
?!
THEN I HAVE COMMITTED A GRAVE ERROR.
DADOOM
W-WHAT'S WRONG?!
I PUT THAT SCENE IN THE SCRIPT ...
...WHERE THE PRINCESS CONFESSES HER LOVE.
I...
...LIKE YOU.
WHOA... SERI-OUSLY ?!
GLOOOM
I'M SUPER-DUPER SORRY!
WHY ARE YOU TALKING DIFFER-ENTLY?!

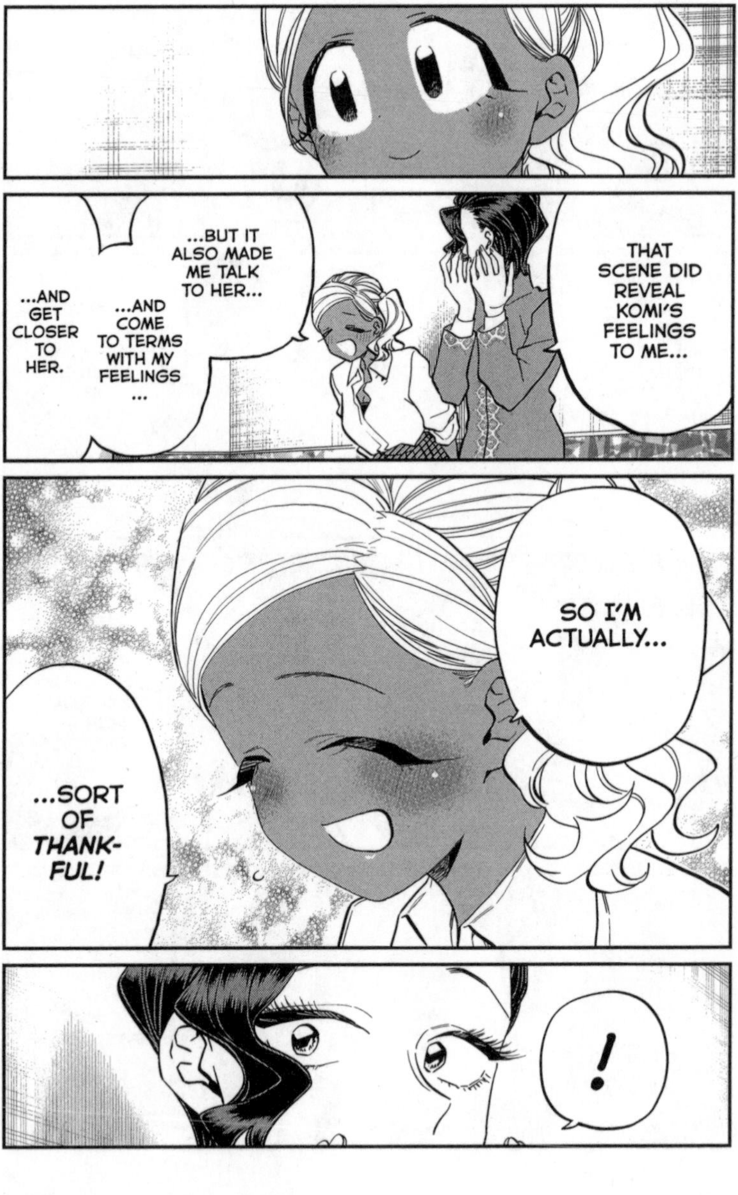
THAT SCENE DID REVEAL KOMI'S FEELINGS TO ME...
...BUT IT ALSO MADE ME TALK TO HER...
...AND COME TO TERMS WITH MY FEELINGS ...
...AND GET CLOSER TO HER.
SO I'M ACTUALLY...
...SORT OF *THANK-FUL!*
!

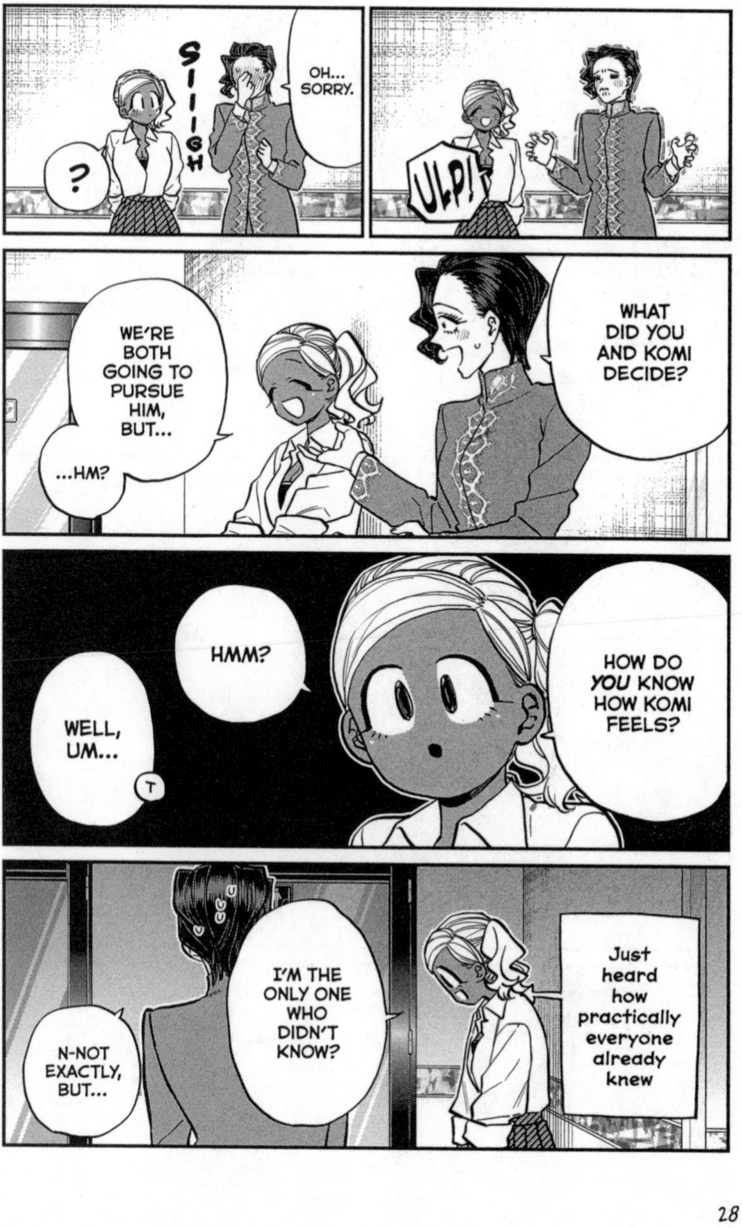
ULP!
OH... SORRY.
SIIIGH
?
WHAT DID YOU AND KOMI DECIDE?
WE'RE BOTH GOING TO PURSUE HIM, BUT...
...HM?
HOW DO *YOU* KNOW HOW KOMI FEELS?
HMM?
WELL, UM...
T
Just heard how practically everyone already knew
I'M THE ONLY ONE WHO DIDN'T KNOW?
N-NOT EXACTLY, BUT...

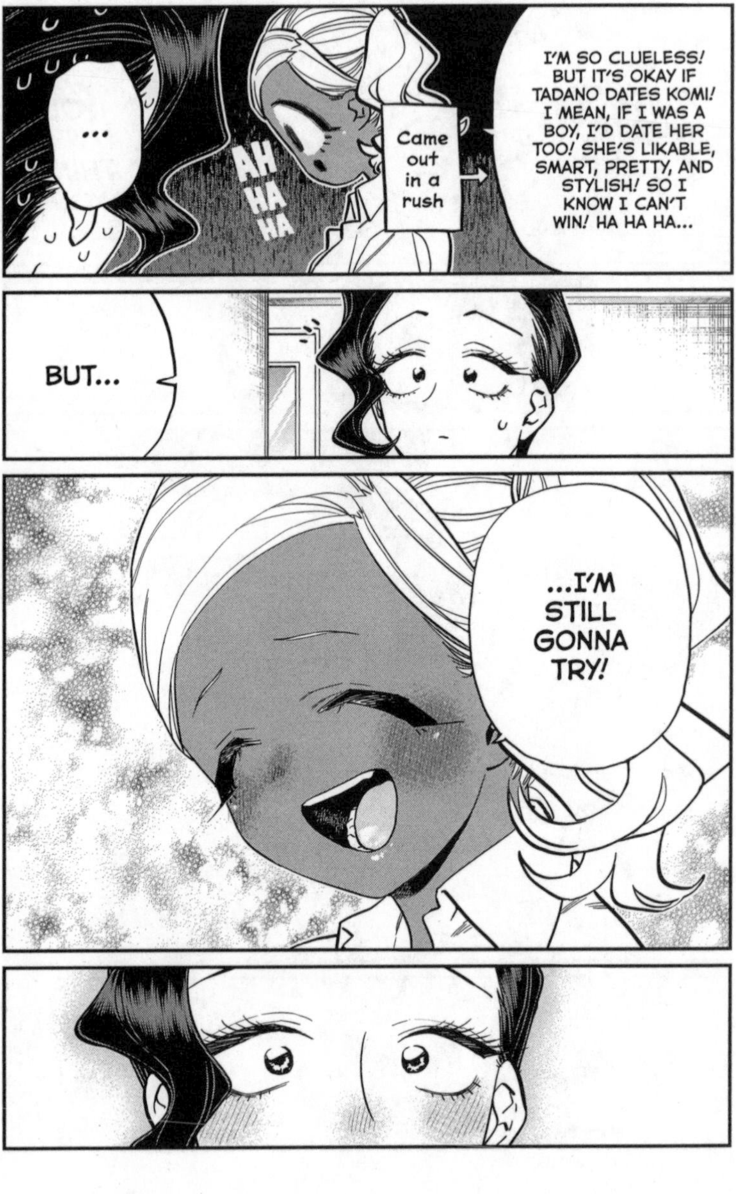
I'M SO CLUELESS! BUT IT'S OKAY IF TADANO DATES KOMI! I MEAN, IF I WAS A BOY, I'D DATE HER TOO! SHE'S LIKABLE, SMART, PRETTY, AND STYLISH! SO I KNOW I CAN'T WIN! HA HA HA...
Came out in a rush
AH HA HA
...
BUT...
...I'M STILL GONNA TRY!

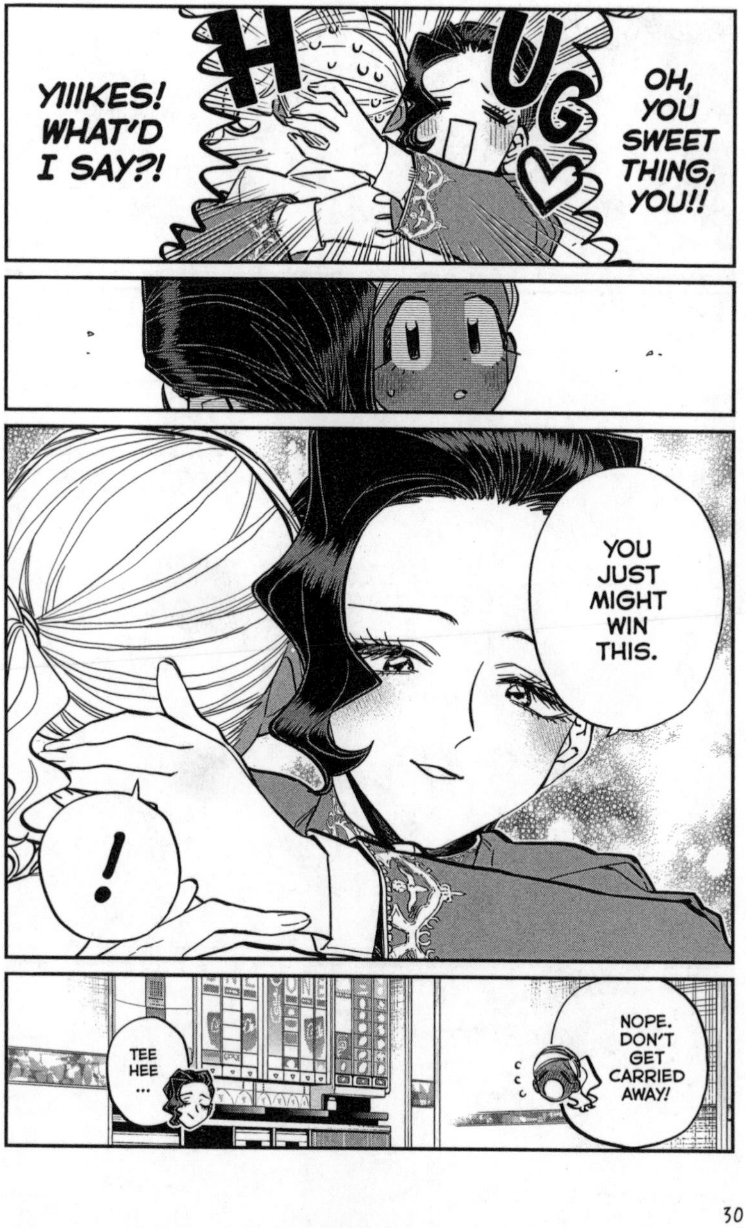
OH, YOU SWEET THING, YOU!!
HUG
YIIIKES! WHAT'D I SAY?!
YOU JUST MIGHT WIN THIS.
!
NOPE. DON'T GET CARRIED AWAY!
TEE HEE ...

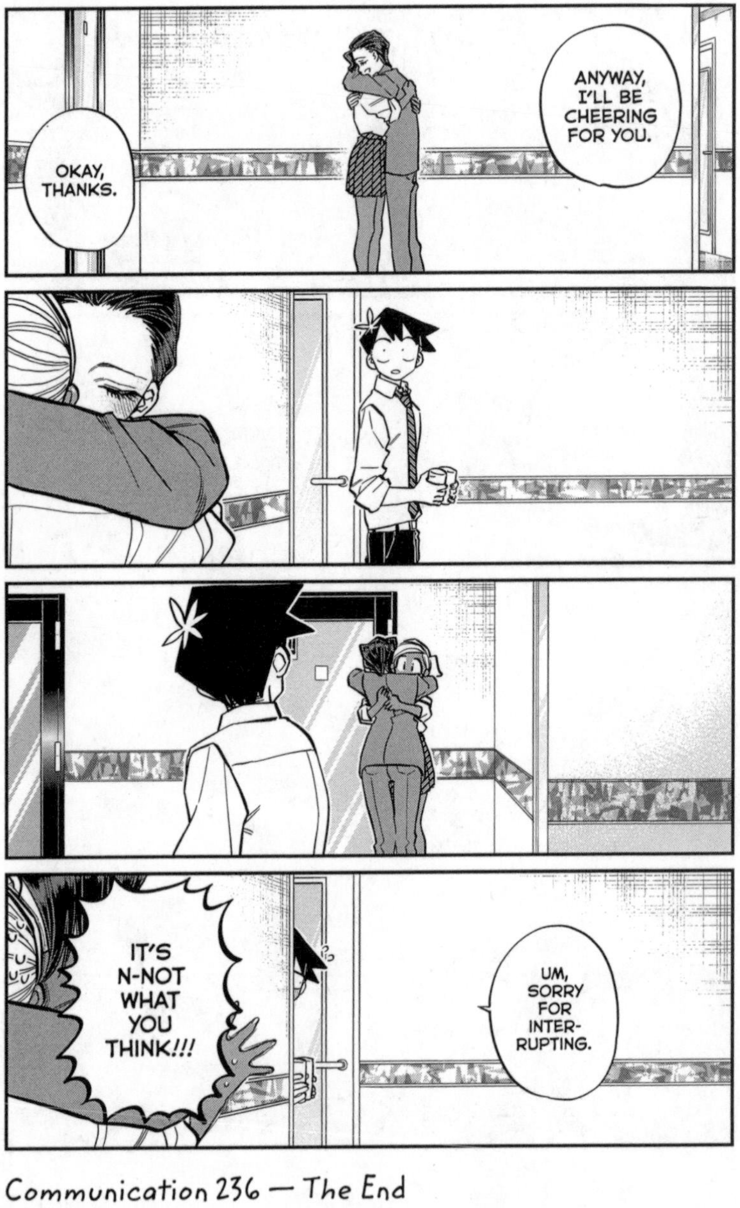
ANYWAY, I'LL BE CHEERING FOR YOU.
OKAY, THANKS.
UM, SORRY FOR INTER-RUPTING.
IT'S N-NOT WHAT YOU THINK!!!

Communication 236 — The End

Communication 237: Making a Play

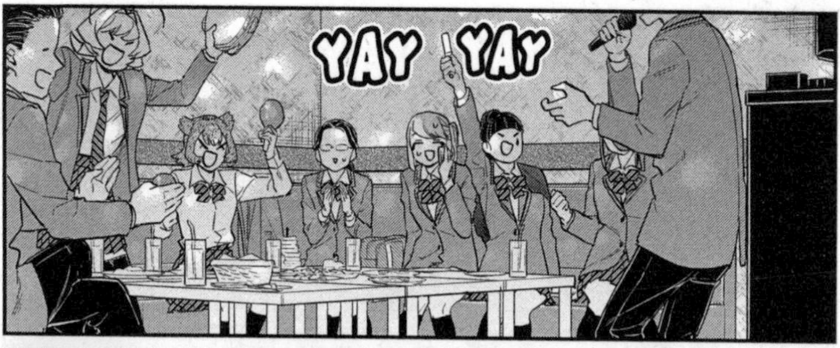
YAY YAY

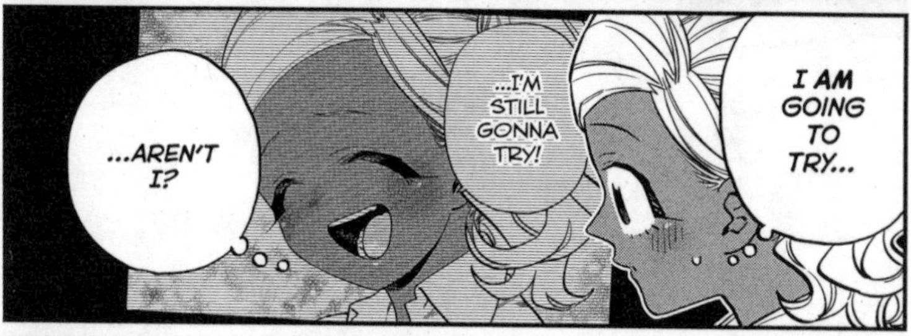
I AM GOING TO TRY...
...I'M STILL GONNA TRY!
...AREN'T I?

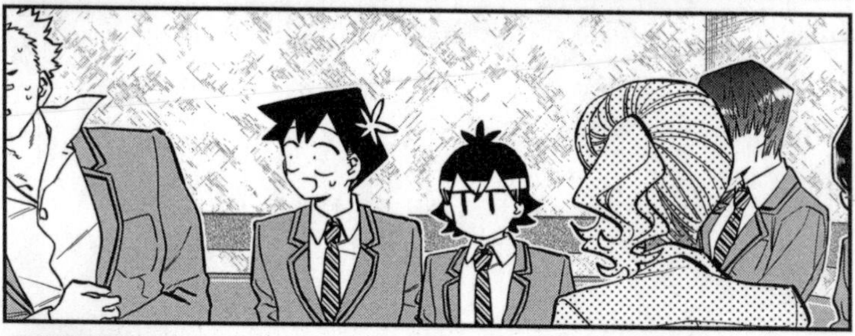

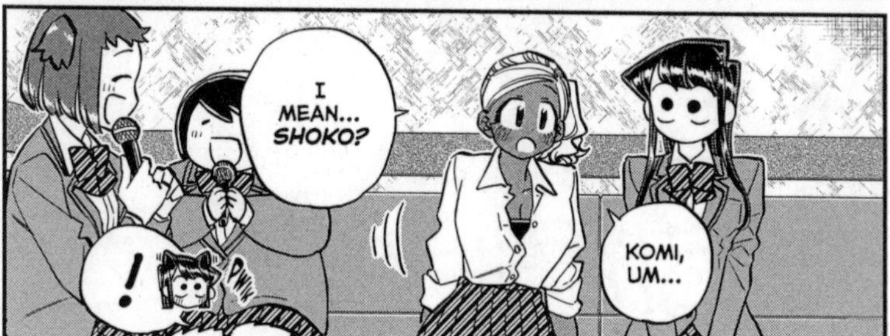
KOMI, UM...
I MEAN... SHOKO?
!

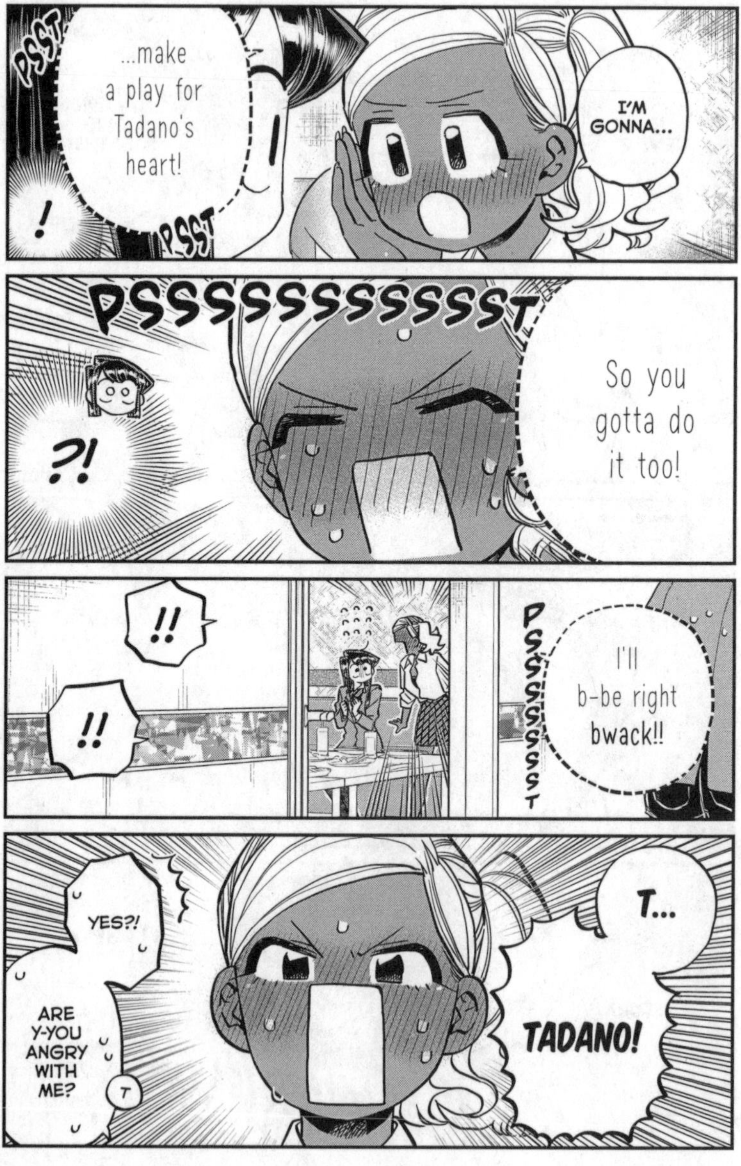
I'M GONNA...
...make a play for Tadano's heart!
PSST
PSST
!
PSSSSSSSSSSST
So you gotta do it too!
?!
I'll b-be right bwack!!
PSSSSSSSSST
!!
!!
T...
TADANO!
YES?!
ARE Y-YOU ANGRY WITH ME?

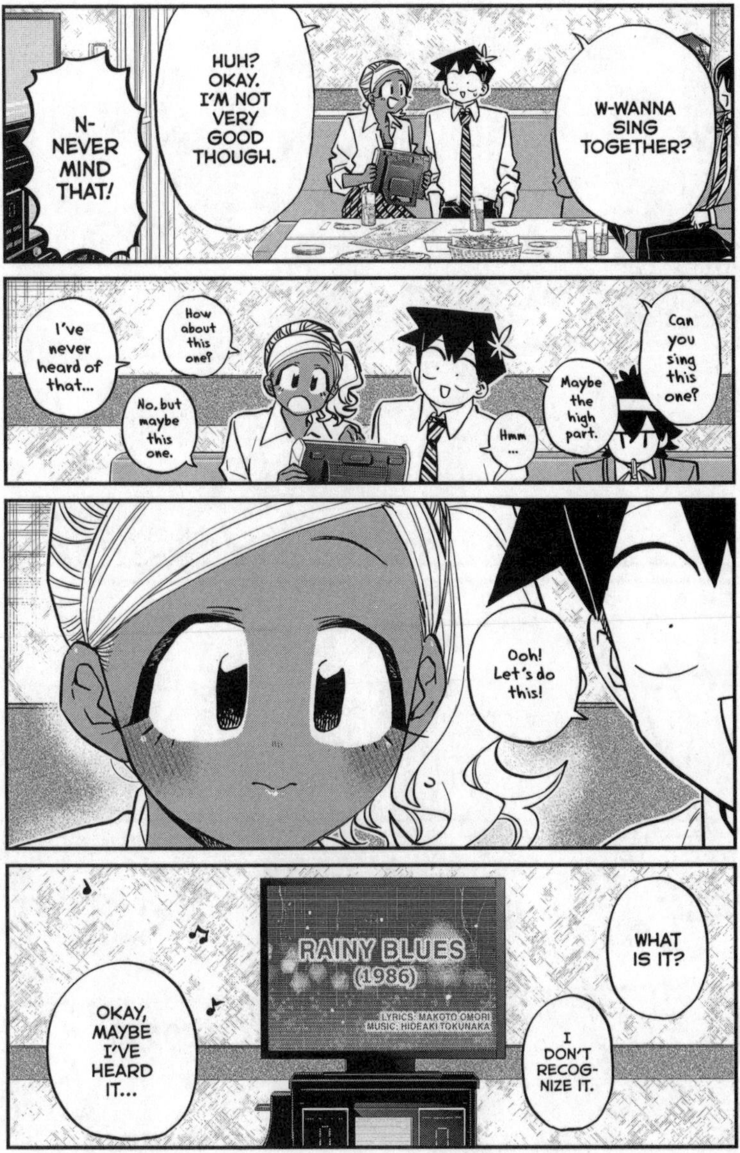
W-WANNA SING TOGETHER?
HUH? OKAY. I'M NOT VERY GOOD THOUGH.
N- NEVER MIND THAT!
Can you sing this one?
Maybe the high part.
Hmm ...
How about this one?
I've never heard of that...
No, but maybe this one.
Ooh! Let's do this!
WHAT IS IT?
I DON'T RECOG- NIZE IT.
RAINY BLUES
(1986)
LYRICS: MAKOTO OMORI
MUSIC: HIDEAKI TOKUNAKA
OKAY, MAYBE I'VE HEARD IT...

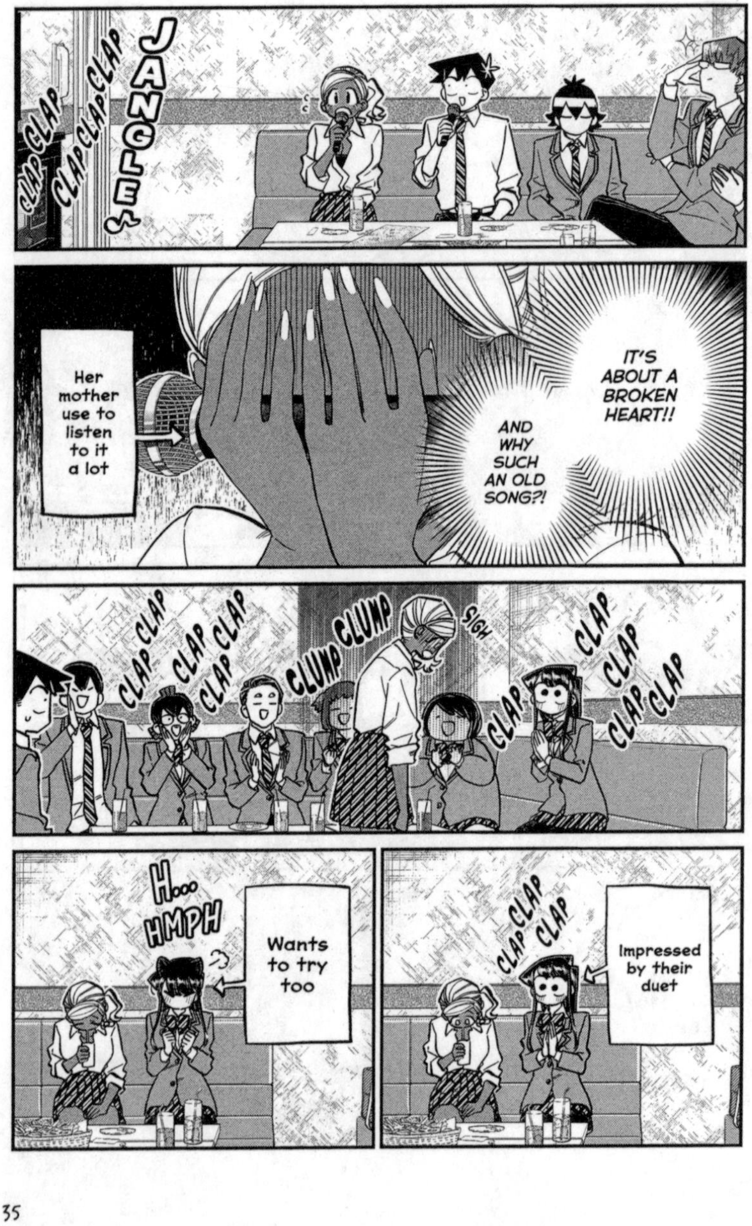
JANGLE
CLAP CLAP CLAP
CLAP CLAP
IT'S ABOUT A BROKEN HEART!!
AND WHY SUCH AN OLD SONG?!
Her mother use to listen to it a lot
CLAP CLAP CLAP CLAP
CLAP
SIGH
CLUMP CLUMP
CLAP CLAP CLAP
CLAP CLAP
Impressed by their duet
CLAP CLAP CLAP CLAP
Wants to try too
H... HMPH

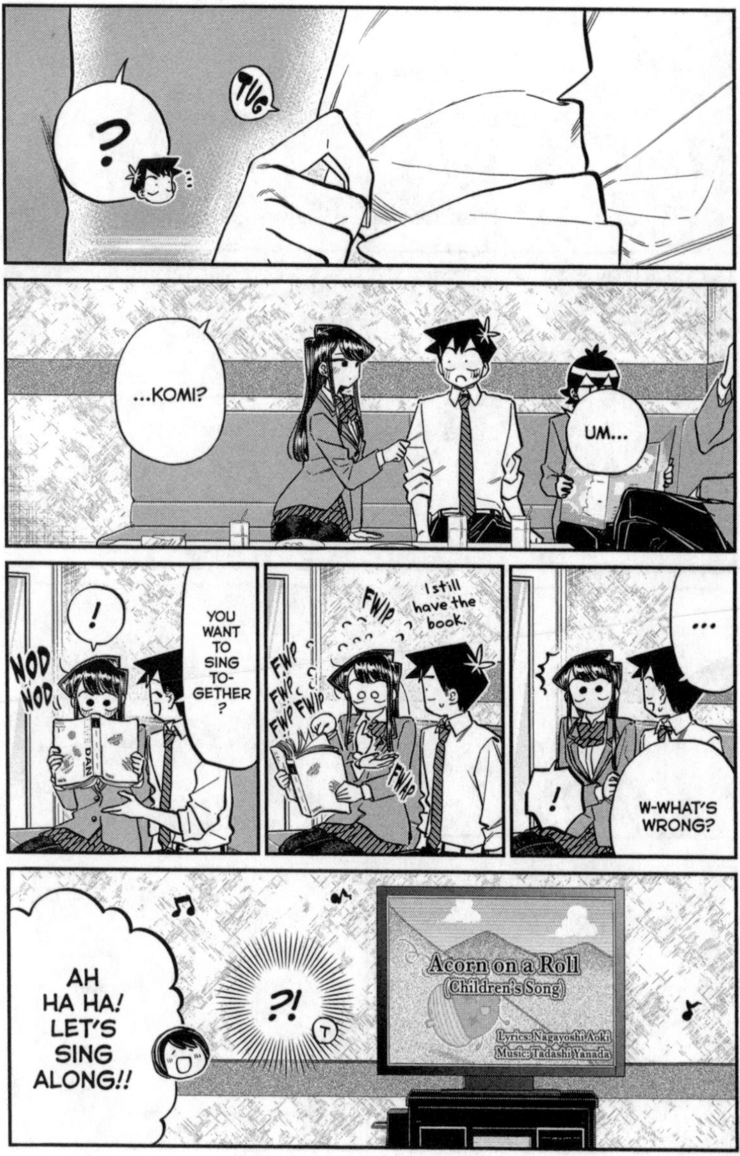
TUG
?
UM...
...KOMI?
...
!
W-WHAT'S WRONG?
I still have the book.
FWIP
FWP FWIP FWP FWIP
FWAP
YOU WANT TO SING TO-GETHER?
!
NOD NOD
Acorn on a Roll
(Children's Song)
Lyrics: Nagayoshi Aoki
Music: Tadashi Yanada
?!
T
AH HA HA! LET'S SING ALONG!!

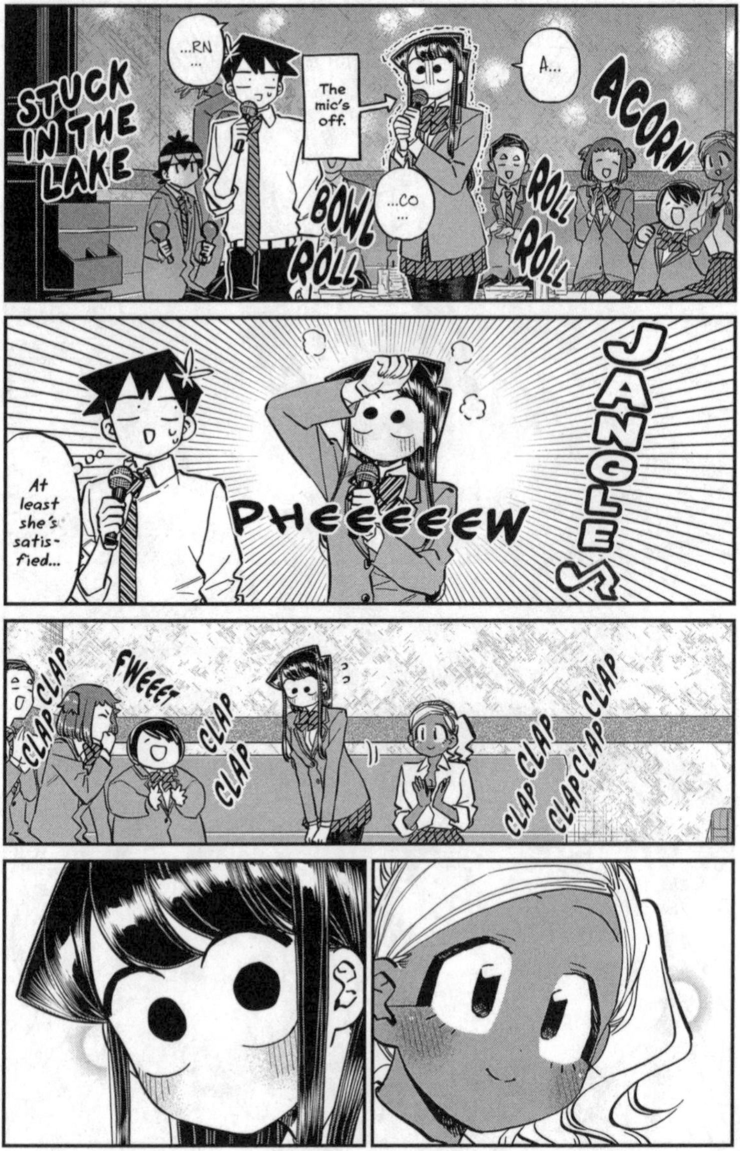
A...
ACORN
ROLL ROLL
...CO...
BOWL ROLL
The mic's off.
...RN...
STUCK IN THE LAKE
JANGLE
PHEEEEEEW
At least she's satis-fied...
CLAP CLAP
CLAP CLAP
CLAP CLAP
FWEEET
CLAP CLAP

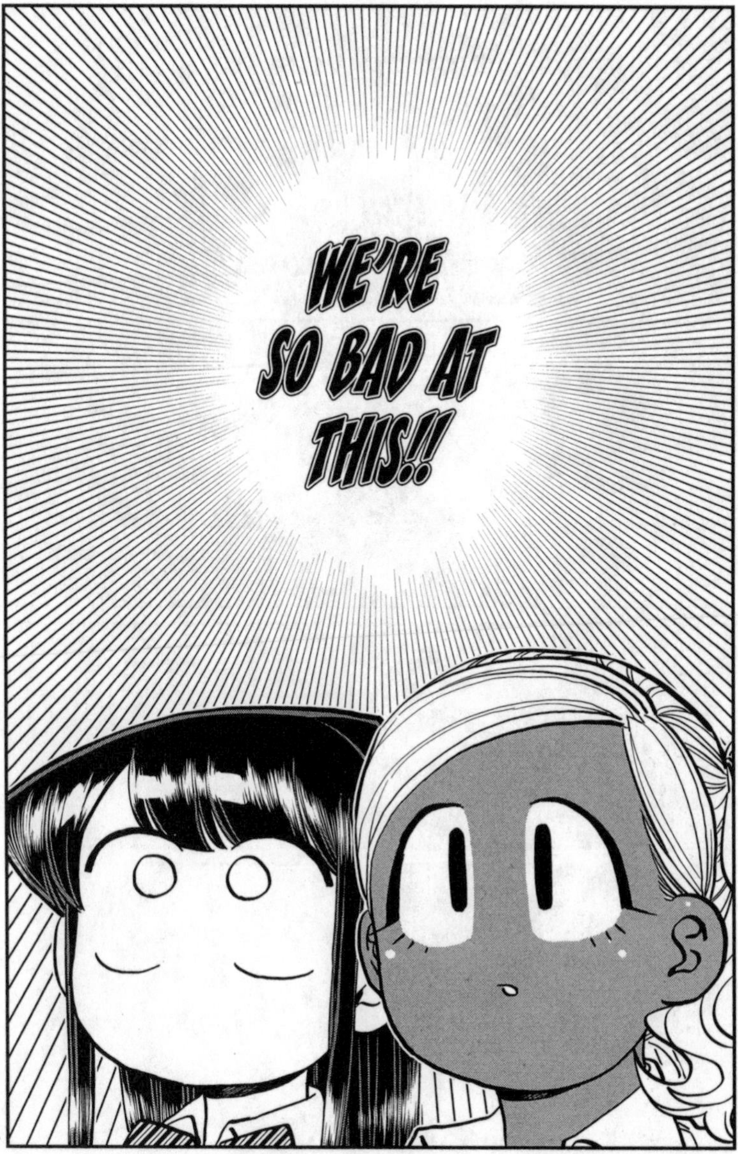
WE'RE SO BAD AT THIS!!
Communication 237 — The End

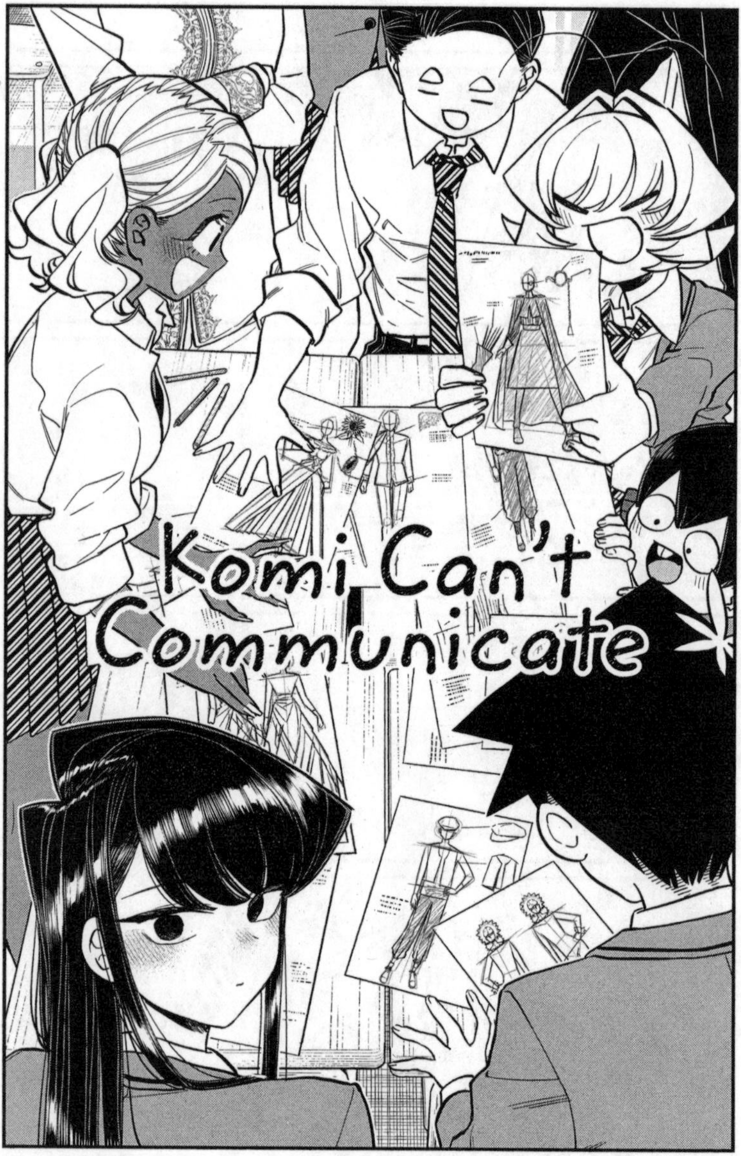
Komi Can't Communicate

Communication 238: Culture Festival Reflections

Repeated Trauma

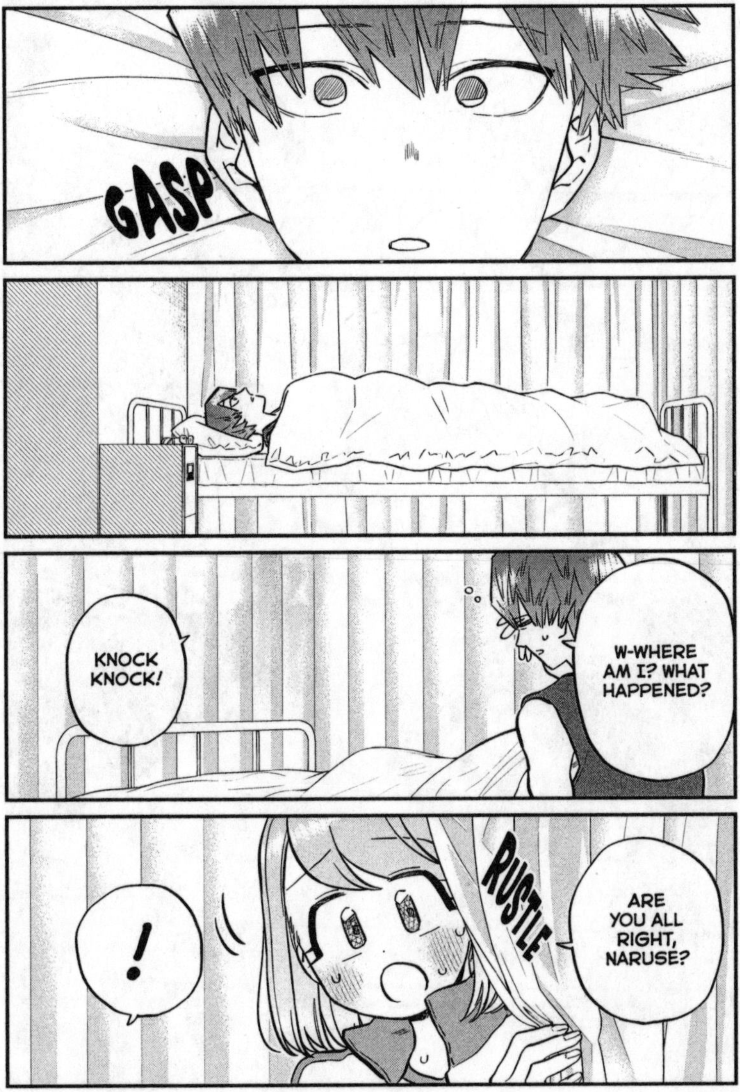
GASP
W-WHERE AM I? WHAT HAPPENED?
KNOCK KNOCK!
ARE YOU ALL RIGHT, NARUSE?
RUSTLE
!

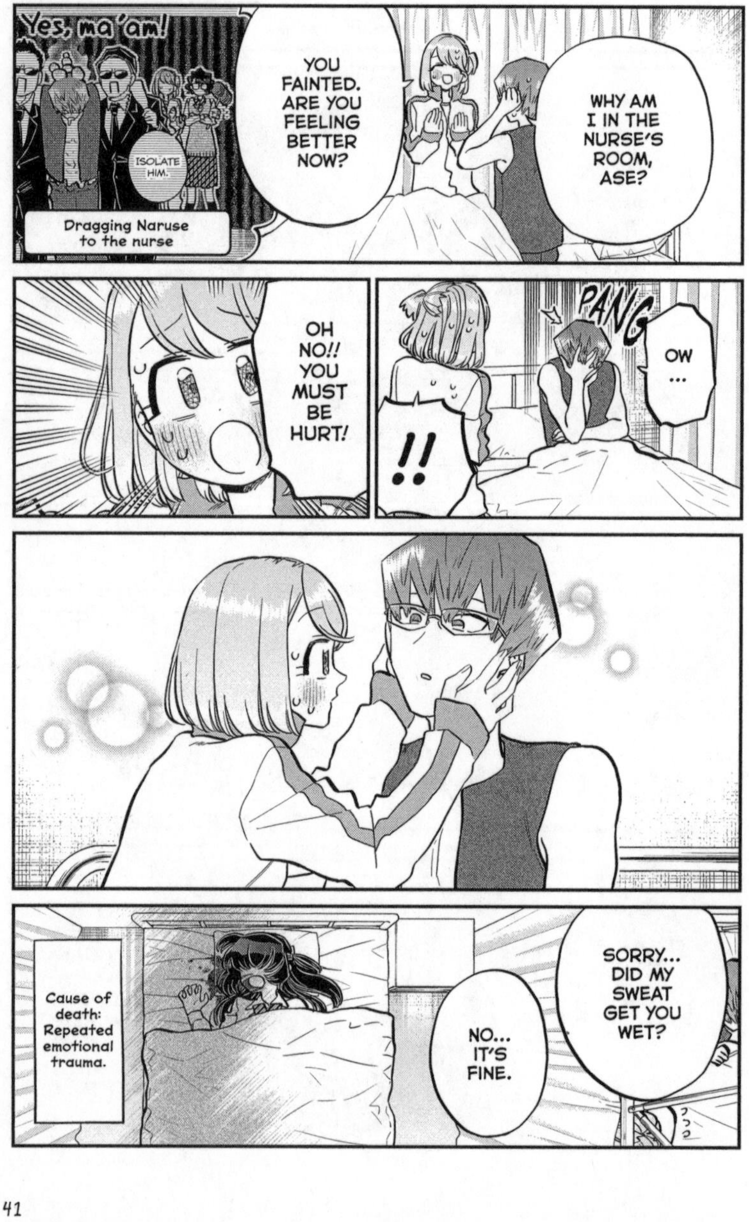
WHY AM I IN THE NURSE'S ROOM, ASE?
YOU FAINTED. ARE YOU FEELING BETTER NOW?
Yes, ma'am!
ISOLATE HIM.
Dragging Naruse to the nurse
PANG
OW ...
!!
OH NO!! YOU MUST BE HURT!
SORRY... DID MY SWEAT GET YOU WET?
NO... IT'S FINE.
Cause of death: Repeated emotional trauma.

Costume Deptartment—Fukusuki's Summer Soft-Spot

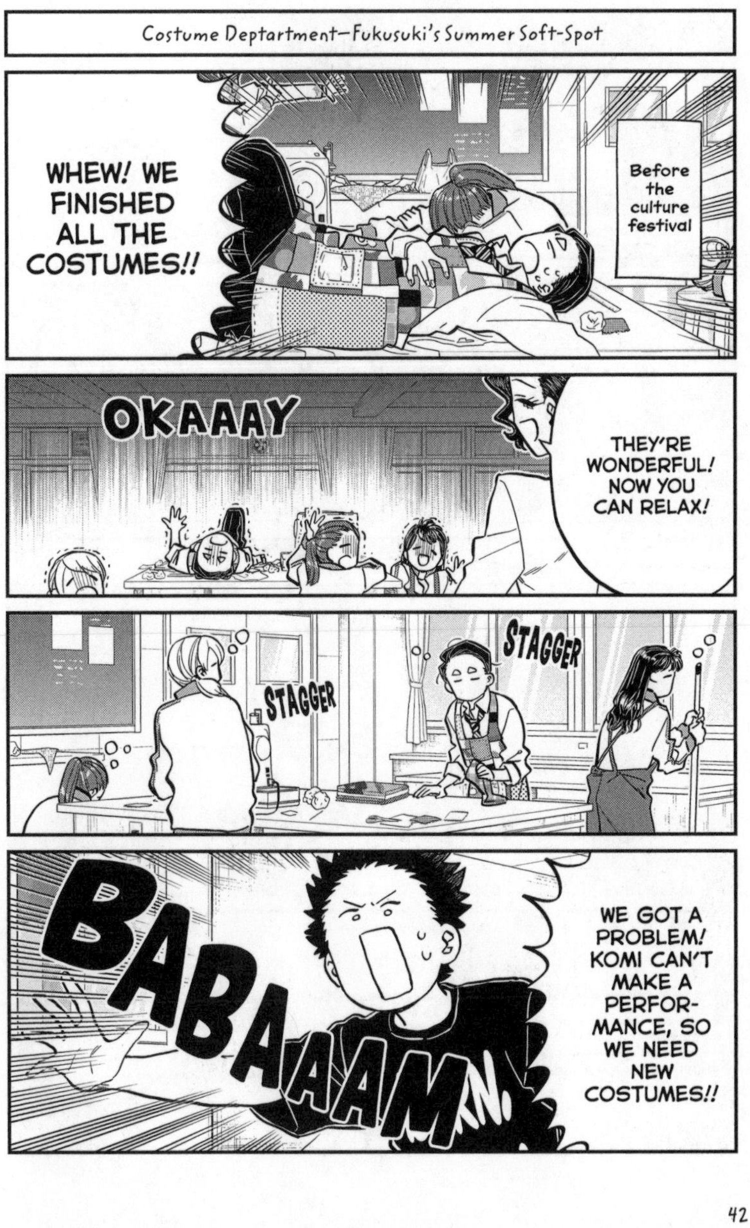
Before the culture festival
WHEW! WE FINISHED ALL THE COSTUMES!!
THEY'RE WONDERFUL! NOW YOU CAN RELAX!
OKAAAY
STAGGER
STAGGER
WE GOT A PROBLEM! KOMI CAN'T MAKE A PERFOR-MANCE, SO WE NEED NEW COSTUMES!!
BABAAAAMN

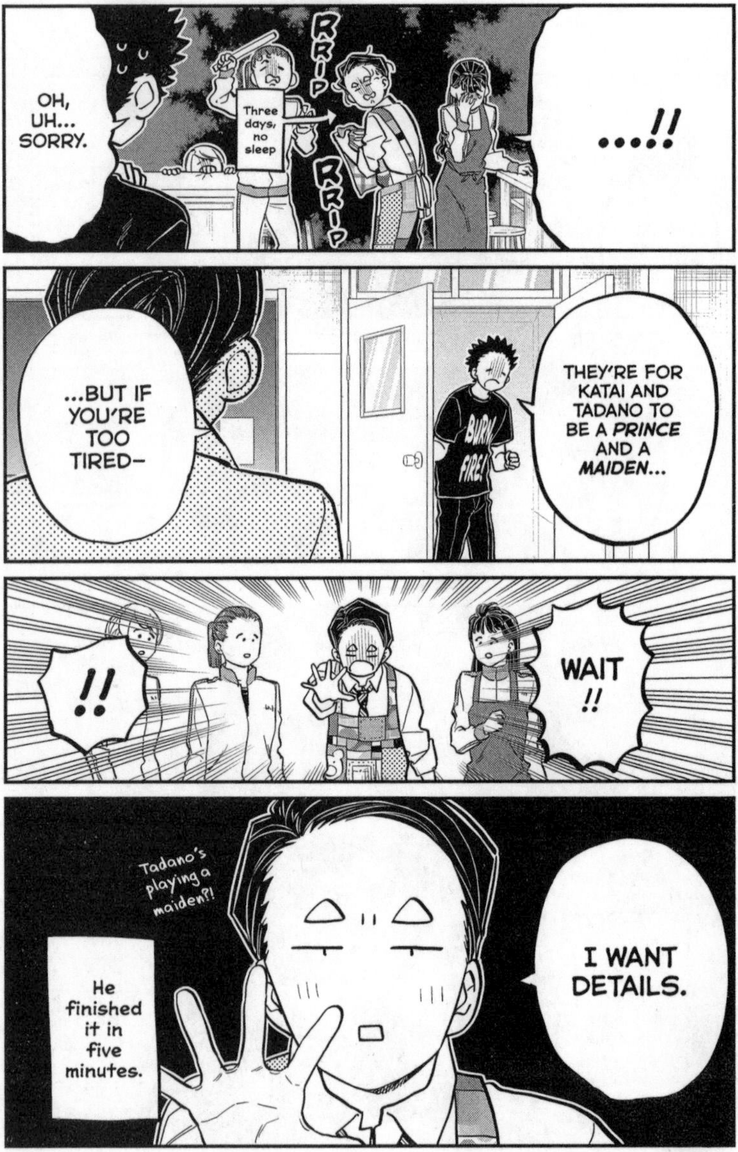
...!!
Three days, no sleep
RRIP
RRIP
OH, UH... SORRY.
THEY'RE FOR KATAI AND TADANO TO BE A *PRINCE* AND A *MAIDEN*...
...BUT IF YOU'RE TOO TIRED—
WAIT !!
!!
I WANT DETAILS.
Tadano's playing a maiden?!
He finished it in five minutes.

The Moment of the Crime

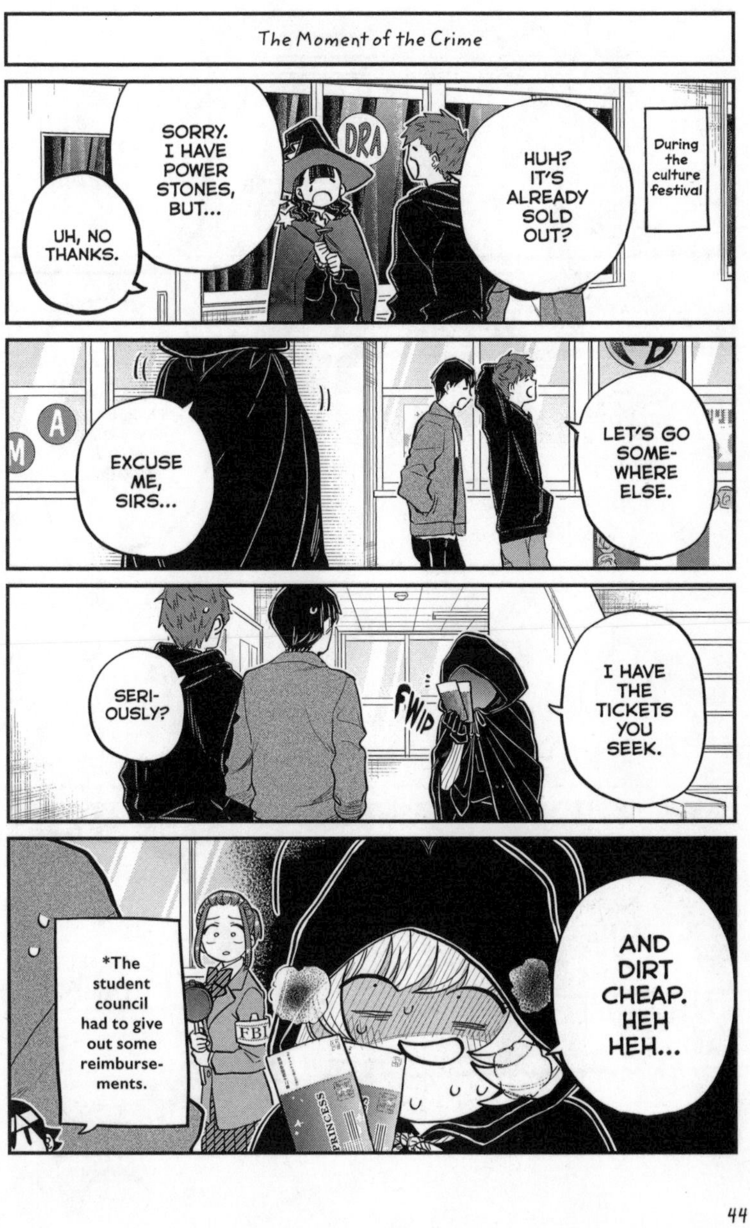
During the culture festival
HUH? IT'S ALREADY SOLD OUT?
DRA
SORRY. I HAVE POWER STONES, BUT...
UH, NO THANKS.
LET'S GO SOME-WHERE ELSE.
EXCUSE ME, SIRS...
I HAVE THE TICKETS YOU SEEK.
FWIP
SERI-OUSLY?
AND DIRT CHEAP. HEH HEH...
*The student council had to give out some reimburse-ments.
FBI
PRINCESS

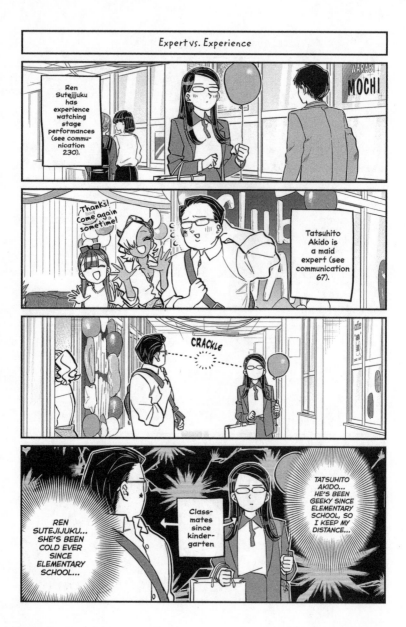

Expert vs. Experience

Ren Sutejijuku has experience watching stage performances (see communication 230).

WARABI MOCHI

Thanks! Come again sometime!

Tatsuhito Akido is a maid expert (see communication 67).

CRACKLE

REN SUTEJIJUKU... SHE'S BEEN COLD EVER SINCE ELEMENTARY SCHOOL...

Classmates since kindergarten

TATSUHITO AKIDO... HE'S BEEN GEEKY SINCE ELEMENTARY SCHOOL, SO I KEEP MY DISTANCE...

45

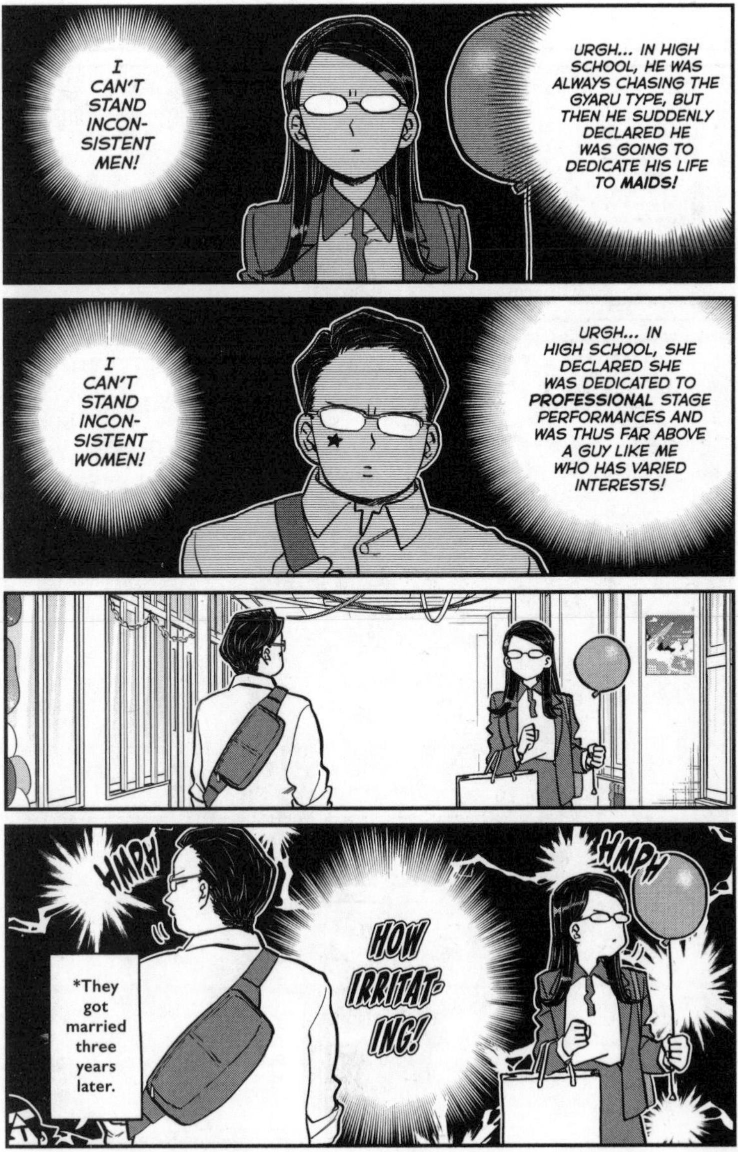
URGH... IN HIGH SCHOOL, HE WAS ALWAYS CHASING THE GYARU TYPE, BUT THEN HE SUDDENLY DECLARED HE WAS GOING TO DEDICATE HIS LIFE TO **MAIDS!**
I CAN'T STAND INCON-SISTENT MEN!
URGH... IN HIGH SCHOOL, SHE DECLARED SHE WAS DEDICATED TO **PROFESSIONAL** STAGE PERFORMANCES AND WAS THUS FAR ABOVE A GUY LIKE ME WHO HAS VARIED INTERESTS!
I CAN'T STAND INCON-SISTENT WOMEN!
HMPH
HOW IRRITAT-ING!
HMPH
*They got married three years later.

A Surprisingly Lovable Personality

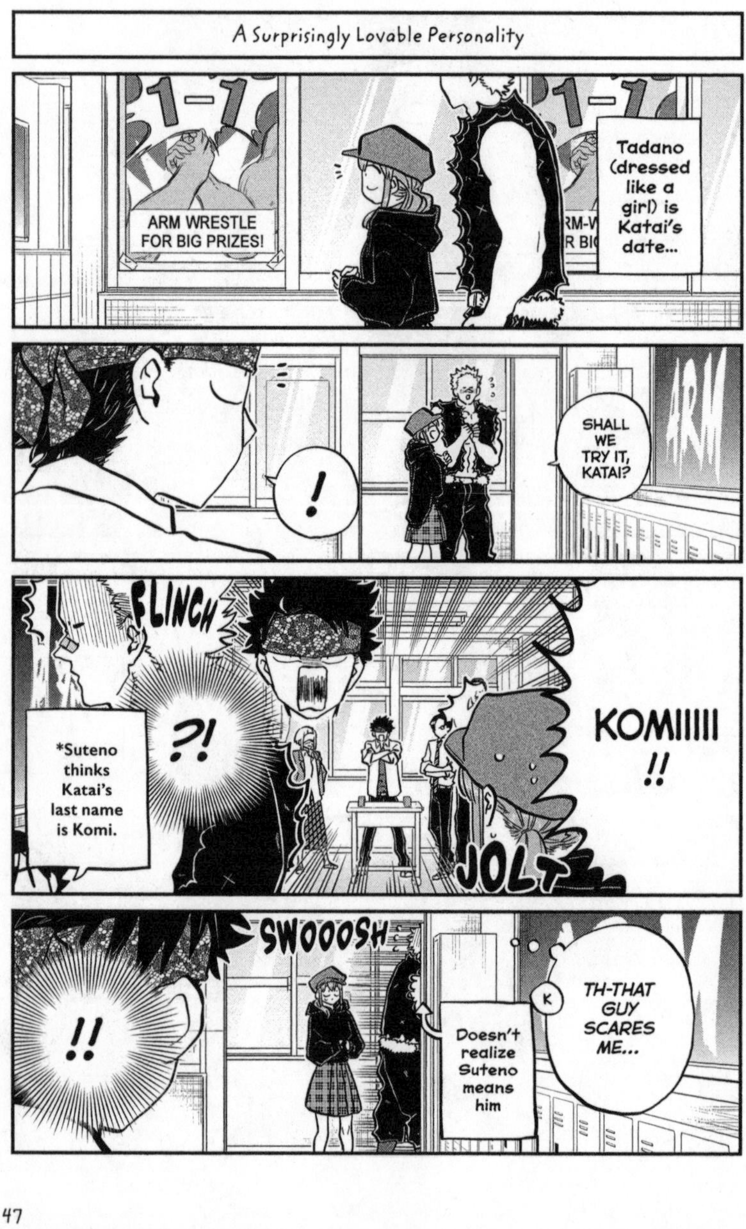
Tadano (dressed like a girl) is Katai's date...
ARM WRESTLE FOR BIG PRIZES!
SHALL WE TRY IT, KATAI?
ARM
!
KOMIIIIII !!
JOLT
?!
FLINCH
*Suteno thinks Katai's last name is Komi.
TH-THAT GUY SCARES ME...
K
Doesn't realize Suteno means him
SWOOOSH
!!

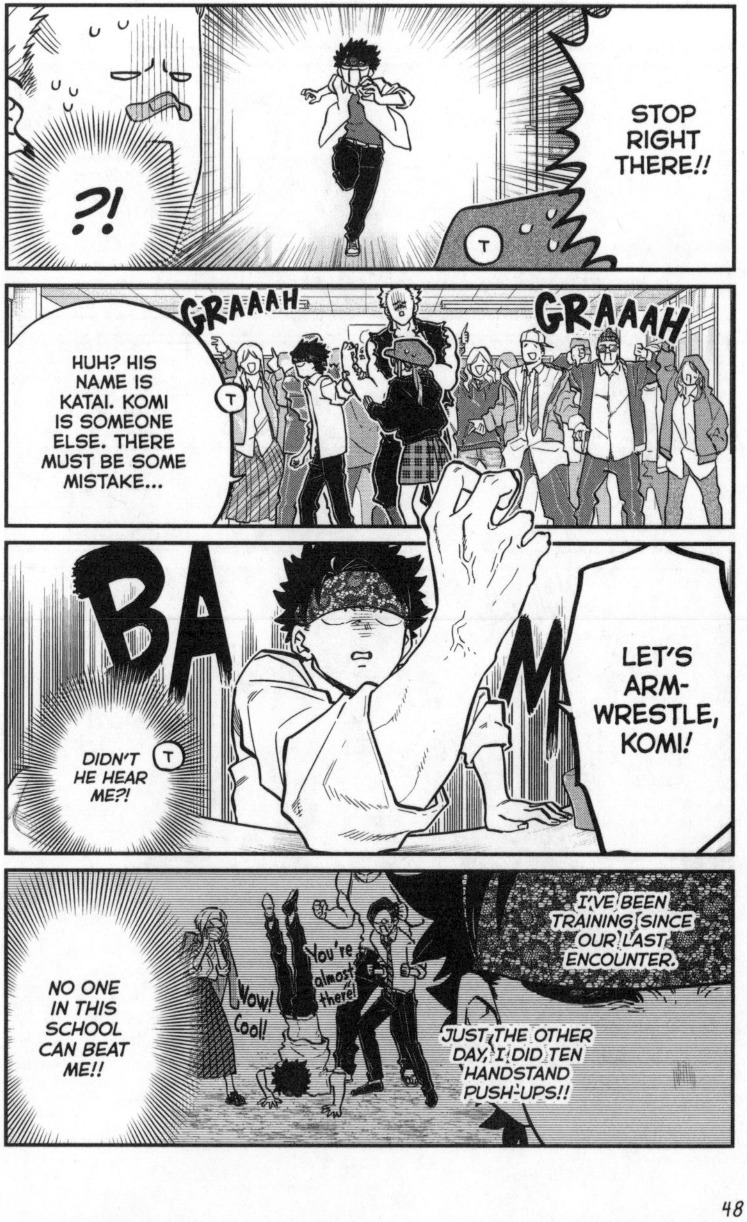
STOP RIGHT THERE!!
?!
GRAAAH
GRAAAH
HUH? HIS NAME IS KATAI. KOMI IS SOMEONE ELSE. THERE MUST BE SOME MISTAKE...
LET'S ARM-WRESTLE, KOMI!
BAM
DIDN'T HE HEAR ME?!
I'VE BEEN TRAINING SINCE OUR LAST ENCOUNTER.
JUST THE OTHER DAY, I DID TEN HANDSTAND PUSH-UPS!!
You're almost there!
Wow! Cool!
NO ONE IN THIS SCHOOL CAN BEAT ME!!

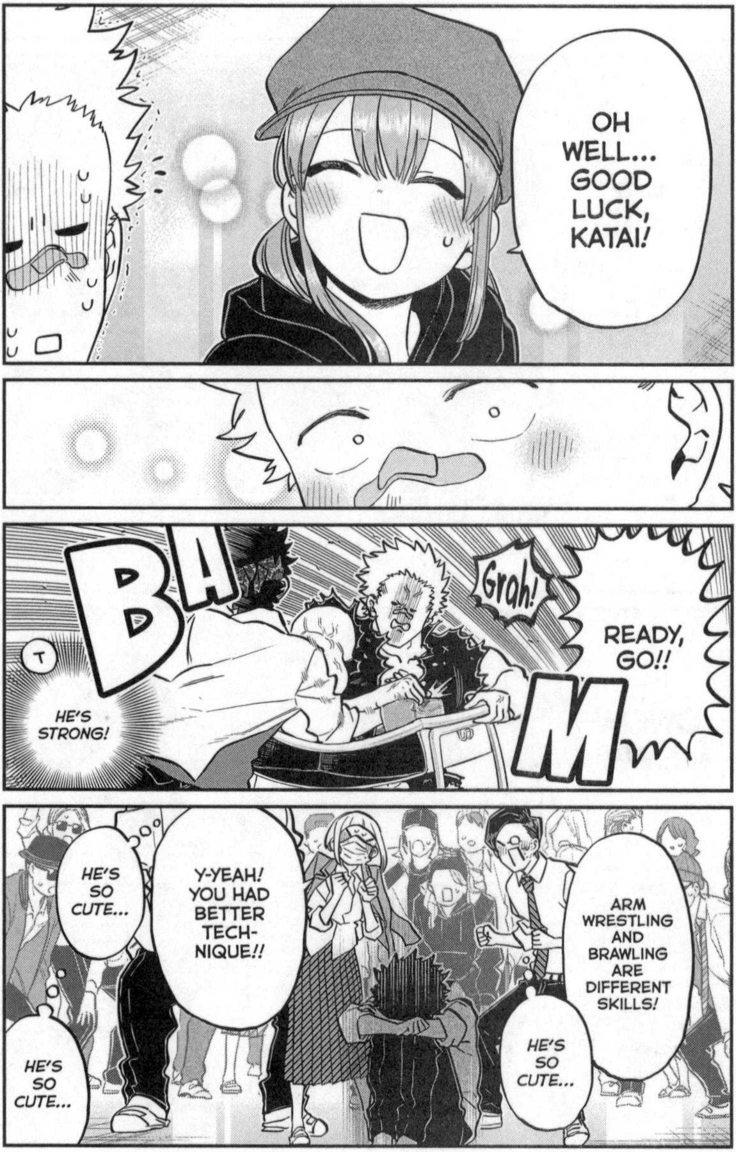
OH WELL... GOOD LUCK, KATAI!
READY, GO!!
Grah!
BAM
HE'S STRONG!
ARM WRESTLING AND BRAWLING ARE DIFFERENT SKILLS!
HE'S SO CUTE...
Y-YEAH! YOU HAD BETTER TECH-NIQUE!!
HE'S SO CUTE...
HE'S SO CUTE...

FBI vs. CIA

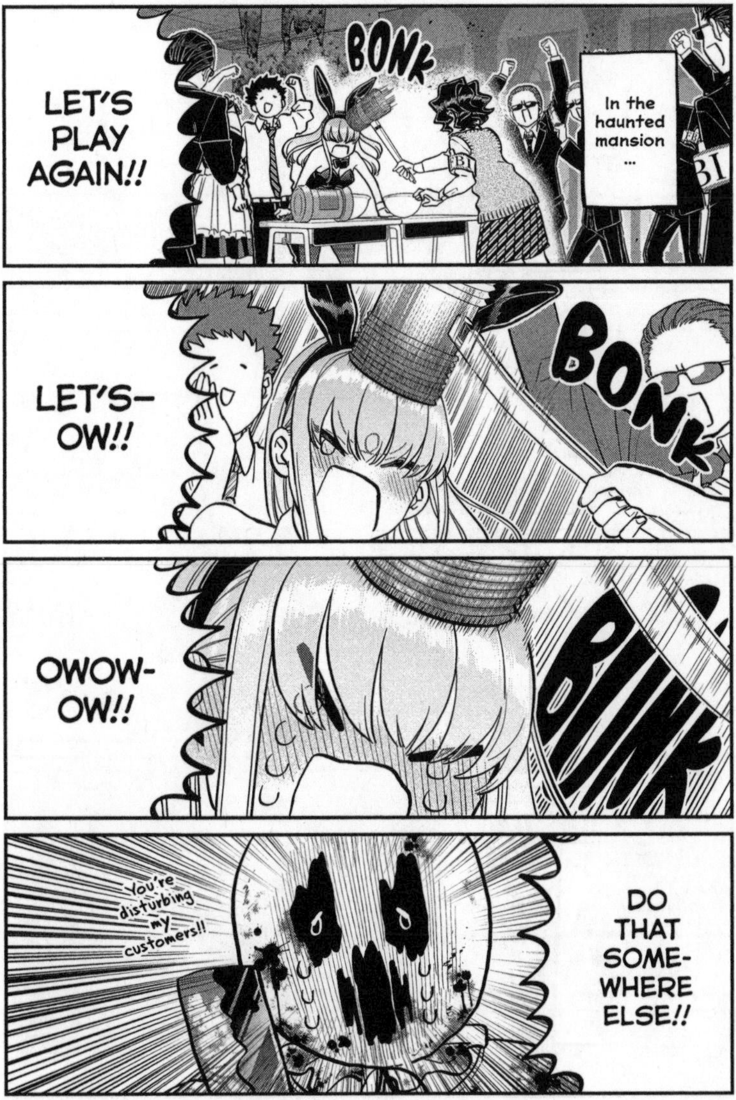
In the haunted mansion ...
BONK
LET'S PLAY AGAIN!!
BONK
LET'S— OW!!
BONK
OWOW-OW!!
DO THAT SOME-WHERE ELSE!!
You're disturbing my customers!!

Legendary

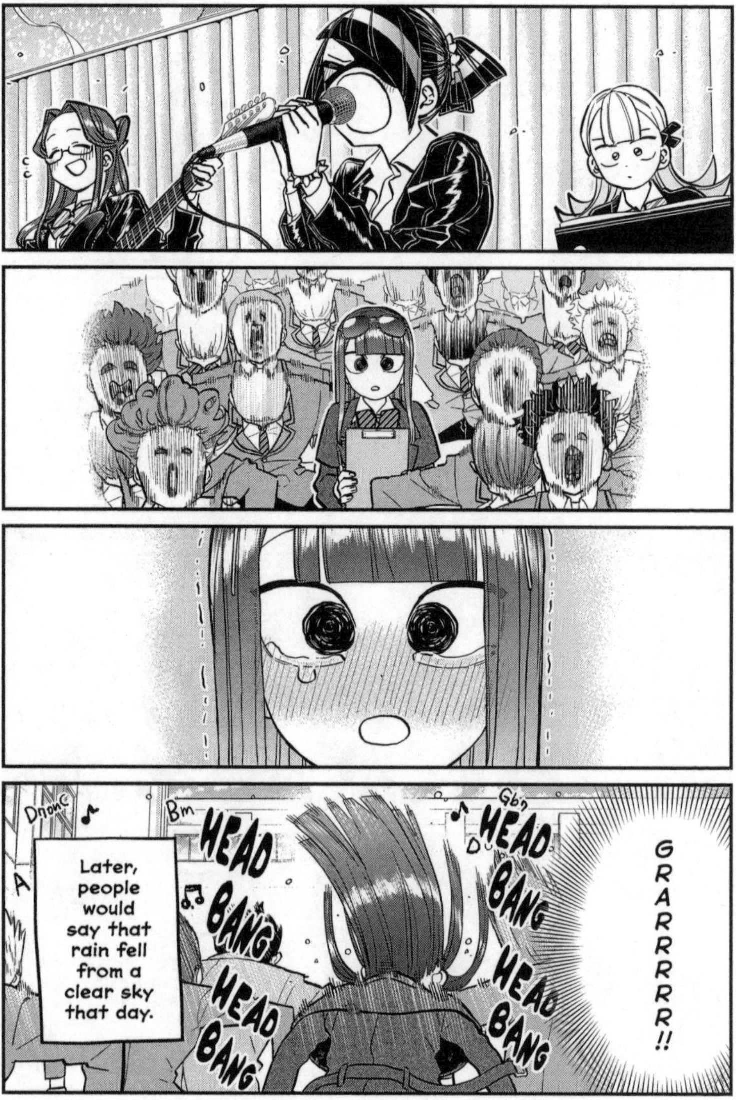
GRARRRRR!!
HEAD BANG
HEAD BANG
Later, people would say that rain fell from a clear sky that day.
HEAD BANG
HEAD BANG
Bm
A

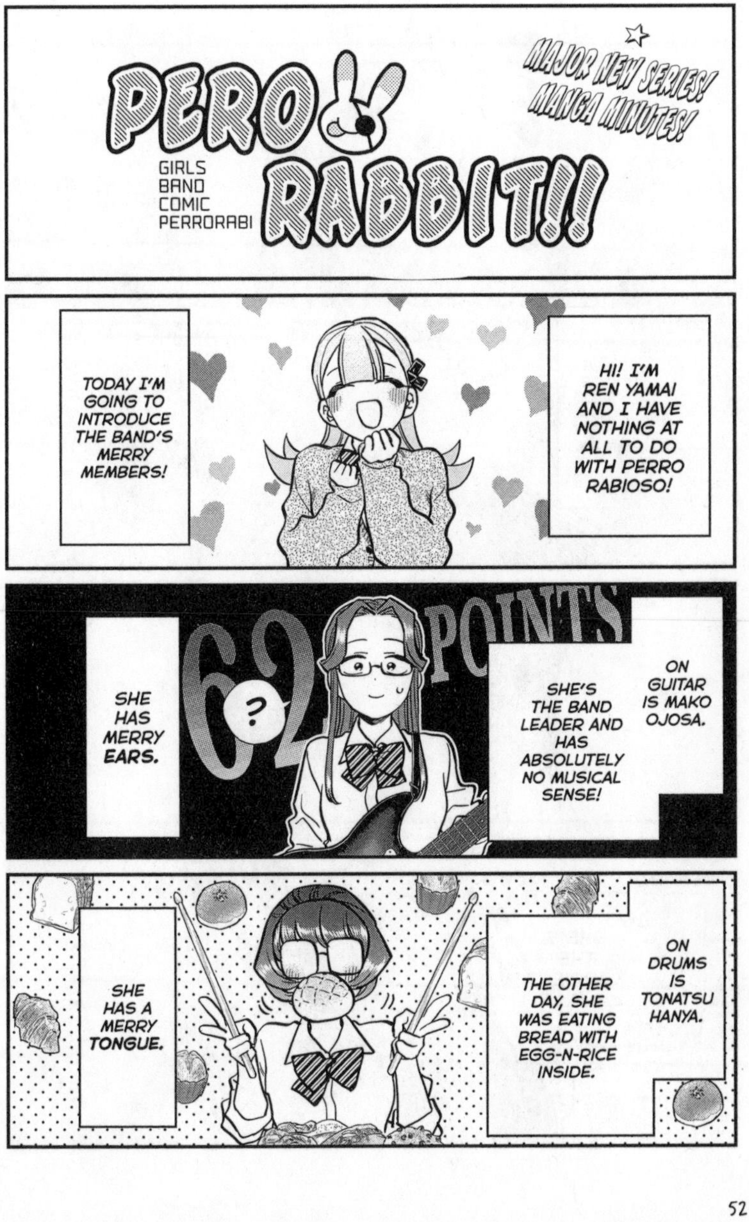
MAJOR NEW SERIES! MANGA MINUTES!
PERO RABBIT!!
GIRLS BAND COMIC PERRORABI
HI! I'M REN YAMAI AND I HAVE NOTHING AT ALL TO DO WITH PERRO RABIOSO!
TODAY I'M GOING TO INTRODUCE THE BAND'S MERRY MEMBERS!
ON GUITAR IS MAKO OJOSA.
SHE'S THE BAND LEADER AND HAS ABSOLUTELY NO MUSICAL SENSE!
62 POINTS
?
SHE HAS MERRY EARS.
ON DRUMS IS TONATSU HANYA.
THE OTHER DAY, SHE WAS EATING BREAD WITH EGG-N-RICE INSIDE.
SHE HAS A MERRY TONGUE.

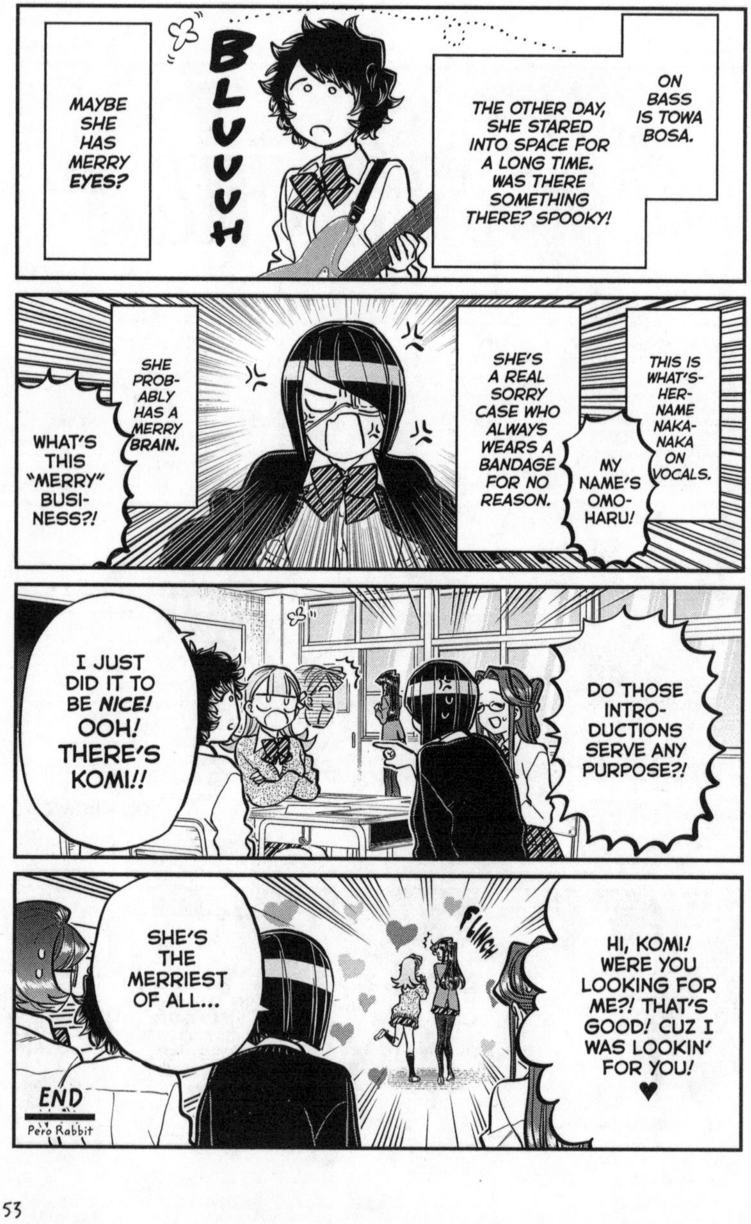
ON BASS IS TOWA BOSA.
THE OTHER DAY, SHE STARED INTO SPACE FOR A LONG TIME. WAS THERE SOMETHING THERE? SPOOKY!
BLUUUH
MAYBE SHE HAS MERRY EYES?
THIS IS WHAT'S-HER-NAME NAKANAKA ON VOCALS.
MY NAME'S OMOHARU!
SHE'S A REAL SORRY CASE WHO ALWAYS WEARS A BANDAGE FOR NO REASON.
SHE PROBABLY HAS A MERRY BRAIN.
WHAT'S THIS "MERRY" BUSINESS?!
DO THOSE INTRODUCTIONS SERVE ANY PURPOSE?!
I JUST DID IT TO BE *NICE!* OOH! THERE'S KOMI!!
HI, KOMI! WERE YOU LOOKING FOR ME?! THAT'S GOOD! CUZ I WAS LOOKIN' FOR YOU! ♥
FLINCH
SHE'S THE MERRIEST OF ALL...
END
Pero Rabbit

Culture Festival Eve

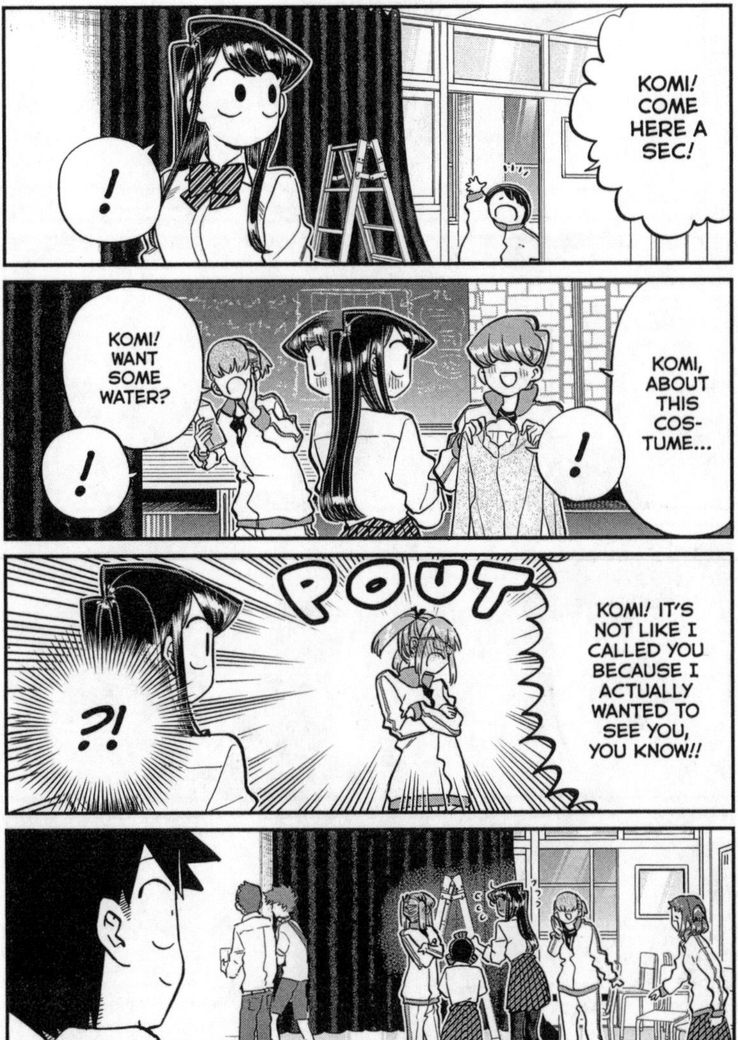
KOMI! COME HERE A SEC!
!
KOMI, ABOUT THIS COS-TUME...
!
KOMI! WANT SOME WATER?
!
KOMI! IT'S NOT LIKE I CALLED YOU BECAUSE I ACTUALLY WANTED TO SEE YOU, YOU KNOW!!
POUT
?!

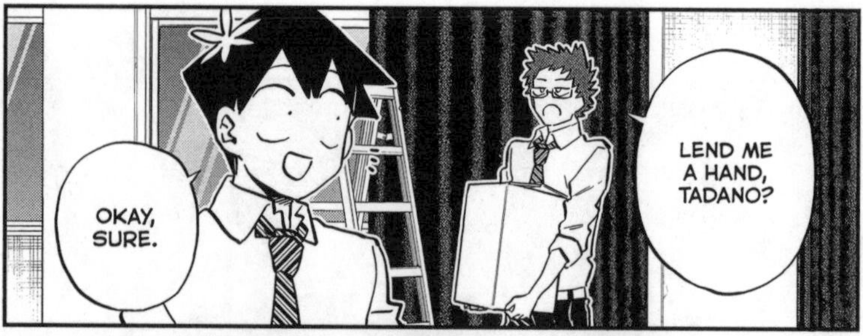
LEND ME A HAND, TADANO?
OKAY, SURE.

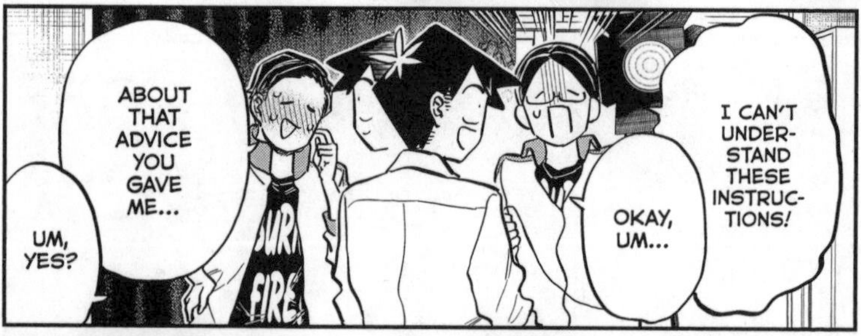
I CAN'T UNDER-STAND THESE INSTRUC-TIONS!
OKAY, UM...
ABOUT THAT ADVICE YOU GAVE ME...
UM, YES?

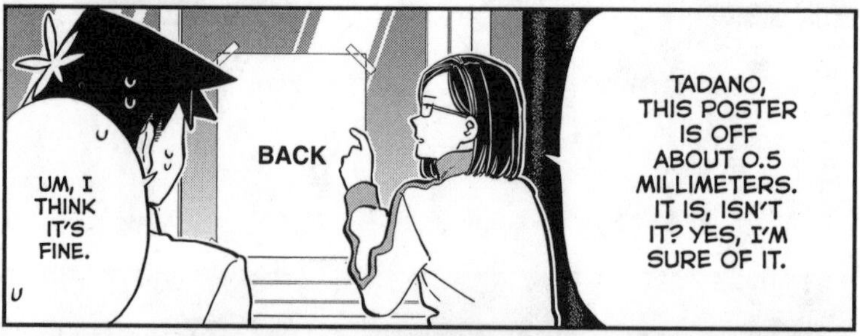
TADANO, THIS POSTER IS OFF ABOUT 0.5 MILLIMETERS. IT IS, ISN'T IT? YES, I'M SURE OF IT.
BACK
UM, I THINK IT'S FINE.

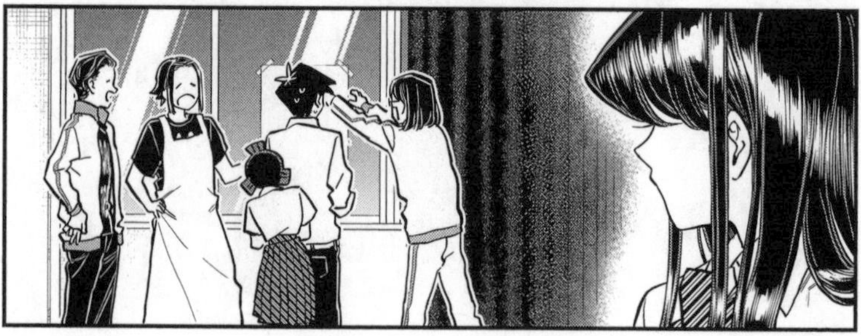

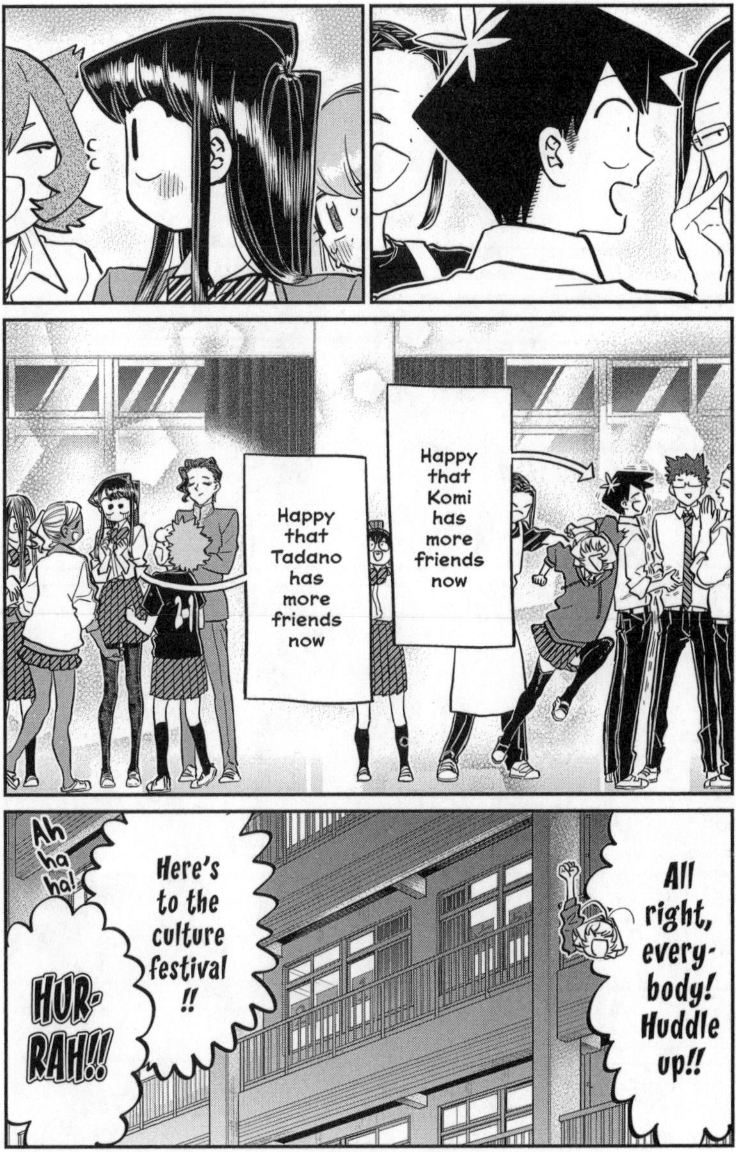
Happy that Komi has more friends now
Happy that Tadano has more friends now
All right, every-body! Huddle up!!
Here's to the culture festival!!
Ah ha ha!
HUR-RAH!!

Communication 238 — The End

Komi Can't Communicate

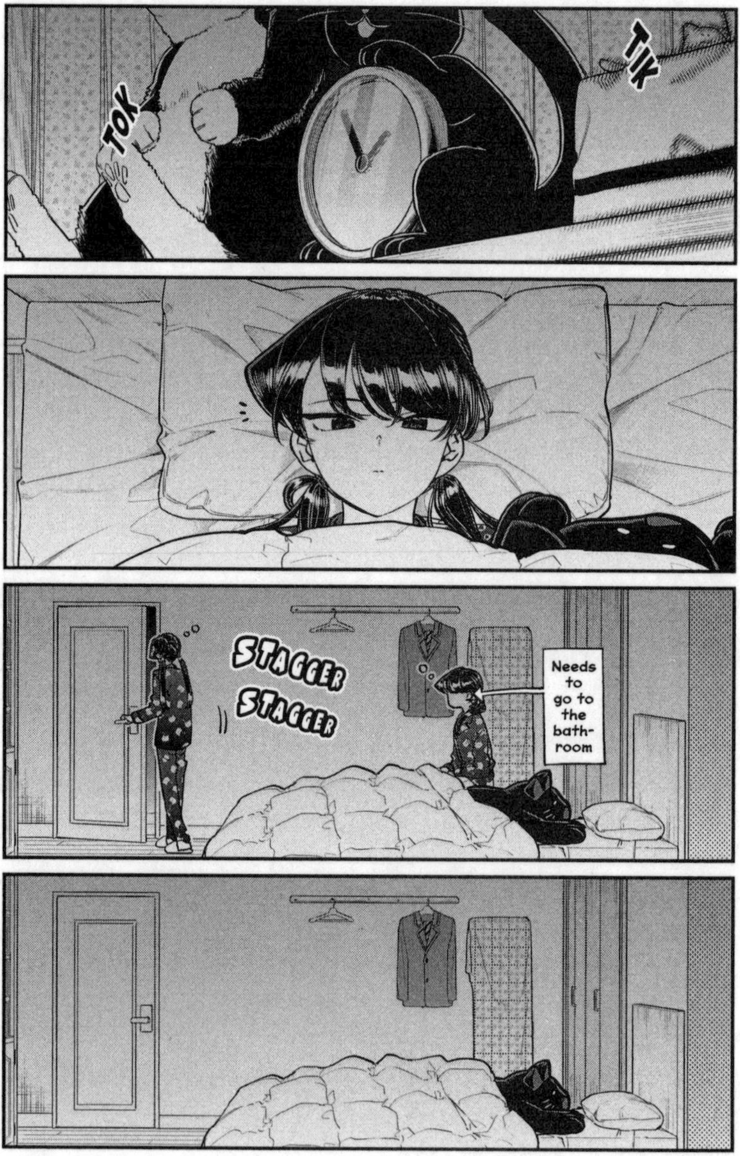
TIK
TOK
Needs to go to the bathroom
STAGGER STAGGER

Communication 239: Rice Balls and Miso Soup

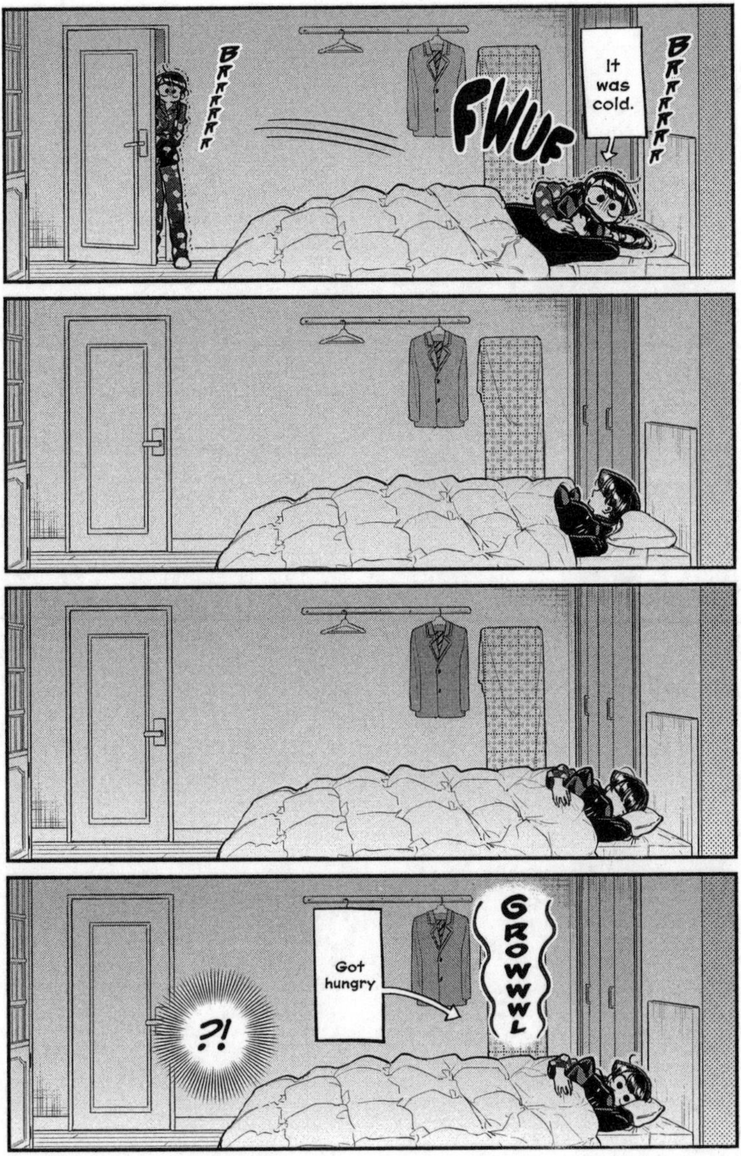
BRRRRRR
It was cold.
FWUF
BRRRRRR
GROWWWL
Got hungry
?!

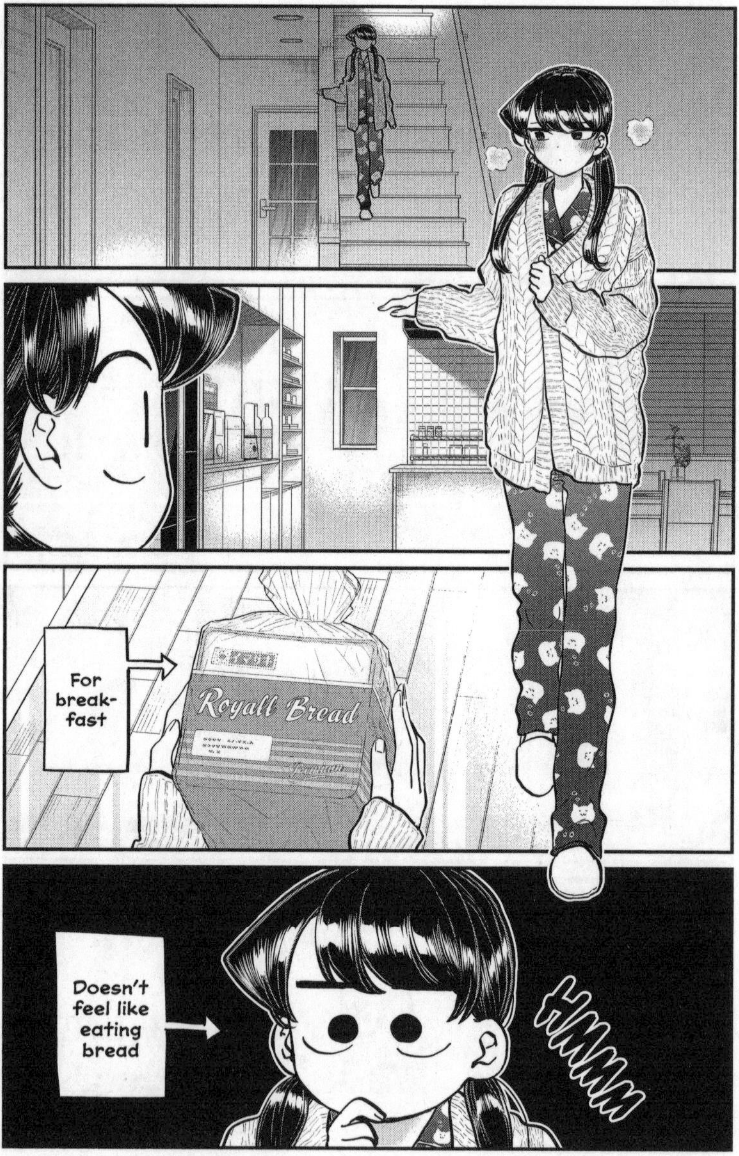
For break-
fast
Royall Bread
Doesn't feel like eating bread
HMMMM

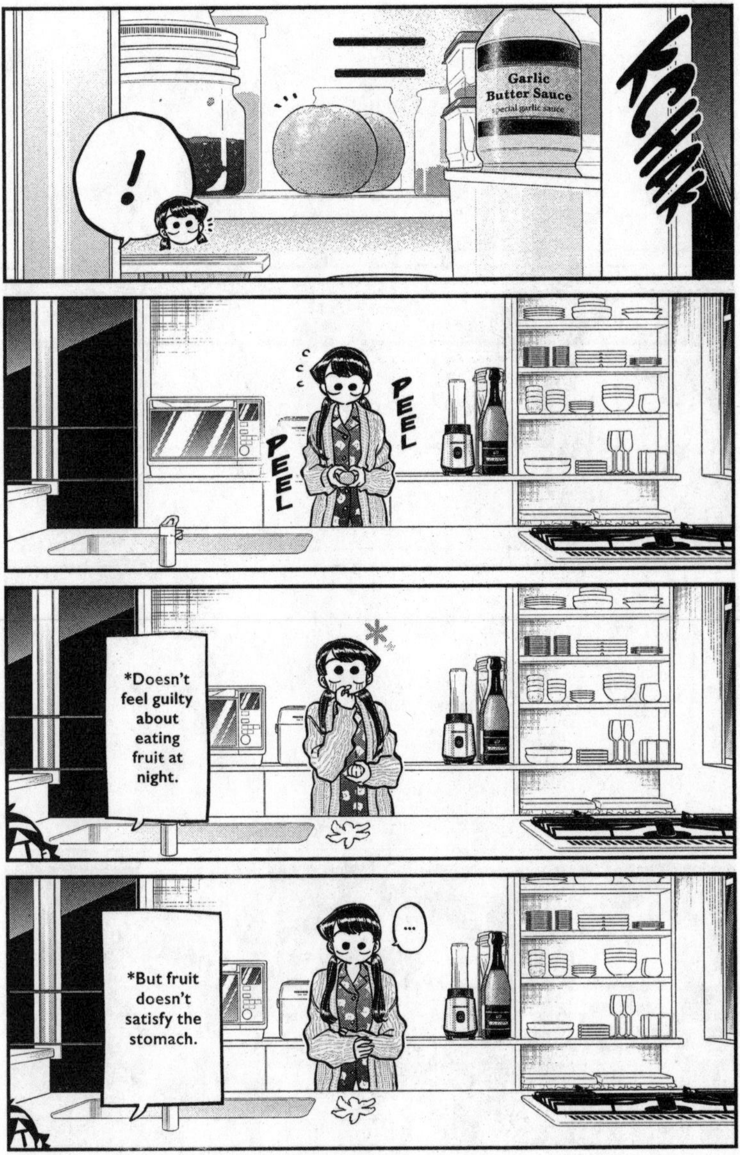
KCHAK
Garlic
Butter Sauce
special garlic sauce
!
PEEL
PEEL
*Doesn't feel guilty about eating fruit at night.
...
*But fruit doesn't satisfy the stomach.

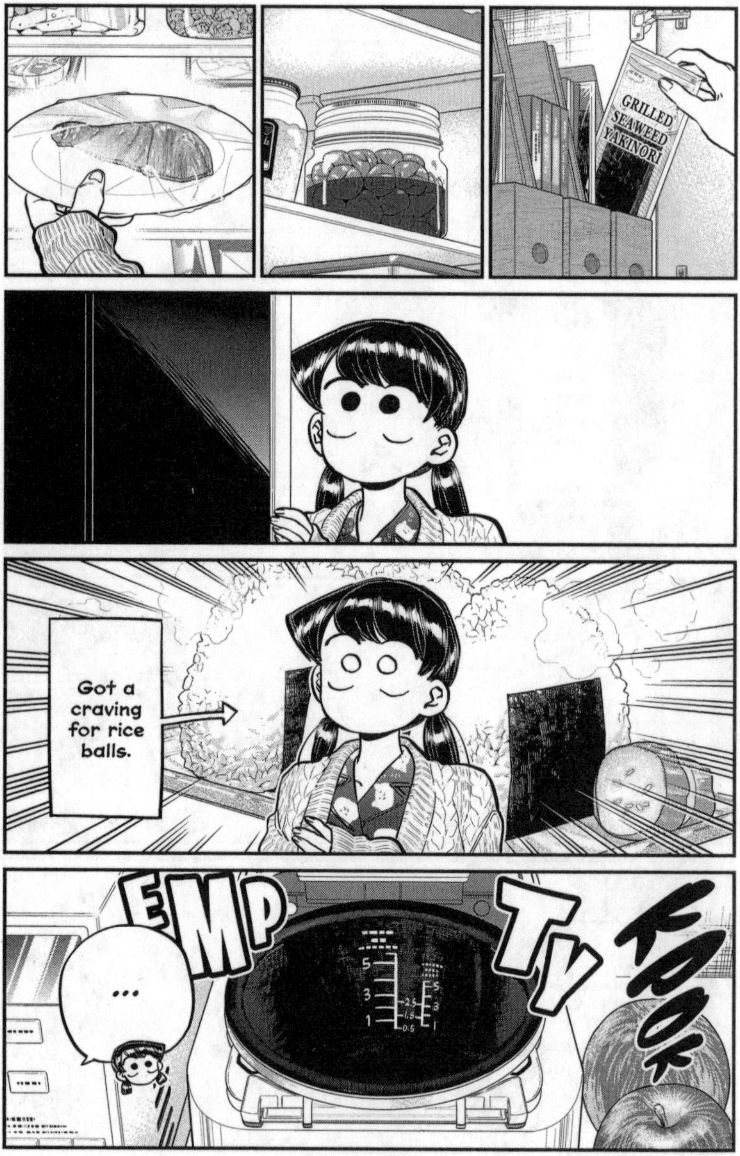
GRILLED SEAWEED YAKINORI
Got a craving for rice balls.
KPOK
EMPTY
...

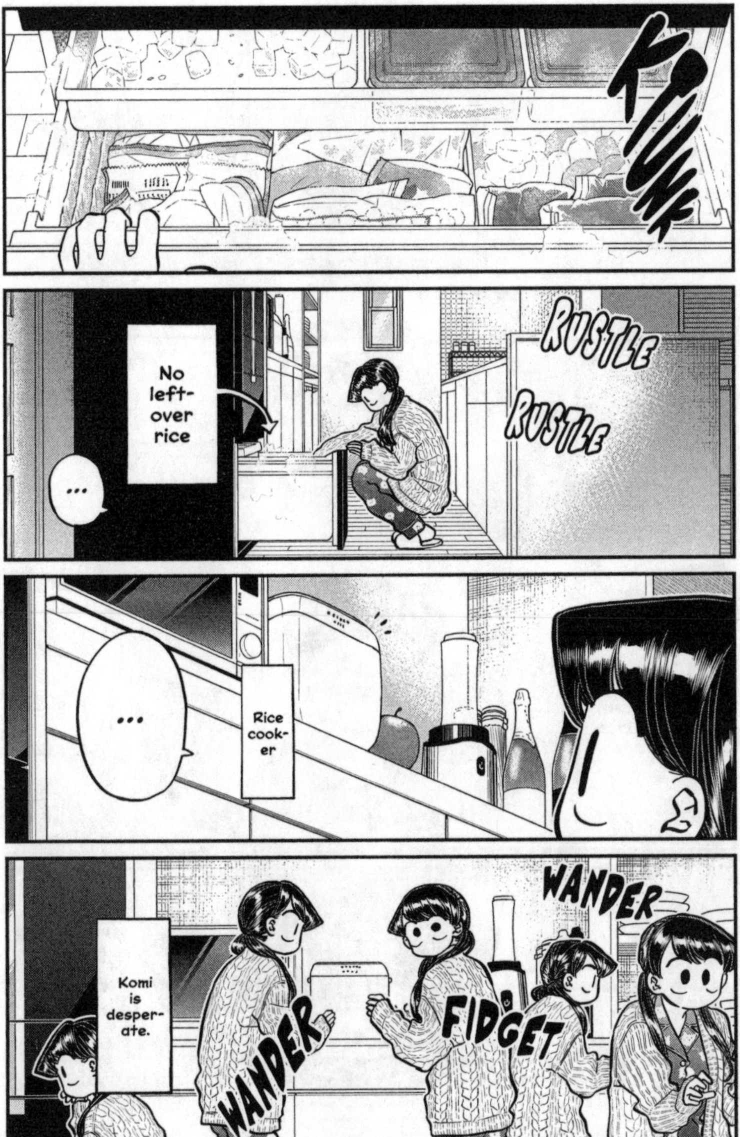
KPUNK
RUSTLE
RUSTLE
No leftover rice
...
Rice cooker
...
WANDER
FIDGET
WANDER
Komi is desperate.

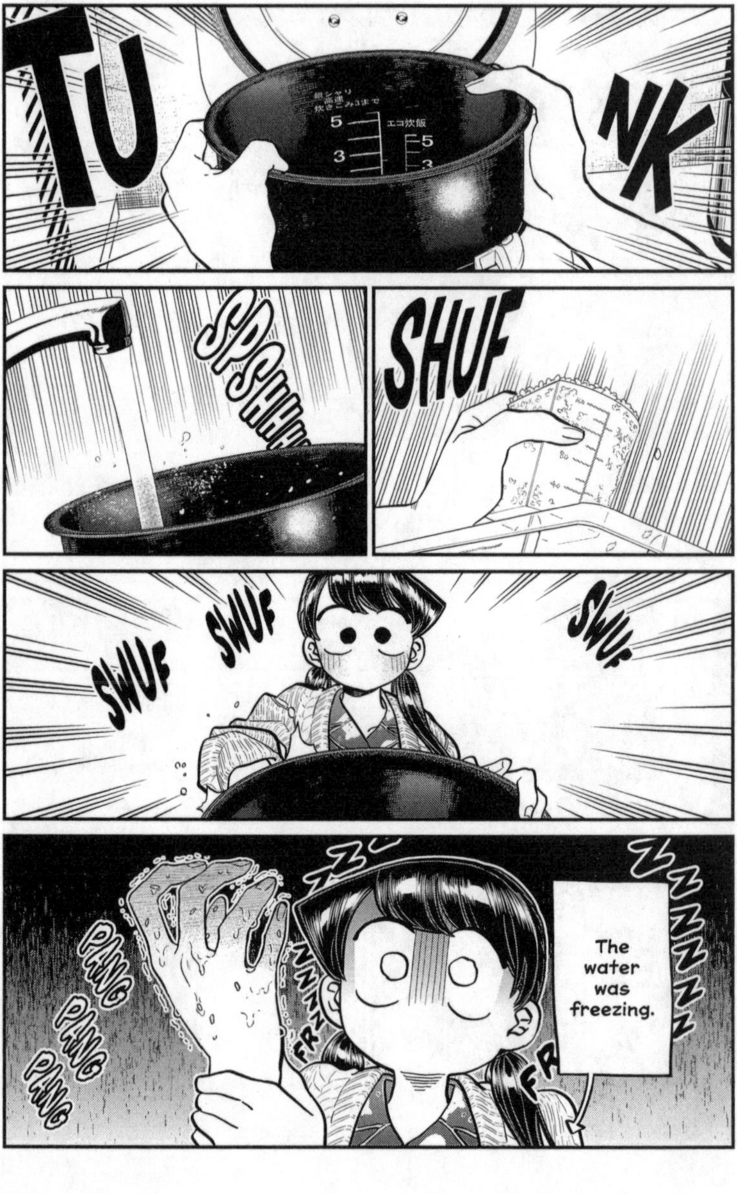
TU
NK
SHUF
SPSHHHH
SWUF
SWUF
SWUF
The water was freezing.
FR
FR
PANG
PANG
PANG

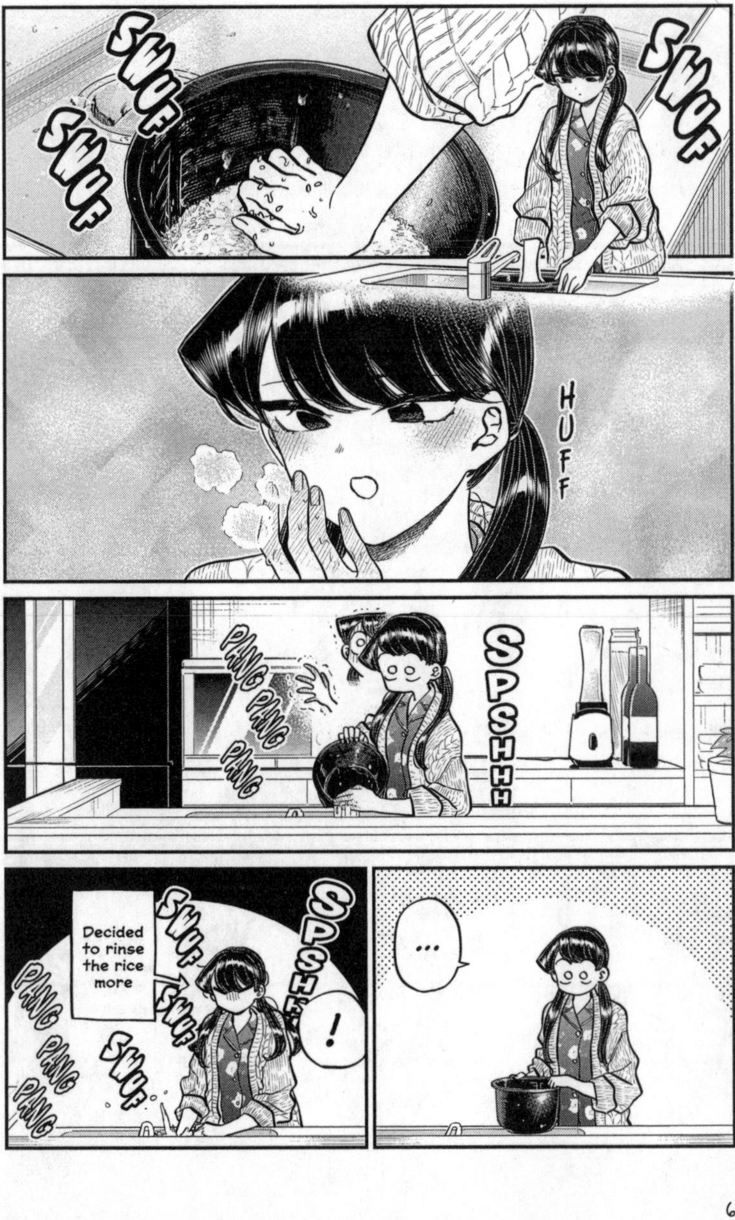
SWUF
SWUF
SWUF
HUFF
SPSHHH
PANG PANG PANG PANG
...
SPSHH
SWUF
Decided to rinse the rice more
SWUF
SWUF
PANG PANG PANG PANG
!

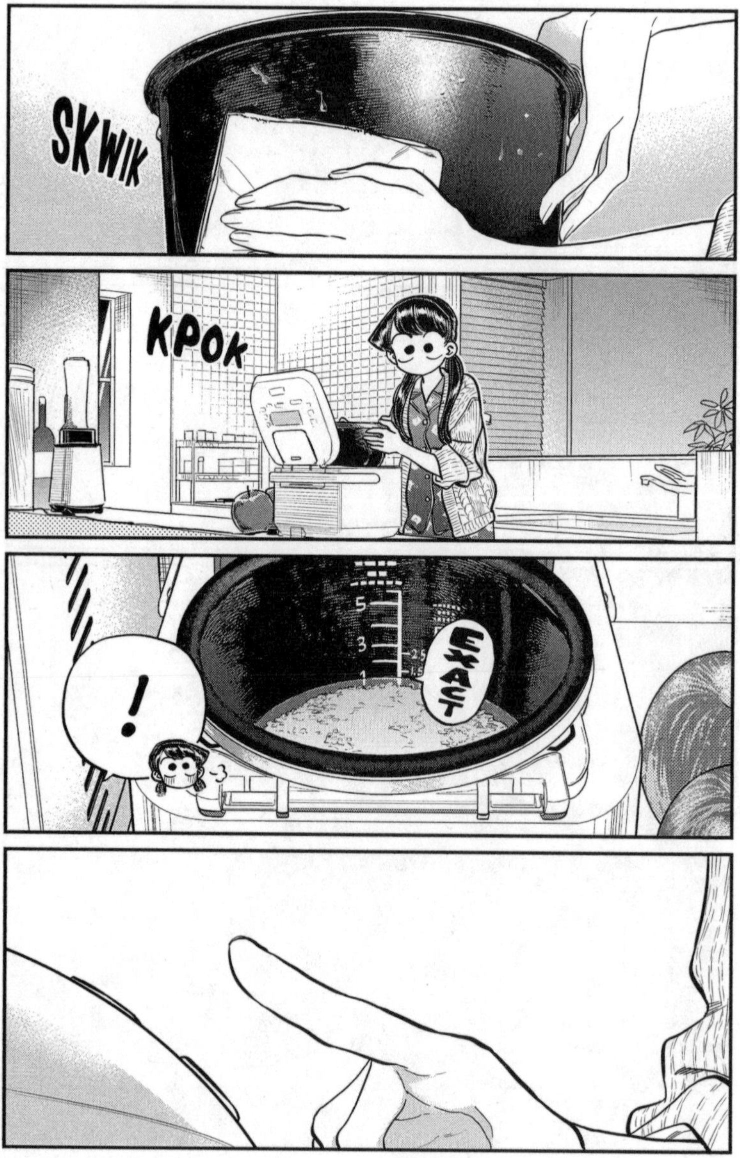
SKWIK
KPOK
EXACT
!

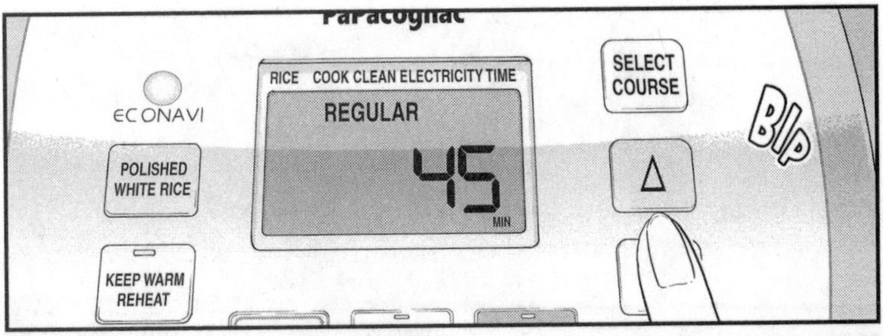
RICE COOK CLEAN ELECTRICITY TIME
REGULAR
45
MIN
SELECT COURSE
ECONAVI
POLISHED WHITE RICE
KEEP WARM REHEAT
Blip

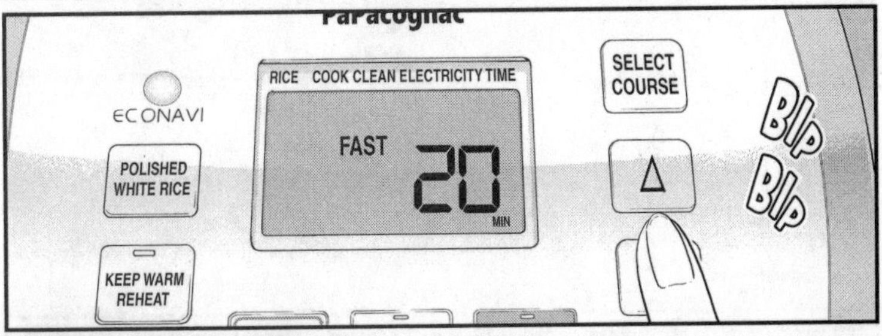
RICE COOK CLEAN ELECTRICITY TIME
FAST
20
MIN
SELECT COURSE
ECONAVI
POLISHED WHITE RICE
KEEP WARM REHEAT
Blip
Blip

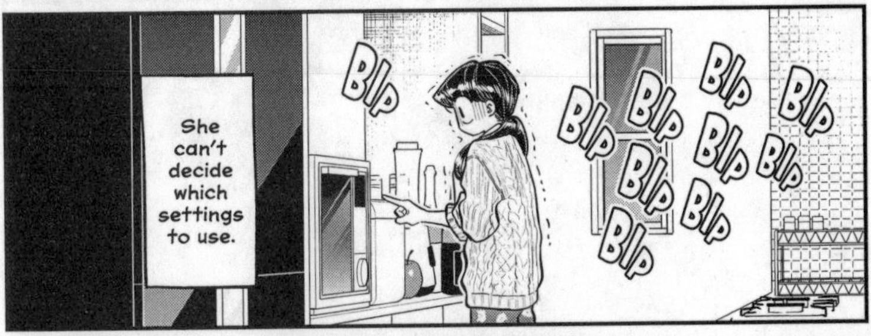
Blip Blip Blip Blip Blip Blip Blip Blip Blip Blip
Blip
She can't decide which settings to use.

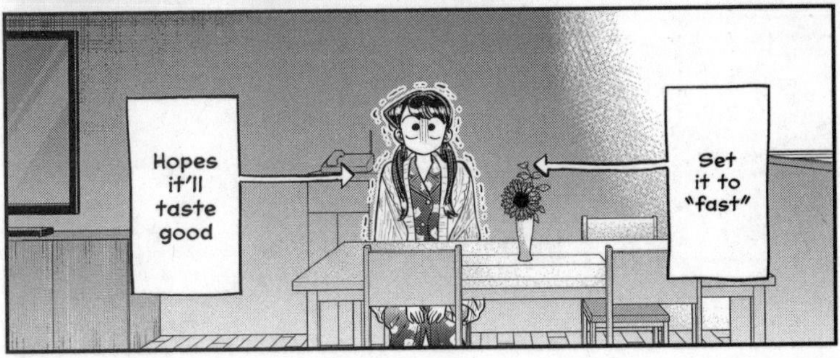
Set it to "fast"
Hopes it'll taste good

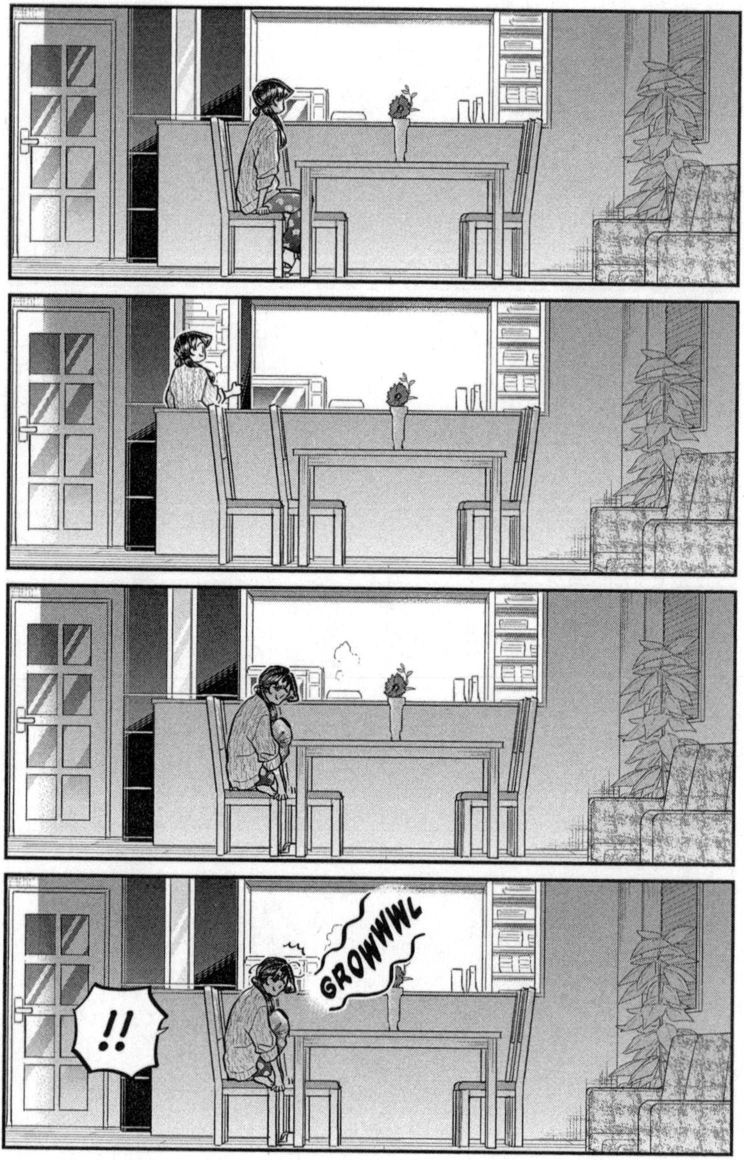
GROWWWL
!!

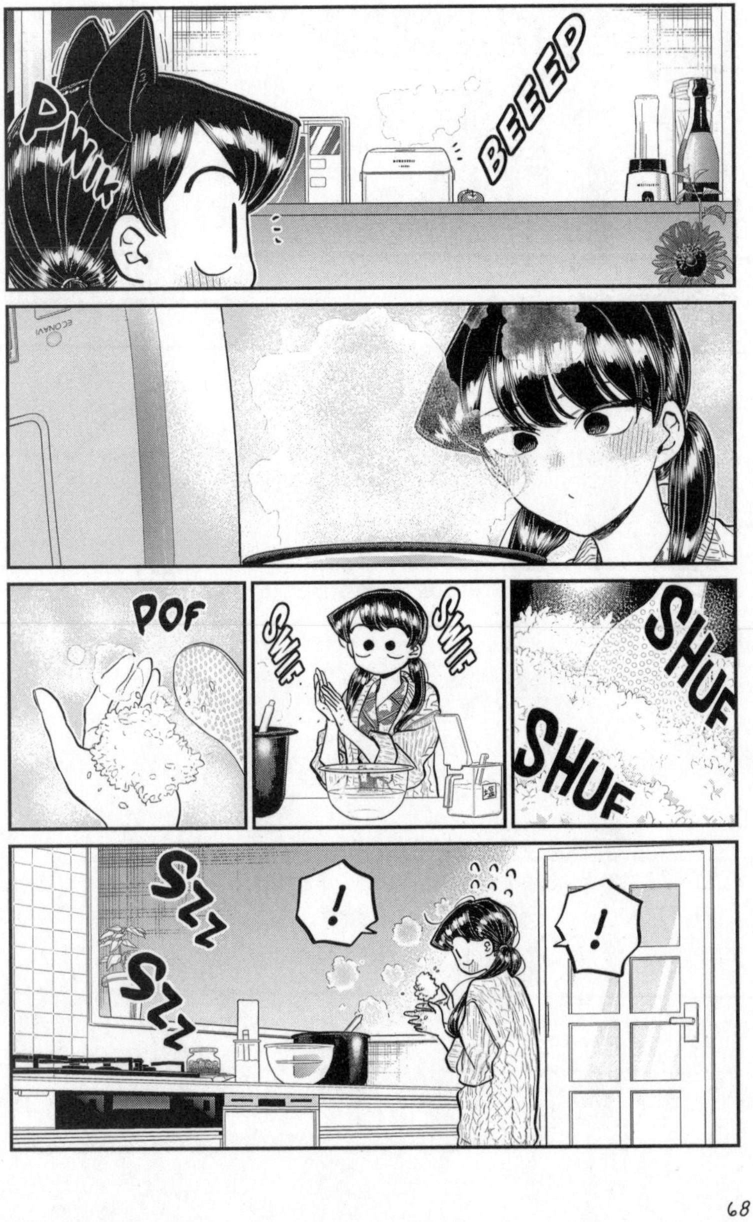
BEEEP
PWIK
SHUF
SHUF
SWIF
SWIF
POF
!
!
SZZ
SZZ

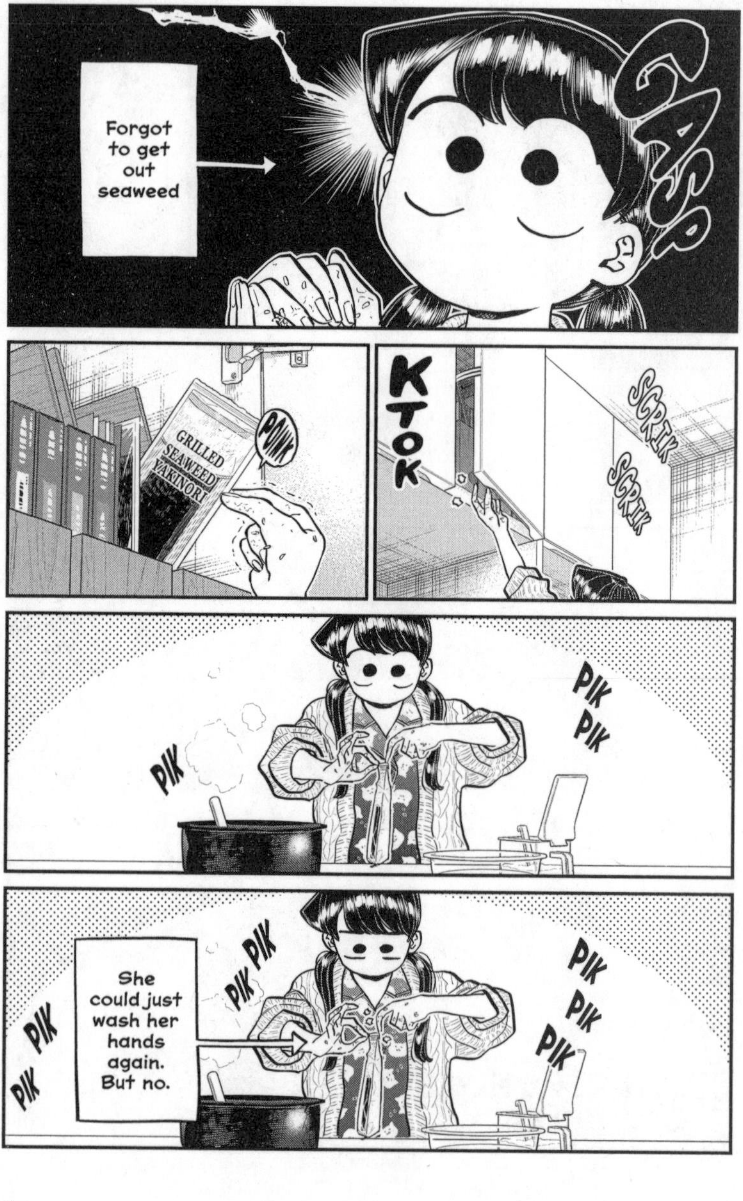
GASP
Forgot to get out seaweed
KTOK
SCRIK
SCRIK
POINK
GRILLED SEAWEED YAKINORI
PIK PIK
PIK
PIK PIK PIK
PIK PIK
PIK PIK
She could just wash her hands again. But no.

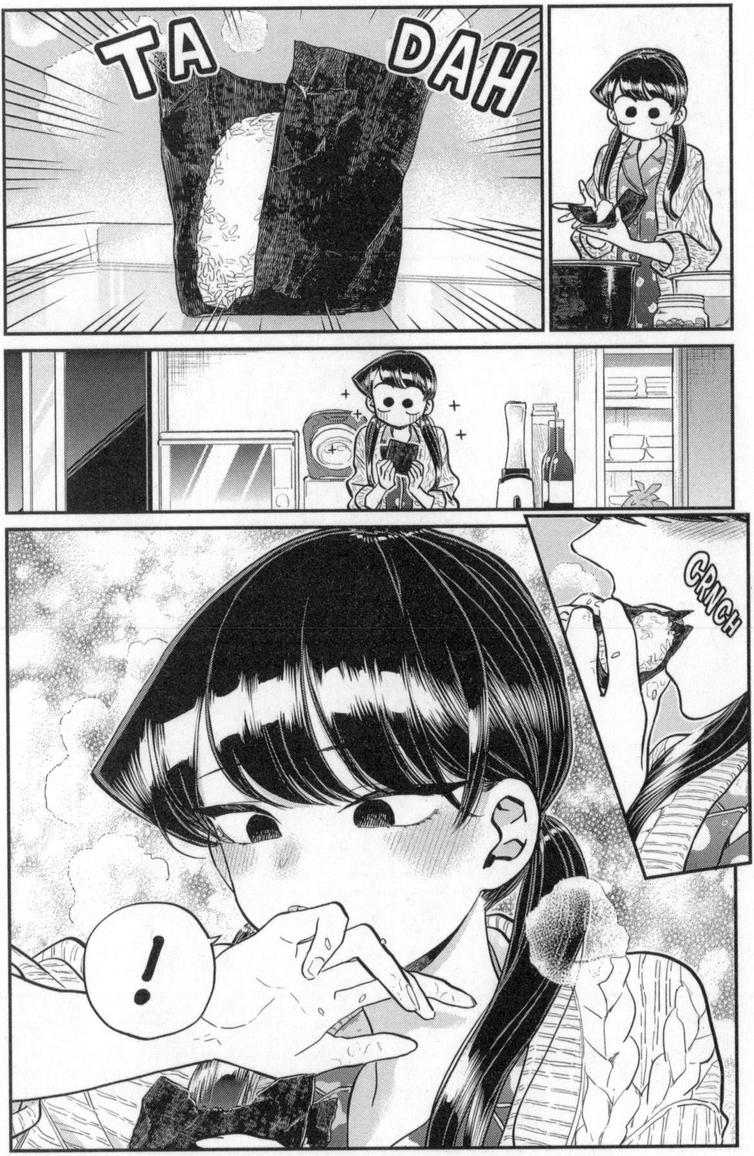
TA DAH
CRNCH
!

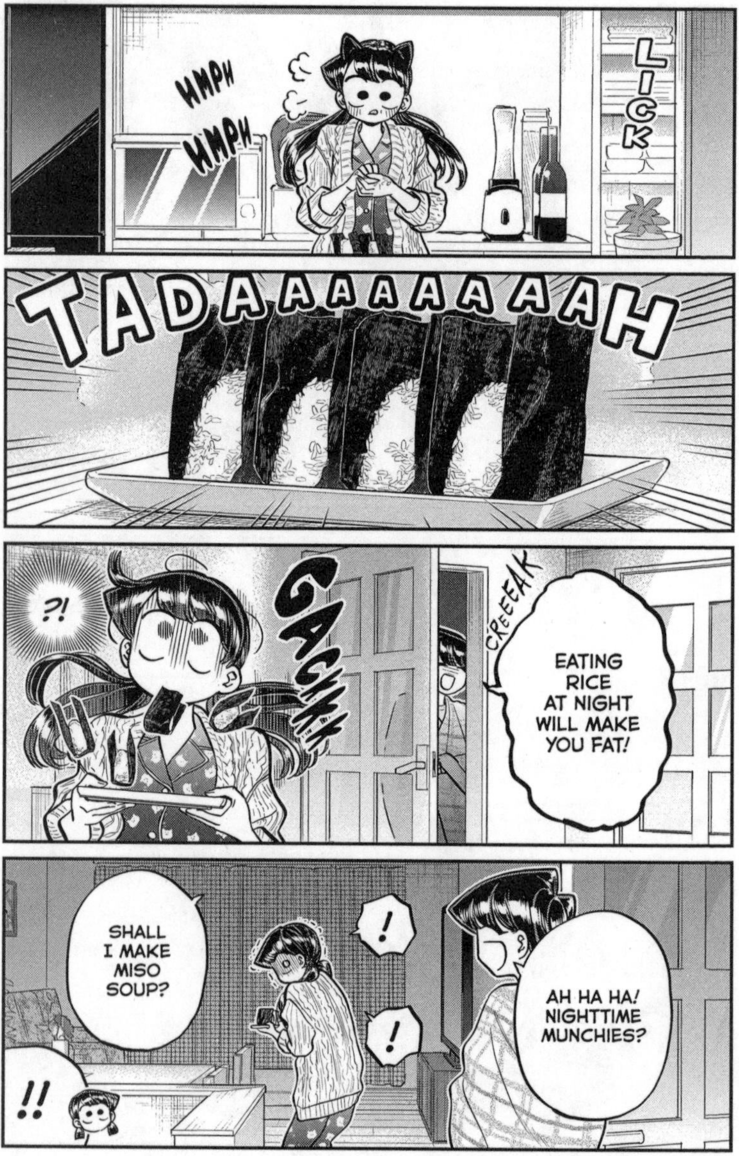
LICK
HMPH
HMPH
TADAAAAAAAAAH
CREEEAK
EATING RICE AT NIGHT WILL MAKE YOU FAT!
GACKKK
?!
AH HA HA! NIGHTTIME MUNCHIES?
!
!
SHALL I MAKE MISO SOUP?
!!

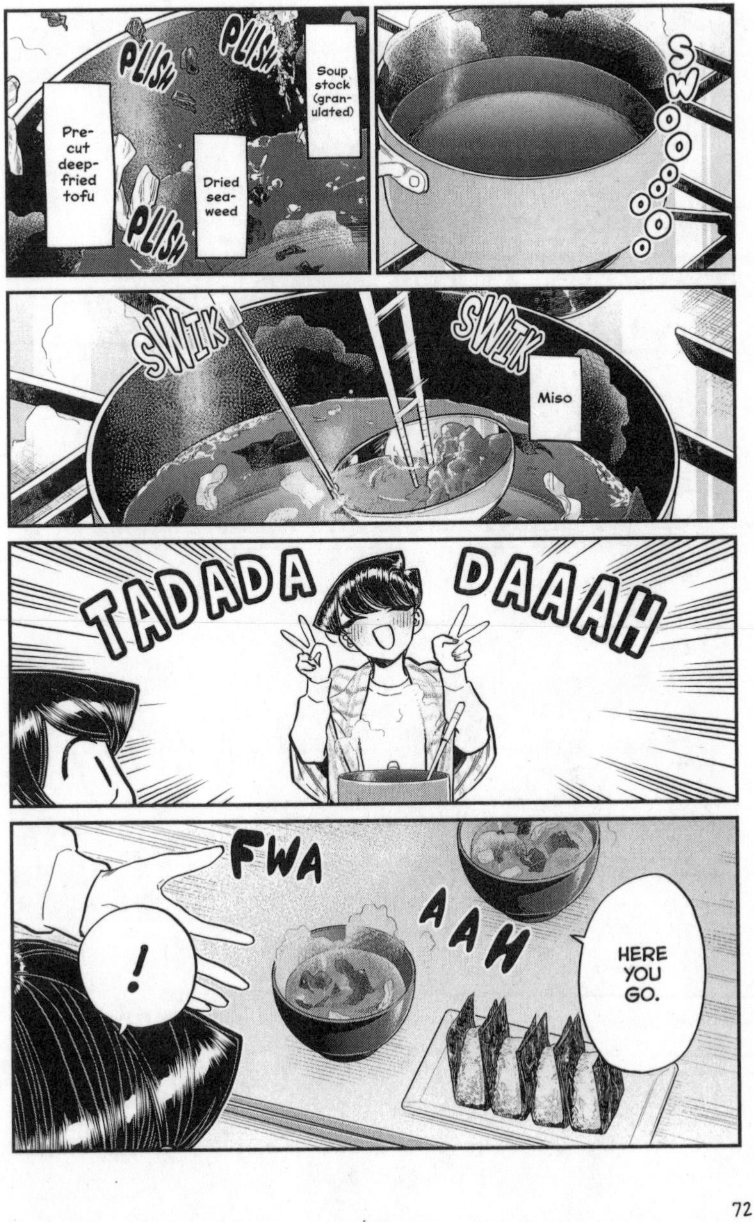
SWOOOOOOO
Soup stock (granulated)
PLISH
Dried seaweed
PLISH
Precut deep-fried tofu
PLISH
SWIK
Miso
SWIK
DAAAAH
TADADA
HERE YOU GO.
FWA
AAH
!

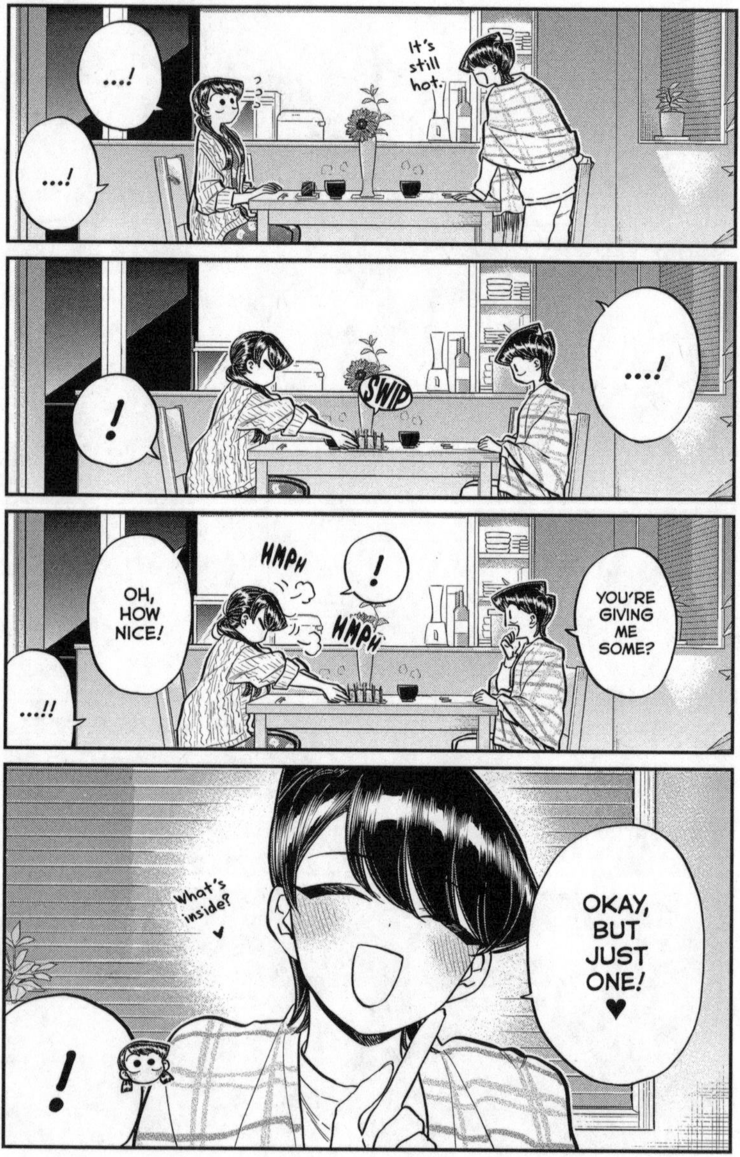
It's still hot.
...!
...!
...!
SWIP
!
YOU'RE GIVING ME SOME?
!
HMPH
HMPH
OH, HOW NICE!
...!!
OKAY, BUT JUST ONE! ♥
What's inside? ♥
!

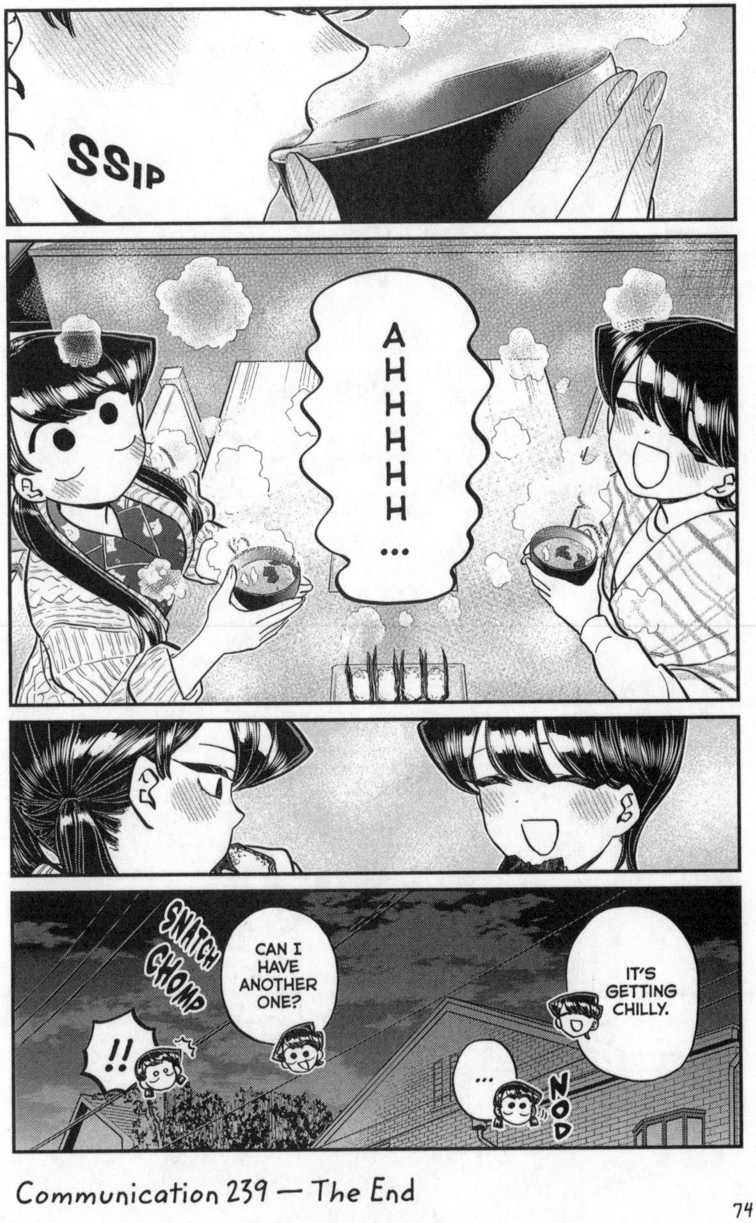
SSIP
AHHHHH...
IT'S GETTING CHILLY.
...
NOD
CAN I HAVE ANOTHER ONE?
SNATCH
CHOMP
!!

Communication 239 — The End

Komi Can't Communicate

OH! HI, KO–
UM... SHOKO! GOOD MORNING!
!
...
...
...
G...
!

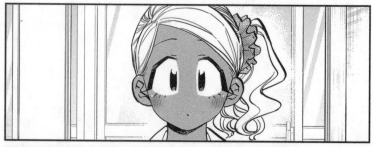

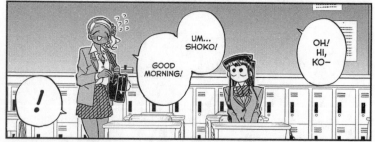

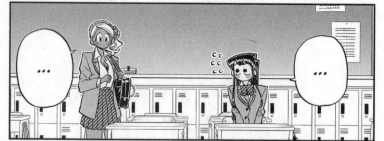

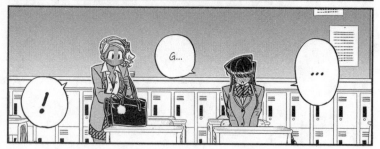

Communication 240: Technique

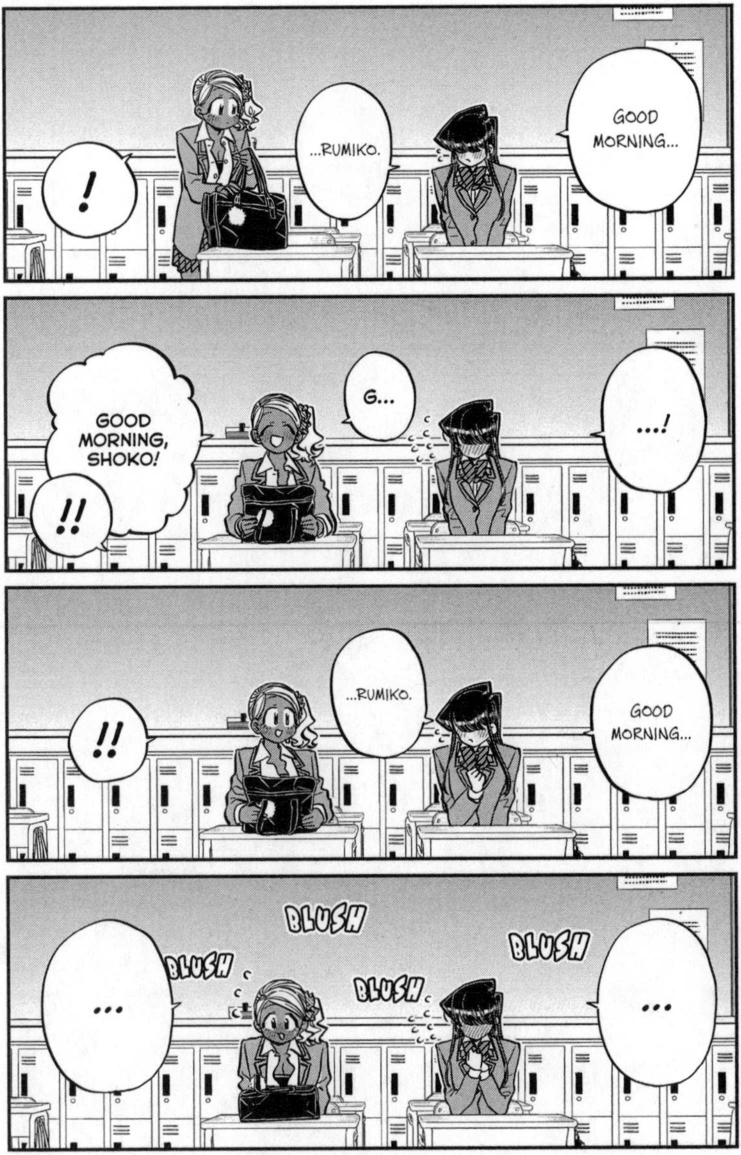
GOOD MORNING...
...RUMIKO.
!
...!
G...
GOOD MORNING, SHOKO!
!!
GOOD MORNING...
...RUMIKO.
!!
...
BLUSH
BLUSH
BLUSH
BLUSH
...

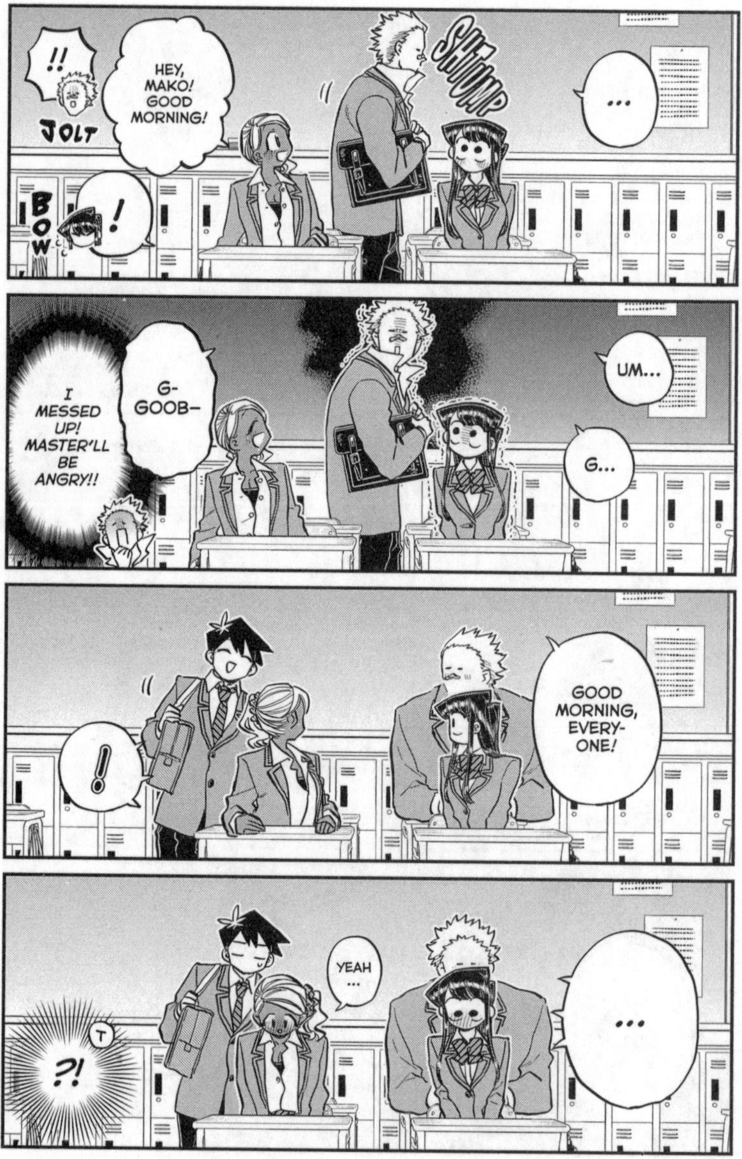
...
SHTOMP
HEY, MAKO! GOOD MORNING!
!!
JOLT
!
BOW
UM...
G...
G- GOOB-
I MESSED UP! MASTER'LL BE ANGRY!!
GOOD MORNING, EVERY-ONE!
!
...
YEAH ...
T
?!

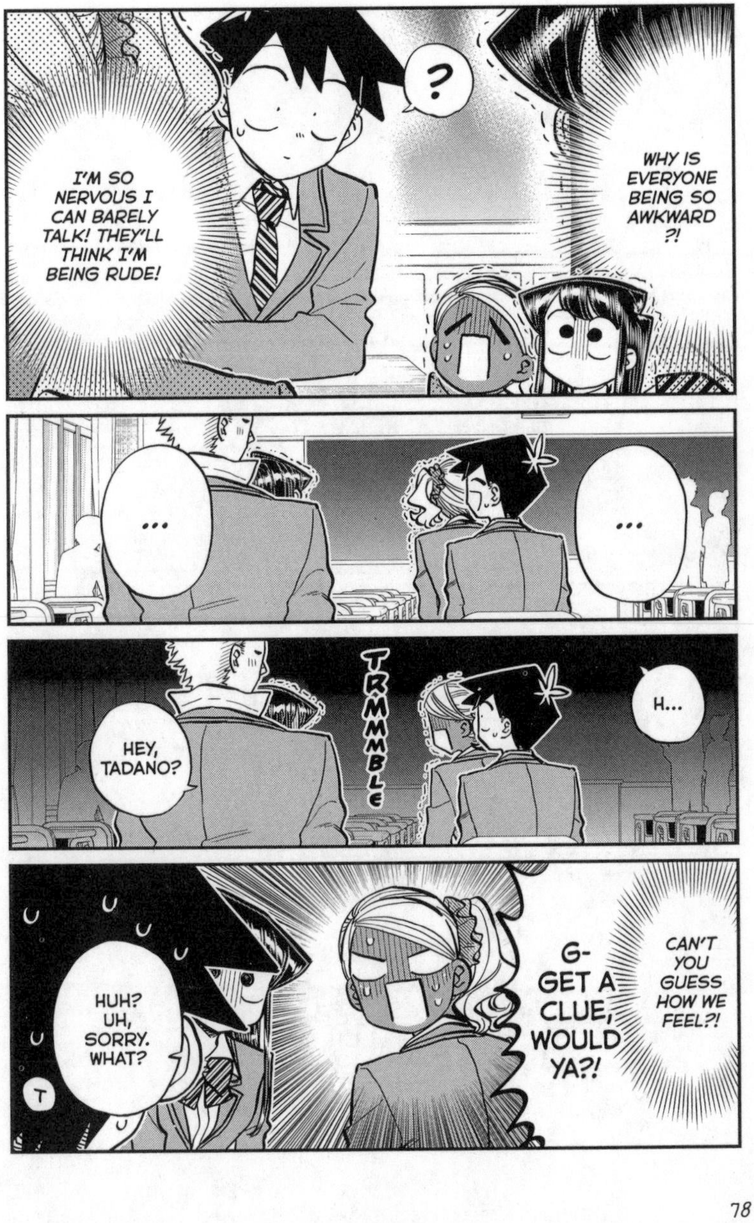
?
WHY IS EVERYONE BEING SO AWKWARD ?!
I'M SO NERVOUS I CAN BARELY TALK! THEY'LL THINK I'M BEING RUDE!
...
...
H...
TRMMMBLE
HEY, TADANO?
CAN'T YOU GUESS HOW WE FEEL?!
G-GET A CLUE, WOULD YA?!
HUH? UH, SORRY. WHAT?
T

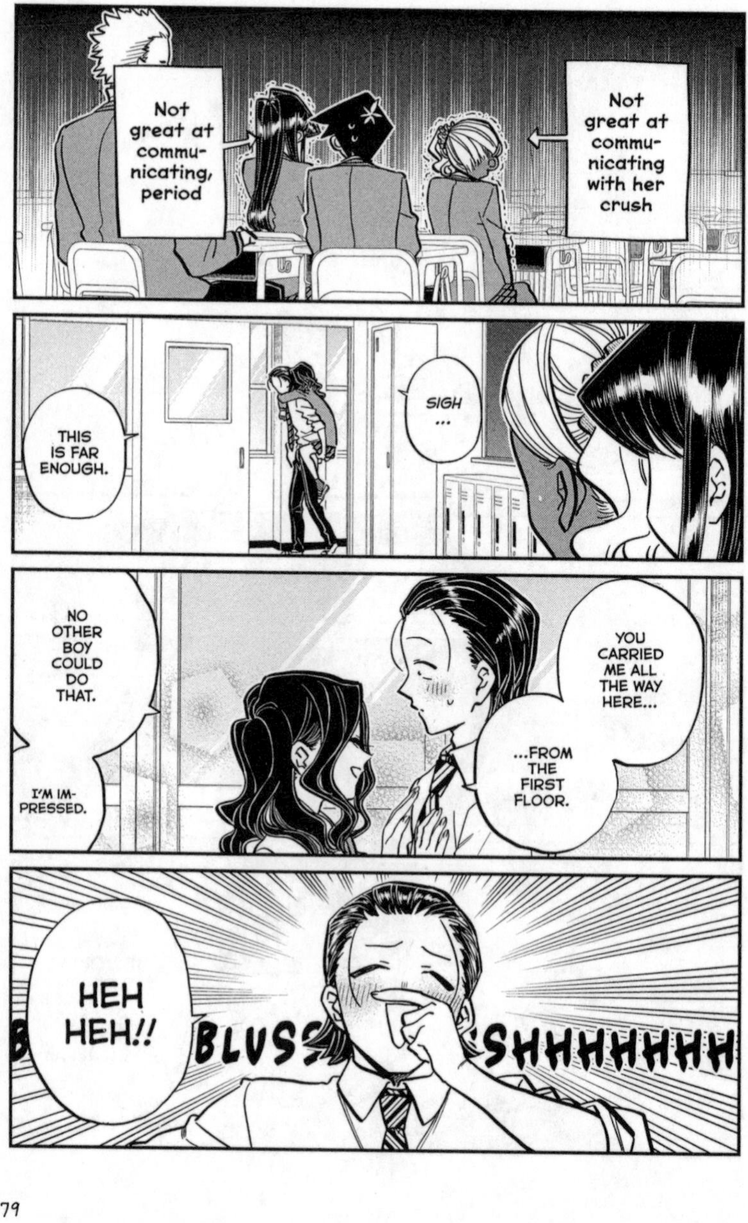
Not great at communicating with her crush
Not great at communicating, period
SIGH...
THIS IS FAR ENOUGH.
YOU CARRIED ME ALL THE WAY HERE...
...FROM THE FIRST FLOOR.
NO OTHER BOY COULD DO THAT.
I'M IMPRESSED.
HEH HEH!!
BLUSS
SHHHHHHH

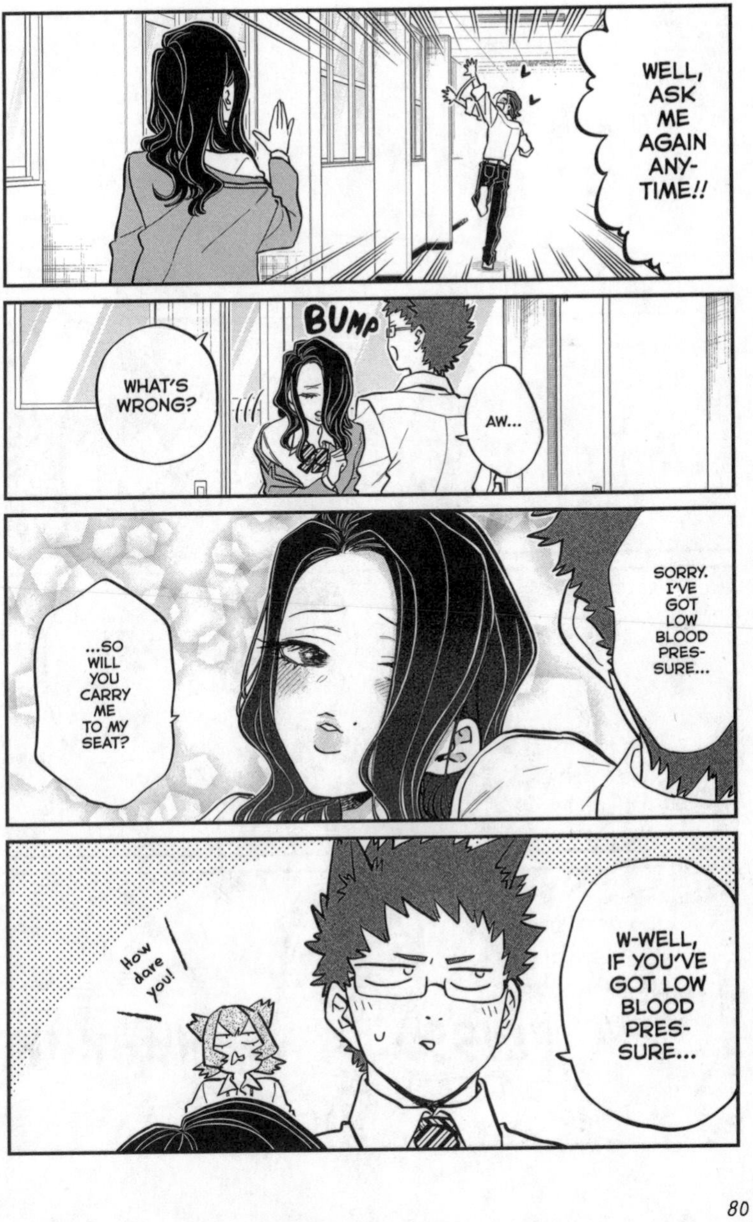

WELL, ASK ME AGAIN ANY-TIME!!
BUMP
AW...
WHAT'S WRONG?
SORRY. I'VE GOT LOW BLOOD PRES-SURE...
...SO WILL YOU CARRY ME TO MY SEAT?
W-WELL, IF YOU'VE GOT LOW BLOOD PRES-SURE...
How dare you!

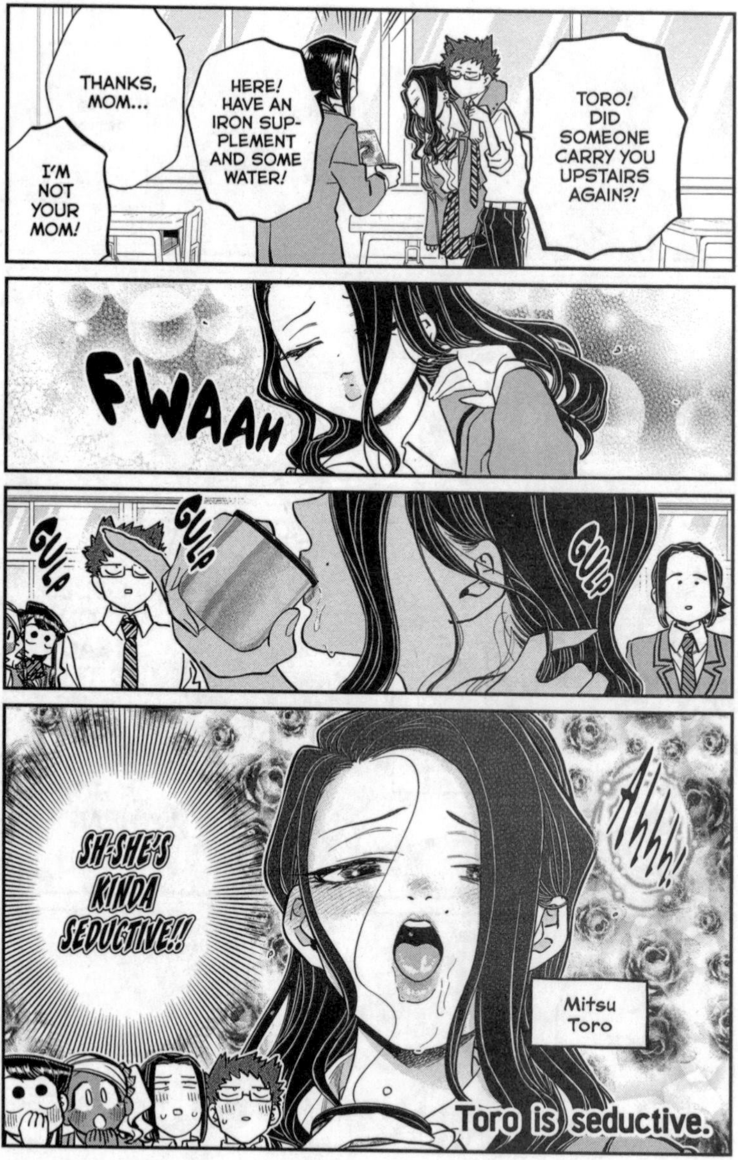
TORO! DID SOMEONE CARRY YOU UPSTAIRS AGAIN?!
HERE! HAVE AN IRON SUPPLEMENT AND SOME WATER!
THANKS, MOM...
I'M NOT YOUR MOM!
FWAAH
GULP
GULP
GULP
Ahhh!
SH-SHE'S KINDA SEDUCTIVE!!
Mitsu Toro
Toro is seductive.

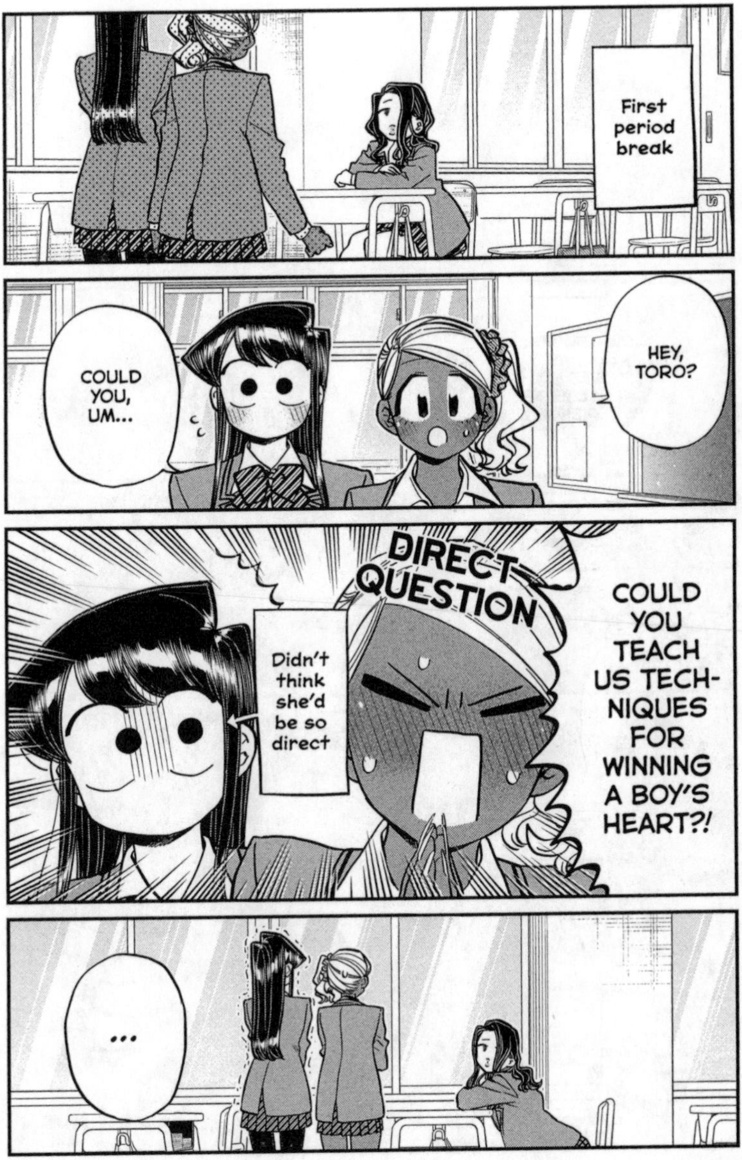
First period break
HEY, TORO?
COULD YOU, UM...
COULD YOU TEACH US TECH-NIQUES FOR WINNING A BOY'S HEART?!
DIRECT QUESTION
Didn't think she'd be so direct
...

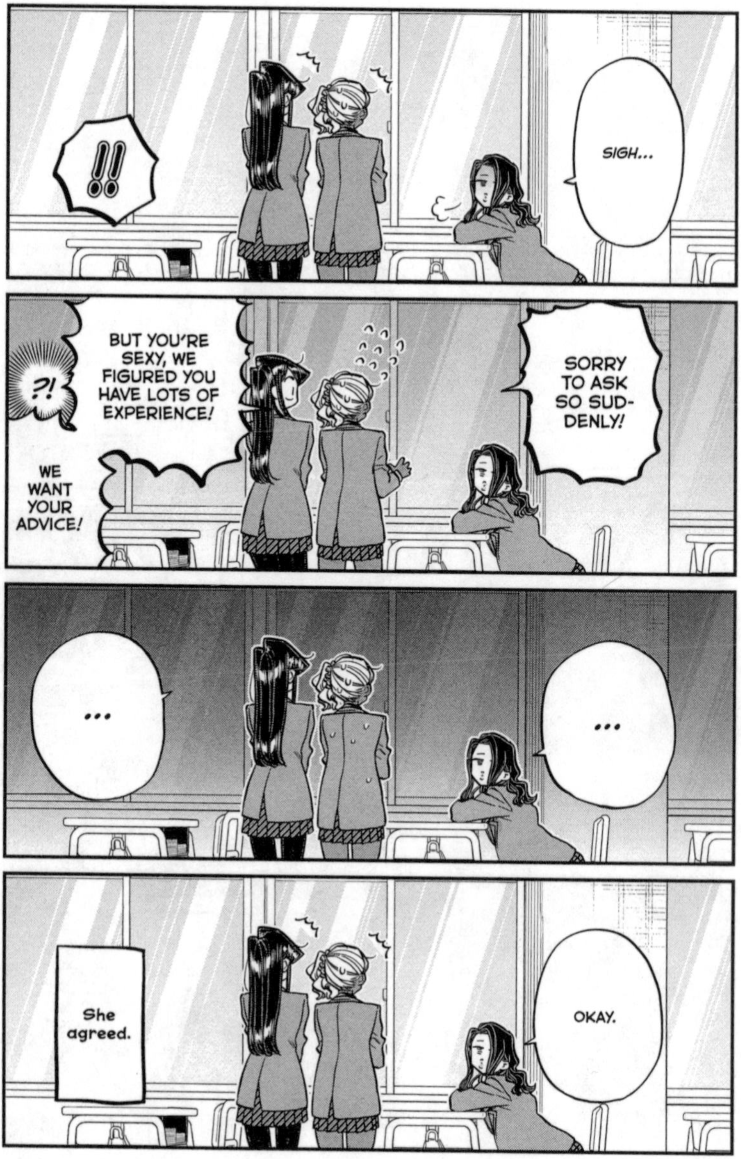
SIGH...
!!
SORRY TO ASK SO SUD-DENLY!
BUT YOU'RE SEXY, WE FIGURED YOU HAVE LOTS OF EXPERIENCE!
?!
WE WANT YOUR ADVICE!
...
...
OKAY.
She agreed.

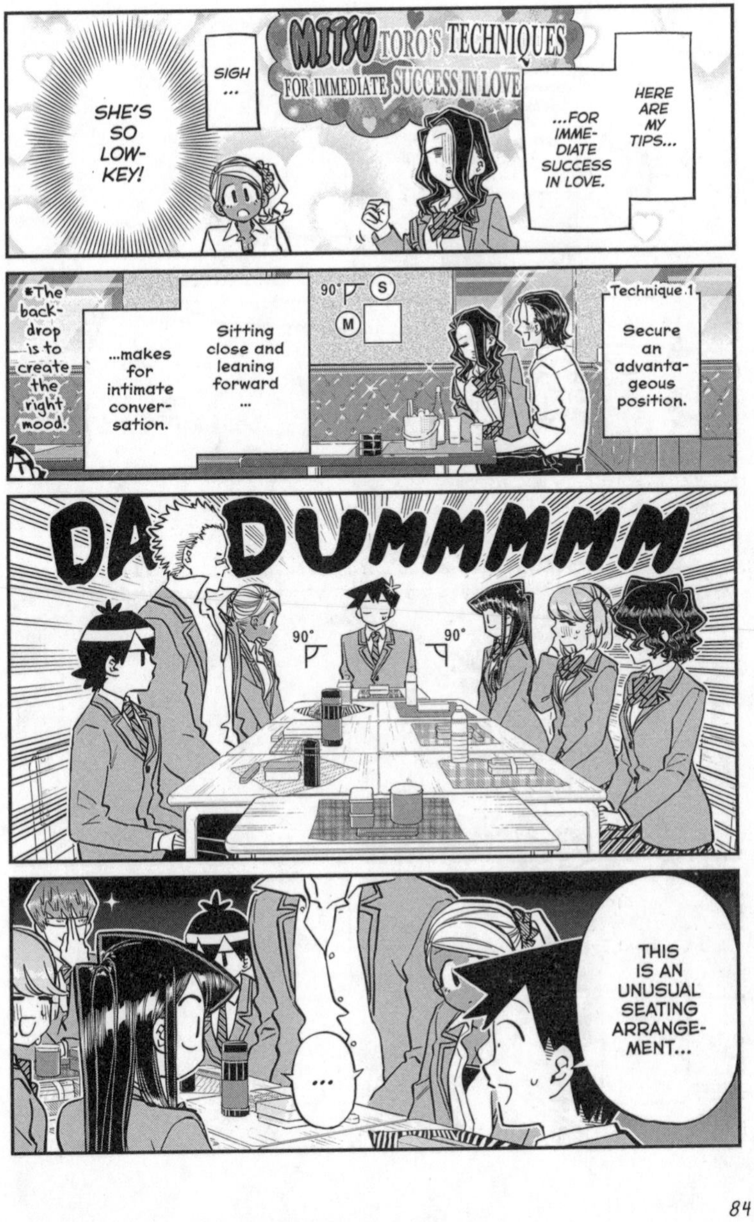
HERE ARE MY TIPS...
...FOR IMMEDIATE SUCCESS IN LOVE.
MITSUTORO'S TECHNIQUES FOR IMMEDIATE SUCCESS IN LOVE
SIGH ...
SHE'S SO LOW-KEY!
Technique 1
Secure an advantageous position.
90°
S
M
Sitting close and leaning forward ...
...makes for intimate conversation.
*The backdrop is to create the right mood.
DA DUMMMMM
90°
90°
THIS IS AN UNUSUAL SEATING ARRANGEMENT...
...

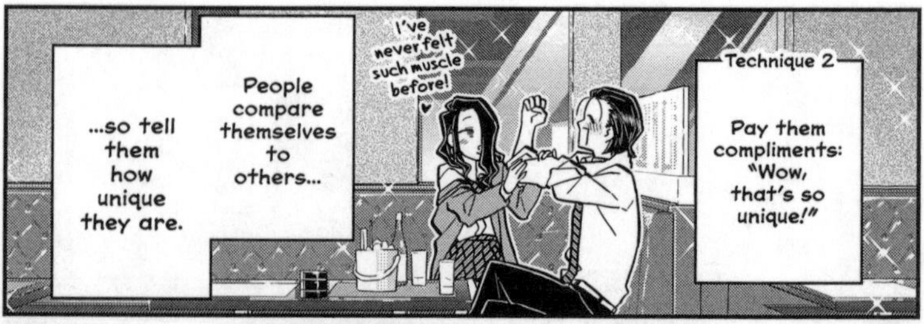
Technique 2
Pay them compliments: "Wow, that's so unique!"
I've never felt such muscle before!
People compare themselves to others...
...so tell them how unique they are.

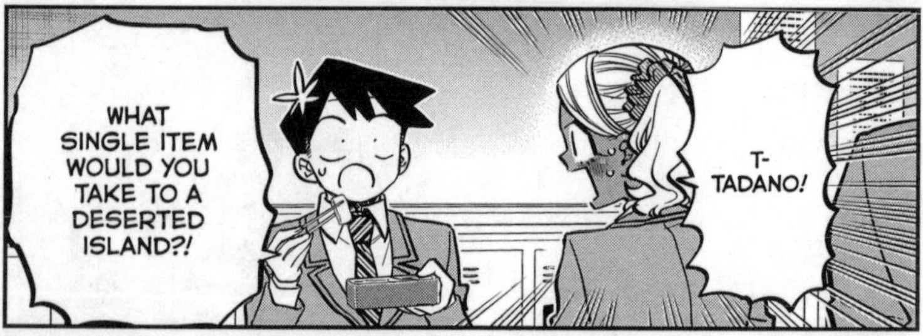
T- TADANO!
WHAT SINGLE ITEM WOULD YOU TAKE TO A DESERTED ISLAND?!

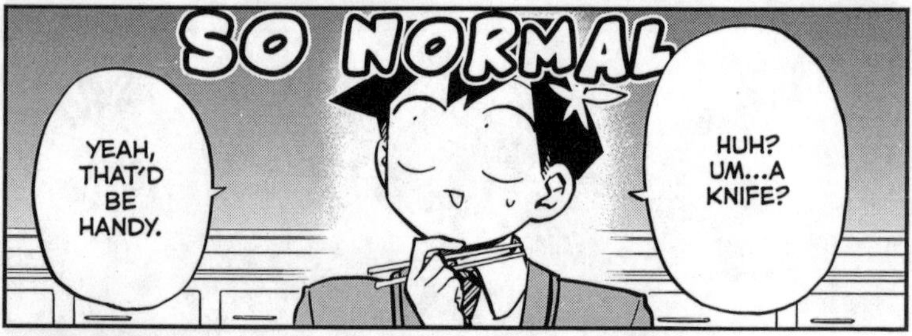
SO NORMAL
HUH? UM...A KNIFE?
YEAH, THAT'D BE HANDY.

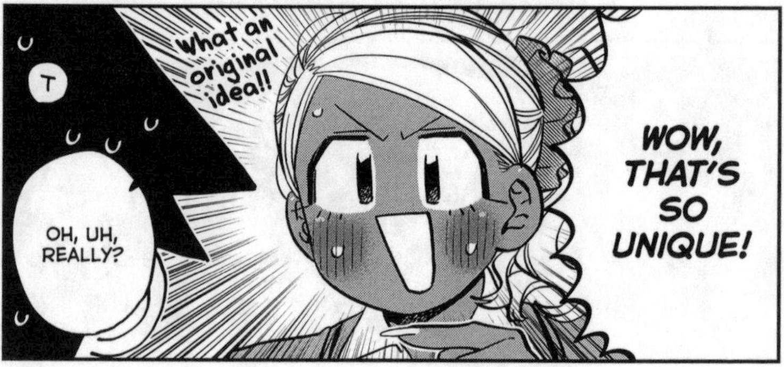
WOW, THAT'S SO UNIQUE!
what an original idea!!
T
OH, UH, REALLY?

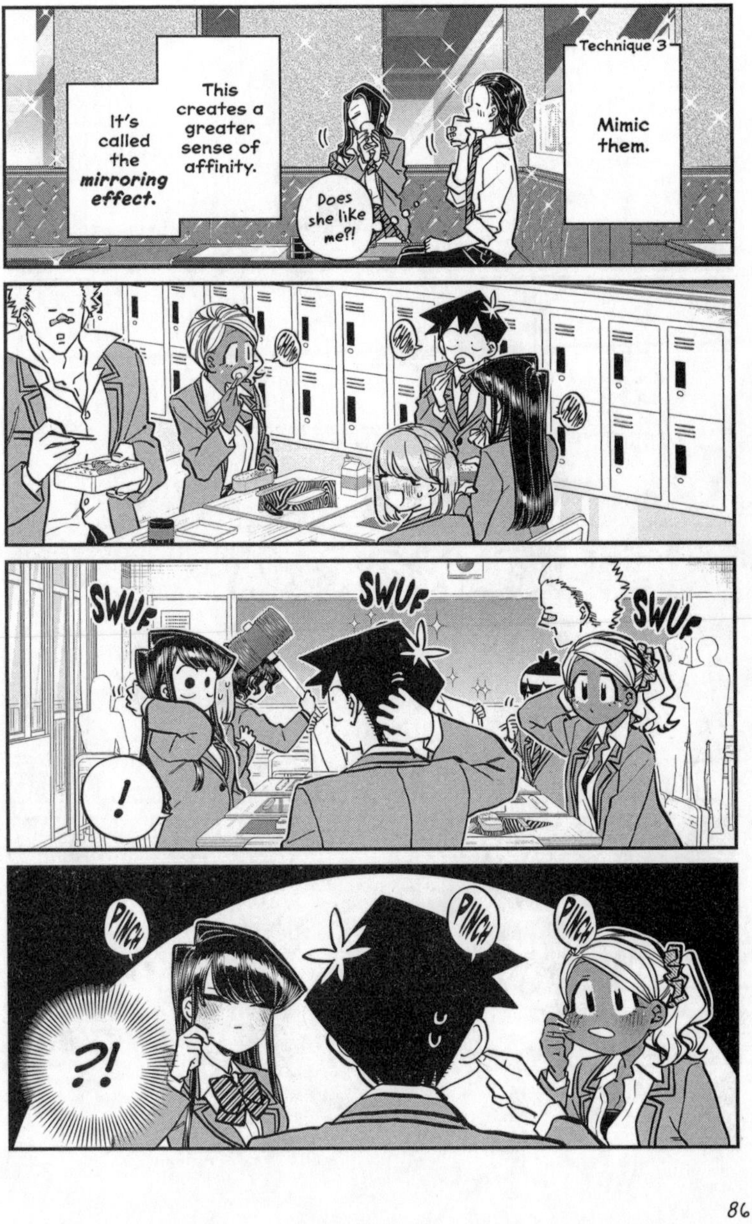
Technique 3
Mimic them.
This creates a greater sense of affinity.
It's called the *mirroring effect.*
Does she like me?!
CHOMP
CHOMP
CHOMP
SWUF
SWUF
SWUF
!
PINCH
PINCH
PINCH
?!

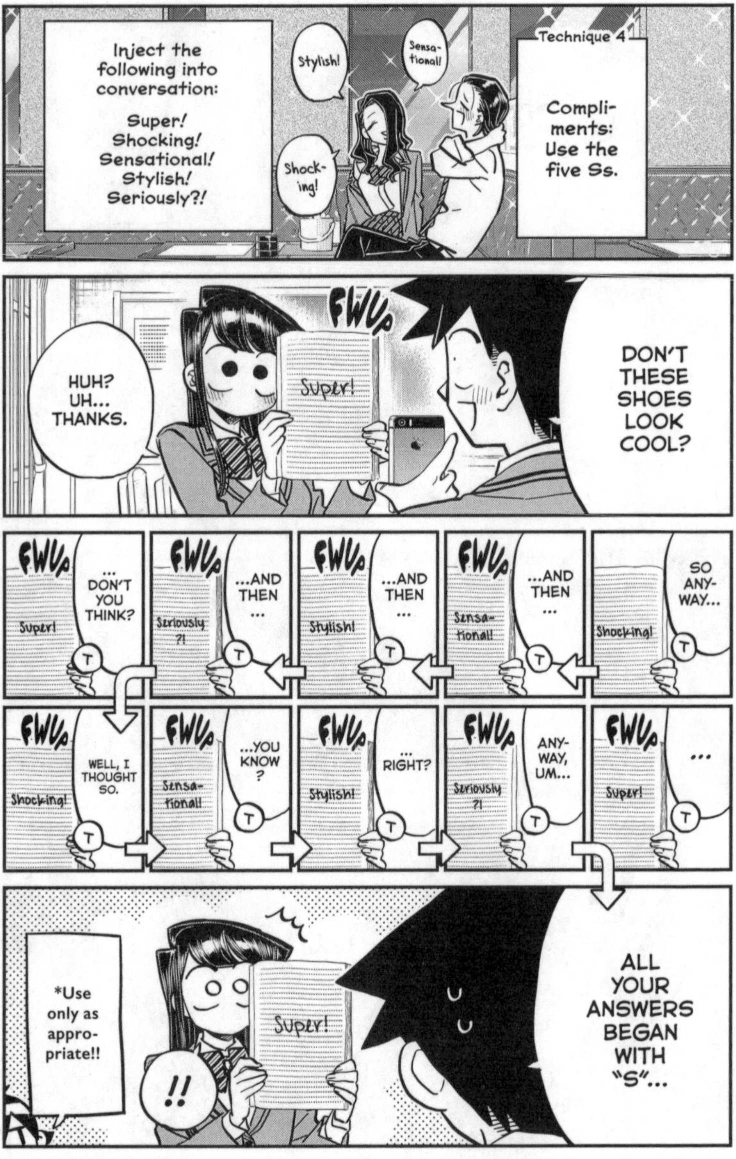
Technique 4
Compli-ments: Use the five Ss.
Sensa-tional!
Stylish!
Shock-ing!
Inject the following into conversation:
Super! Shocking! Sensational! Stylish! Seriously?!
FWUP
DON'T THESE SHOES LOOK COOL?
Super!
HUH? UH... THANKS.
FWUP
SO ANY-WAY...
Shocking!
FWUP
...AND THEN ...
Sensa-tional!
FWUP
...AND THEN ...
Stylish!
FWUP
...AND THEN ...
Seriously ?!
FWUP
... DON'T YOU THINK?
Super!
FWUP
WELL, I THOUGHT SO.
Shocking!
FWUP
...YOU KNOW ?
Sensa-tional!
FWUP
... RIGHT?
Stylish!
FWUP
ANY-WAY, UM...
Seriously ?!
FWUP
...
Super!
ALL YOUR ANSWERS BEGAN WITH "S"...
Super!
!!
*Use only as appro-priate!!

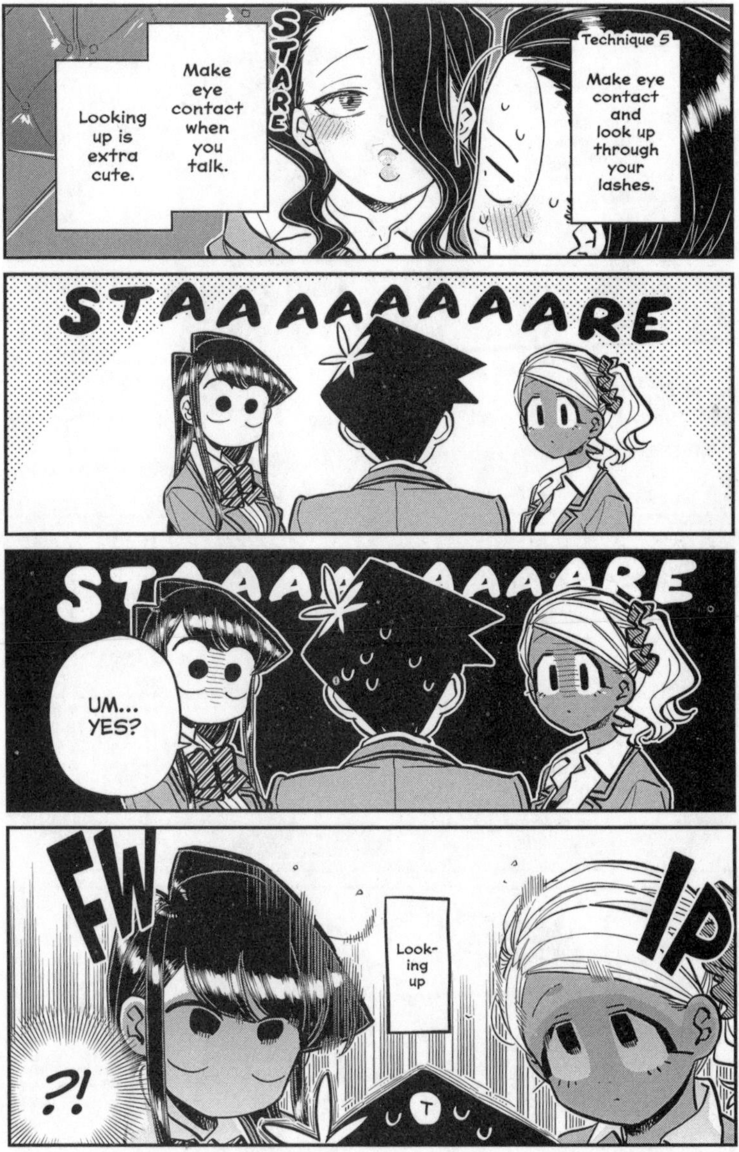
Technique 5
Make eye contact and look up through your lashes.
STARE
Make eye contact when you talk.
Looking up is extra cute.
STAAAAAAAARE
UM... YES?
FWIP
Look-ing up
?!

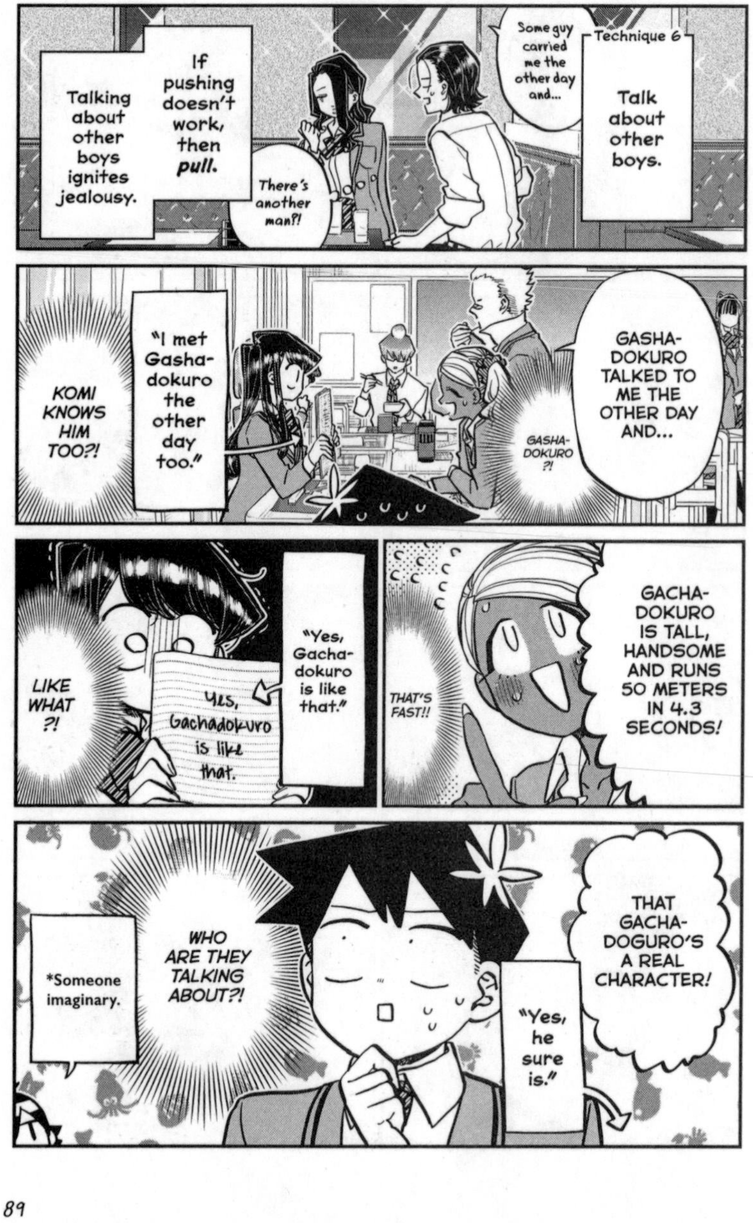
Technique 6
Talk about other boys.
Some guy carried me the other day and...
If pushing doesn't work, then **pull.**
Talking about other boys ignites jealousy.
There's another man?!
GASHA-DOKURO TALKED TO ME THE OTHER DAY AND...
GASHA-DOKURO ?!
"I met Gasha-dokuro the other day too."
KOMI KNOWS HIM TOO?!
GACHA-DOKURO IS TALL, HANDSOME AND RUNS 50 METERS IN 4.3 SECONDS!
THAT'S FAST!!
"Yes, Gacha-dokuro is like that."
Yes, Gachadokuro is like that.
LIKE WHAT ?!
THAT GACHA-DOGURO'S A REAL CHARACTER!
"Yes, he sure is."
WHO ARE THEY TALKING ABOUT?!
*Someone imaginary.

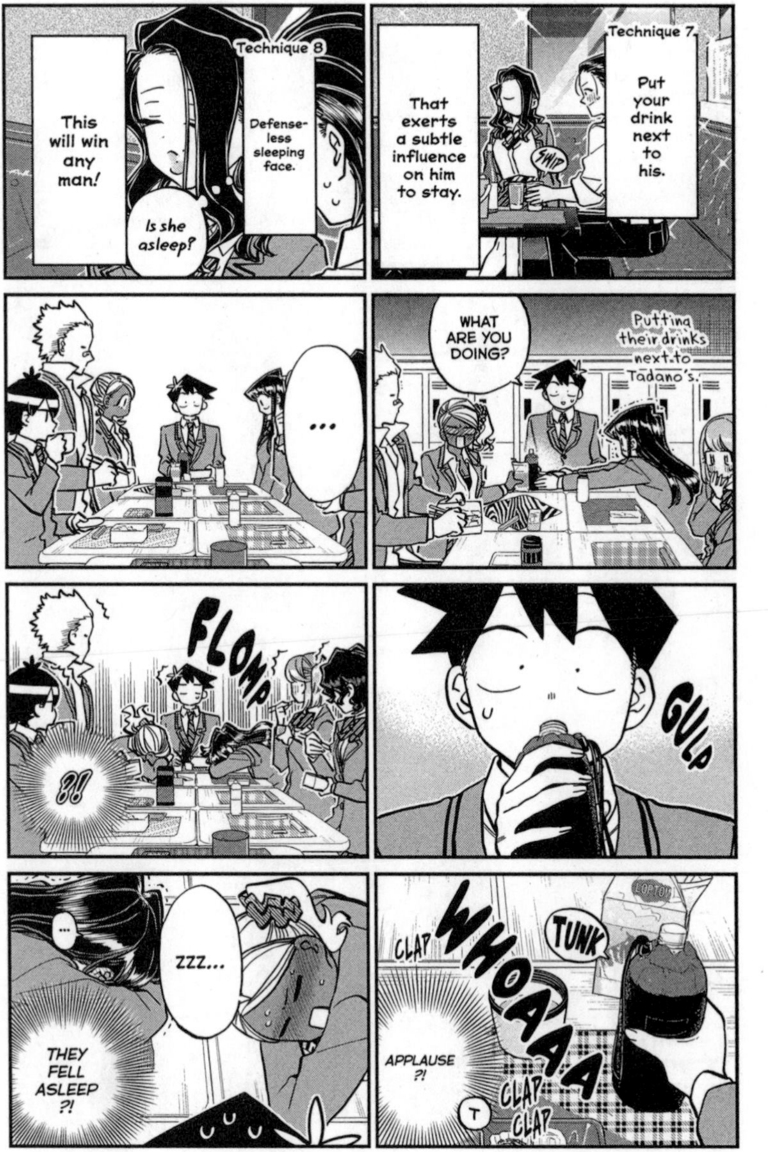
Technique 7
Put your drink next to his.
SWIP
That exerts a subtle influence on him to stay.
Technique 8
Defense-less sleeping face.
Is she asleep?
This will win any man!
WHAT ARE YOU DOING?
Putting their drinks next to Tadano's.
...
GULP
FLOMP
?!
TUNK
WHOAAA
CLAP
APPLAUSE ?!
CLAP CLAP
T
...
ZZZ...
THEY FELL ASLEEP ?!

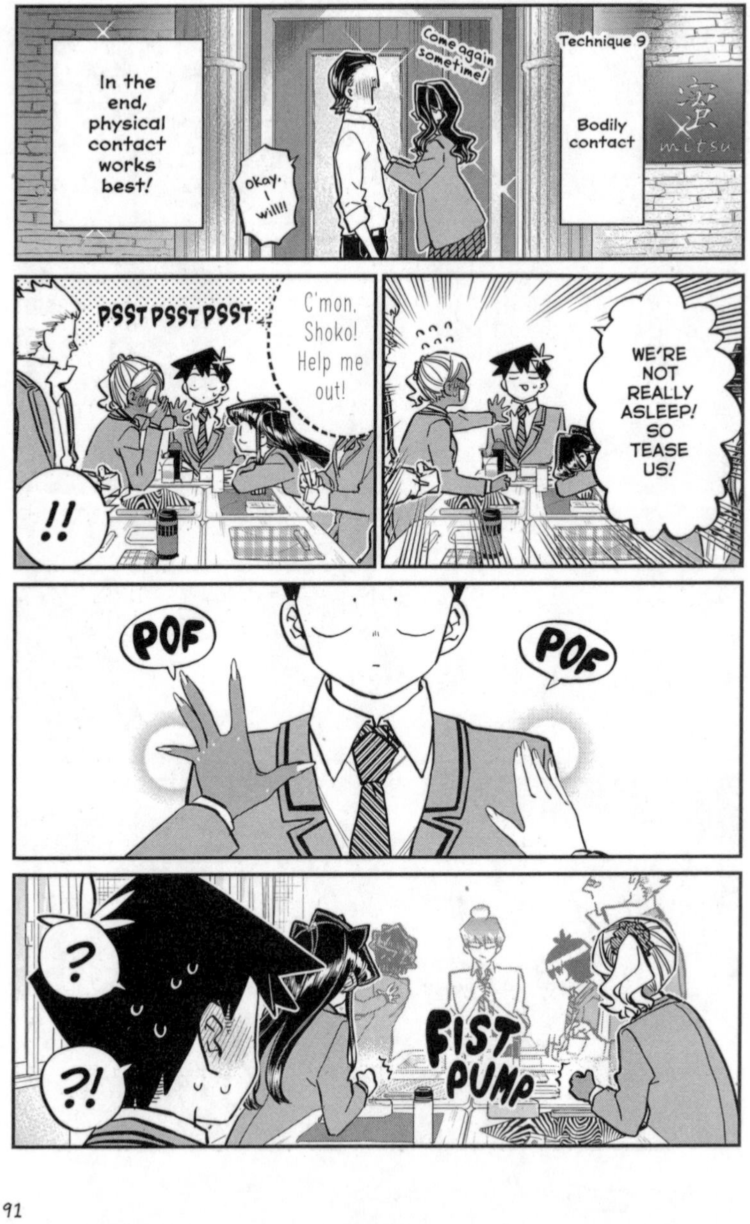
Technique 9
Bodily contact
蜜 mitsu
Come again sometime!
Okay, I will!!
In the end, physical contact works best!
WE'RE NOT REALLY ASLEEP! SO TEASE US!
C'mon, Shoko! Help me out!
PSST PSST PSST
!!
POF
POF
FIST PUMP
?
?!

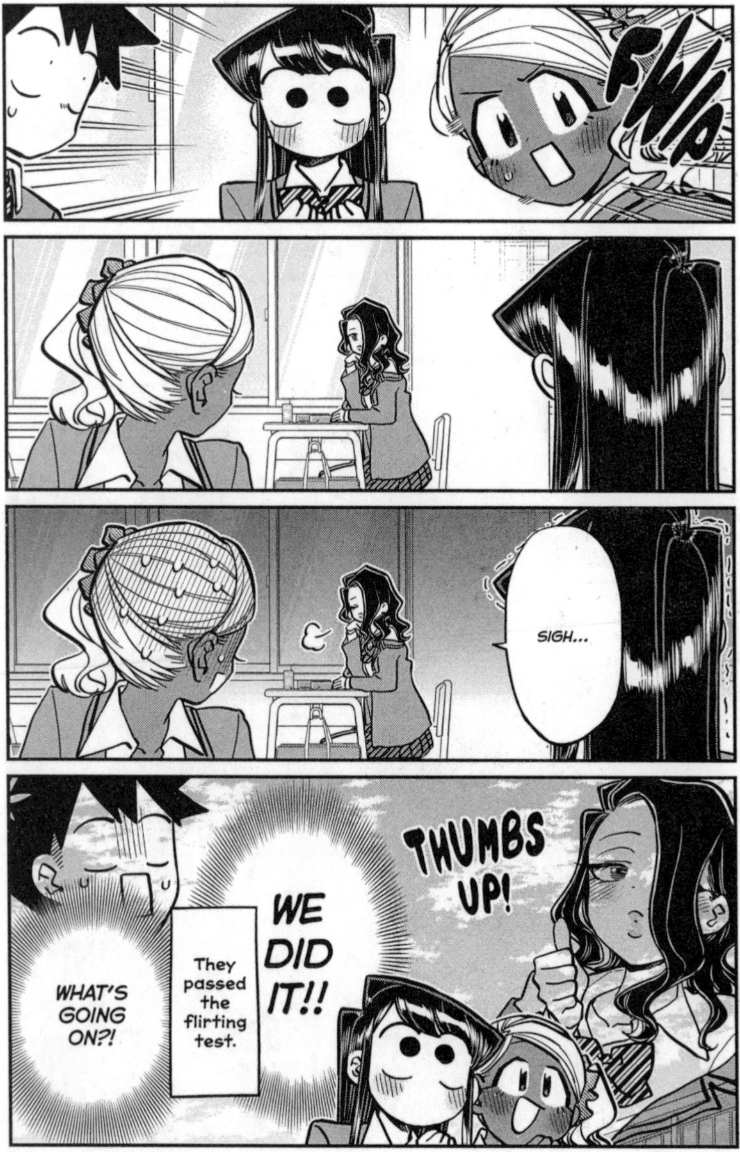
FWIP
SIGH...
THUMBS UP!
WE DID IT!!
They passed the flirting test.
WHAT'S GOING ON?!

Communication 240 — The End

Komi Can't Communicate

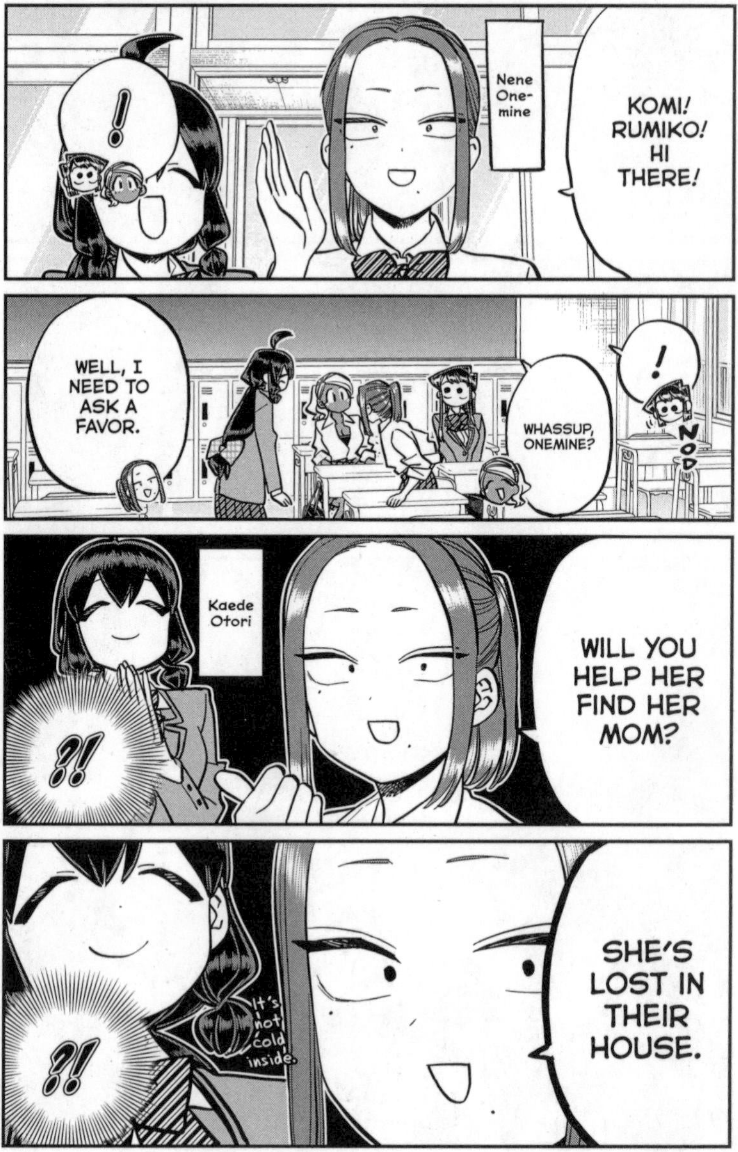
KOMI! RUMIKO! HI THERE!
Nene One-mine
!
!
NOD
WHASSUP, ONEMINE?
WELL, I NEED TO ASK A FAVOR.
WILL YOU HELP HER FIND HER MOM?
Kaede Otori
?!
SHE'S LOST IN THEIR HOUSE.
It's not cold inside.
?!

Chapter 241: The Escape

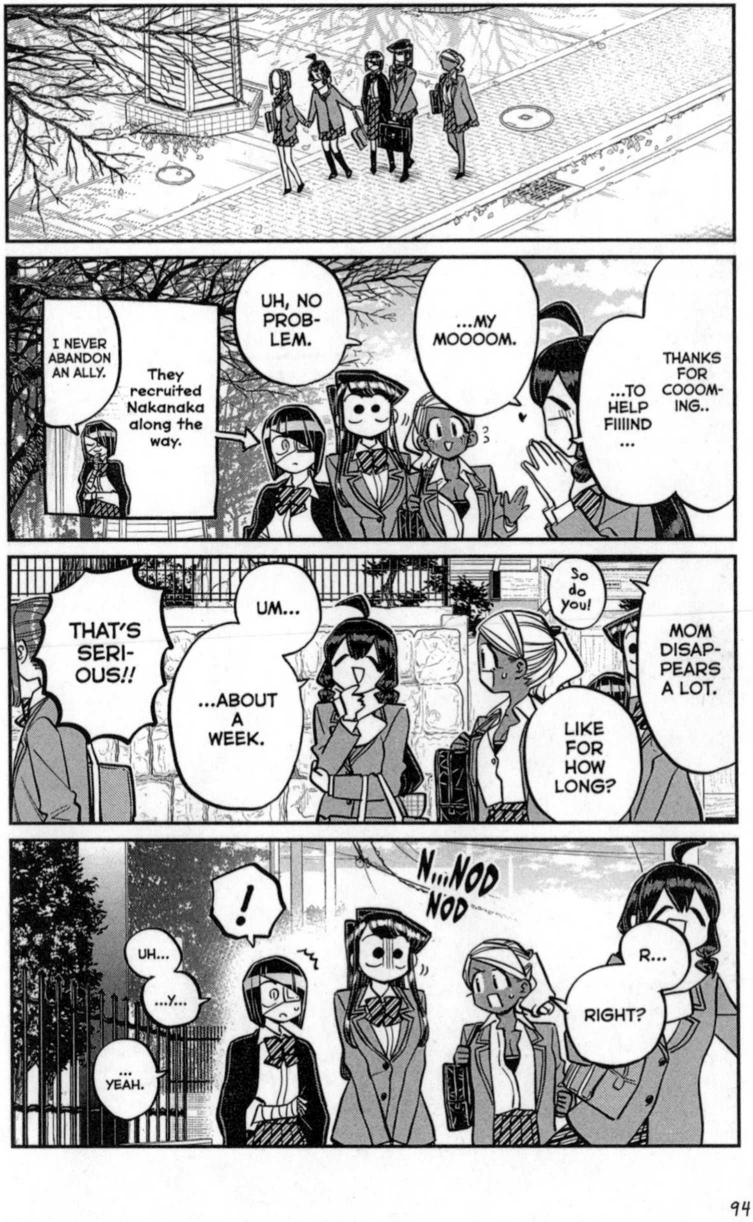
THANKS FOR COOOM-ING..
...TO HELP FIIIIND ...
...MY MOOOOM.
UH, NO PROB-LEM.
I NEVER ABANDON AN ALLY.
They recruited Nakanaka along the way.
MOM DISAP-PEARS A LOT.
So do you!
LIKE FOR HOW LONG?
UM...
...ABOUT A WEEK.
THAT'S SERI-OUS!!
R...
RIGHT?
N...NOD NOD
!
UH...
...Y...
... YEAH.

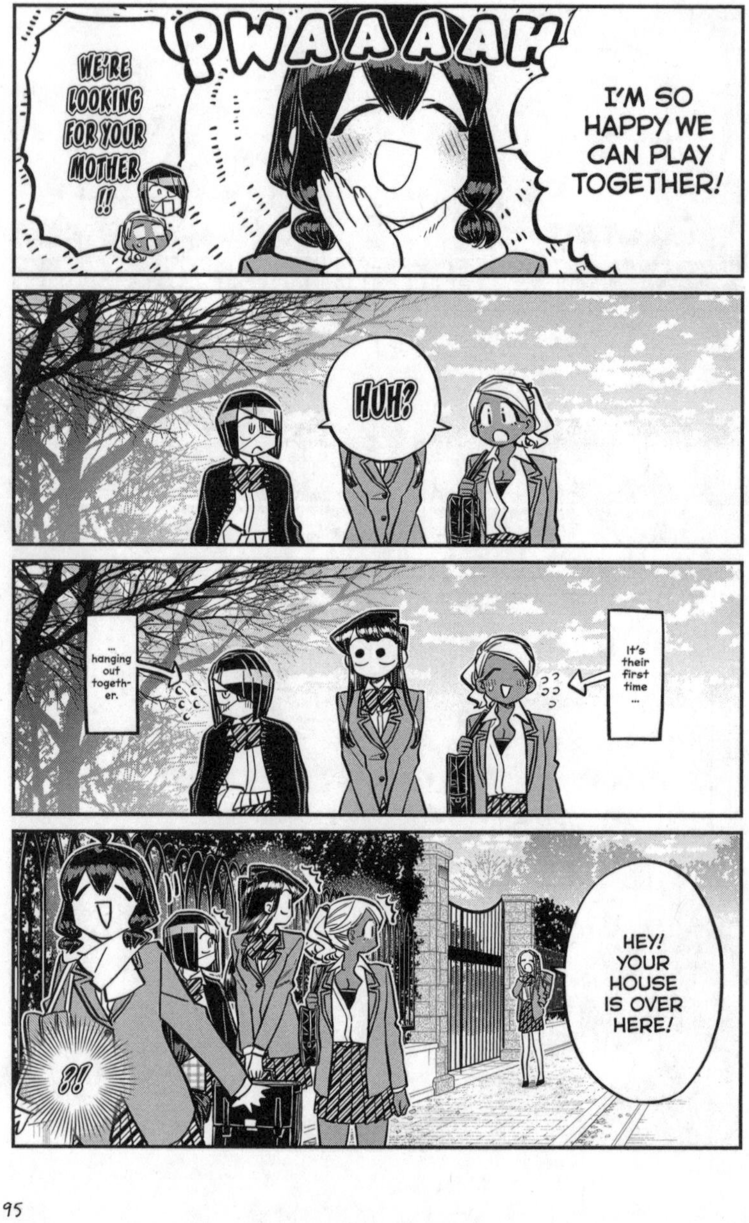
PWAAAAAH
I'M SO HAPPY WE CAN PLAY TOGETHER!
WE'RE LOOKING FOR YOUR MOTHER!!
HUH?
It's their first time...
...hanging out together.
HEY! YOUR HOUSE IS OVER HERE!
?!

Otori's house
IT'S LIKE A CASTLE!
YOU NEED A KEY TO OPEN THIS FROM INSIDE.

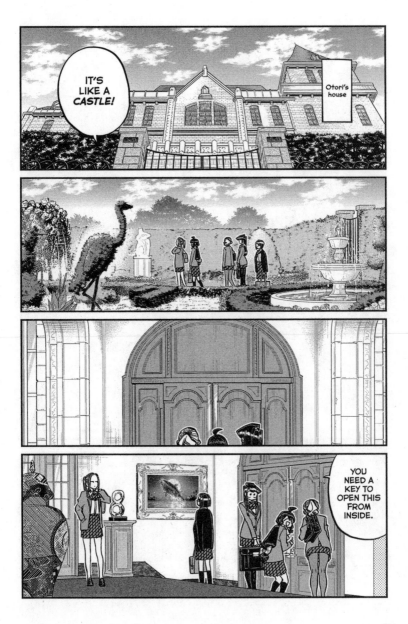

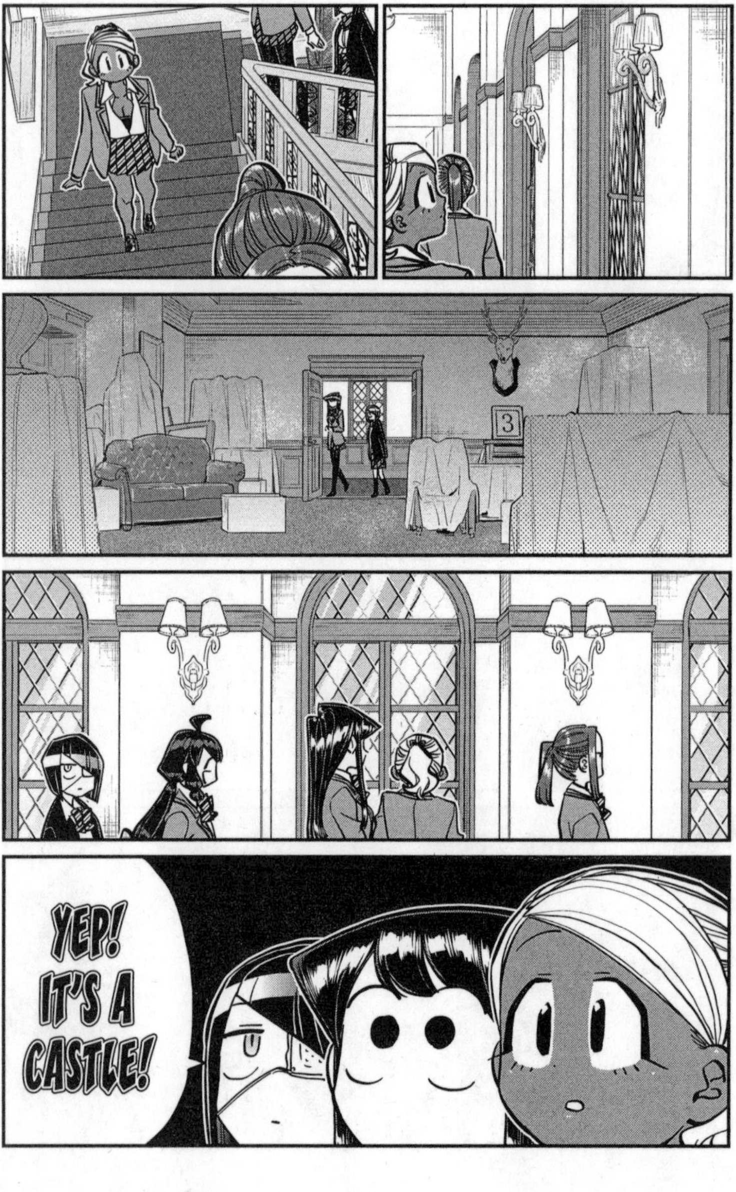
YEP! IT'S A CASTLE!

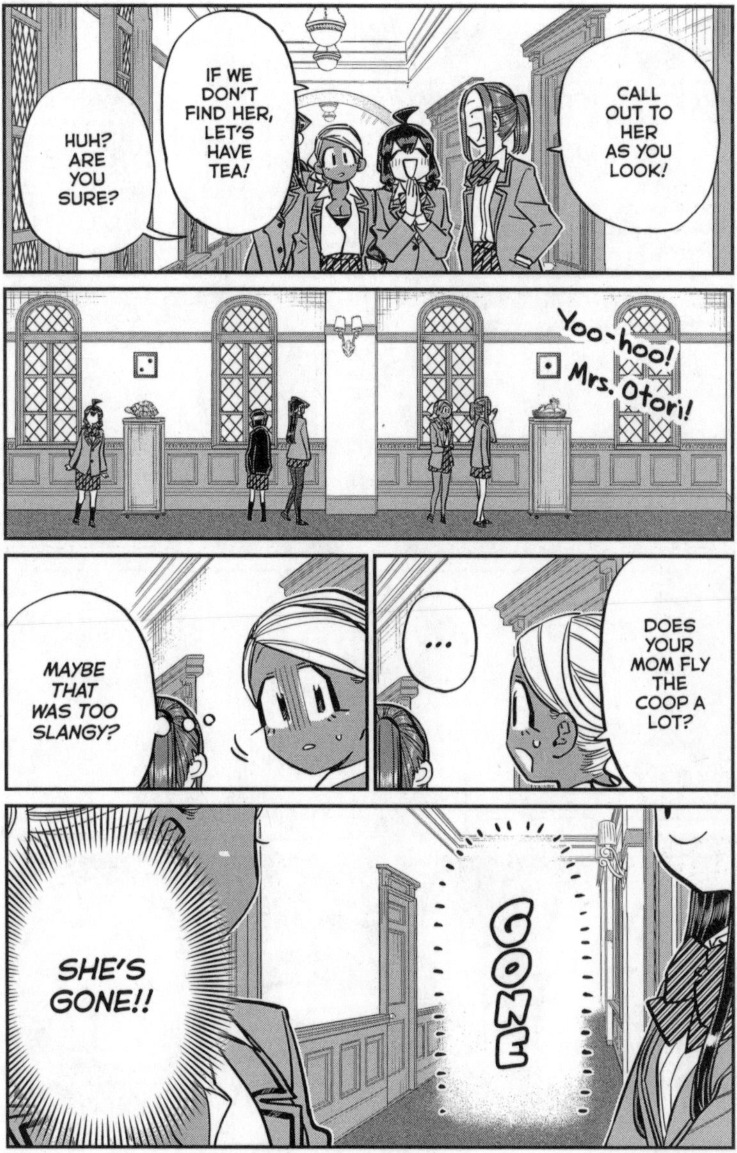
CALL OUT TO HER AS YOU LOOK!
IF WE DON'T FIND HER, LET'S HAVE TEA!
HUH? ARE YOU SURE?
Yoo-hoo! Mrs. Otori!
DOES YOUR MOM FLY THE COOP A LOT?
...
MAYBE THAT WAS TOO SLANGY?
GONE
SHE'S GONE!!

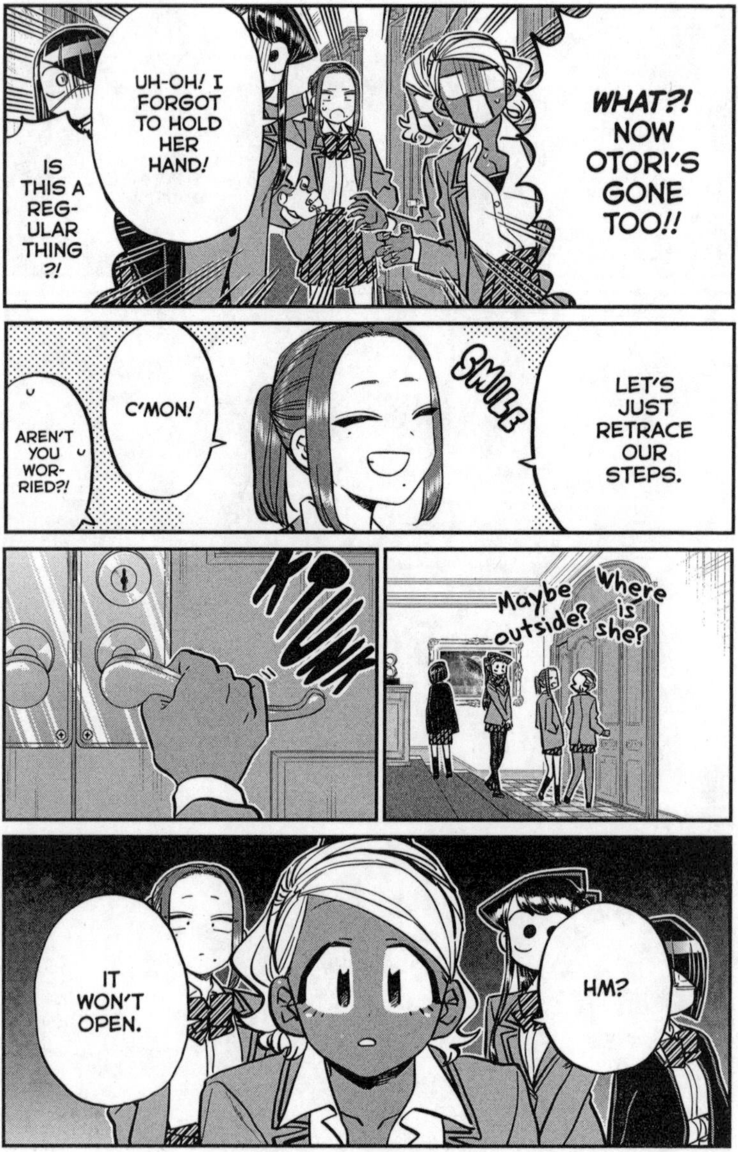
WHAT?! NOW OTORI'S GONE TOO!!
UH-OH! I FORGOT TO HOLD HER HAND!
IS THIS A REG-ULAR THING?!
LET'S JUST RETRACE OUR STEPS.
SMILE
C'MON!
AREN'T YOU WOR-RIED?!
Where is she?
Maybe outside?
KLUNK
HM?
IT WON'T OPEN.

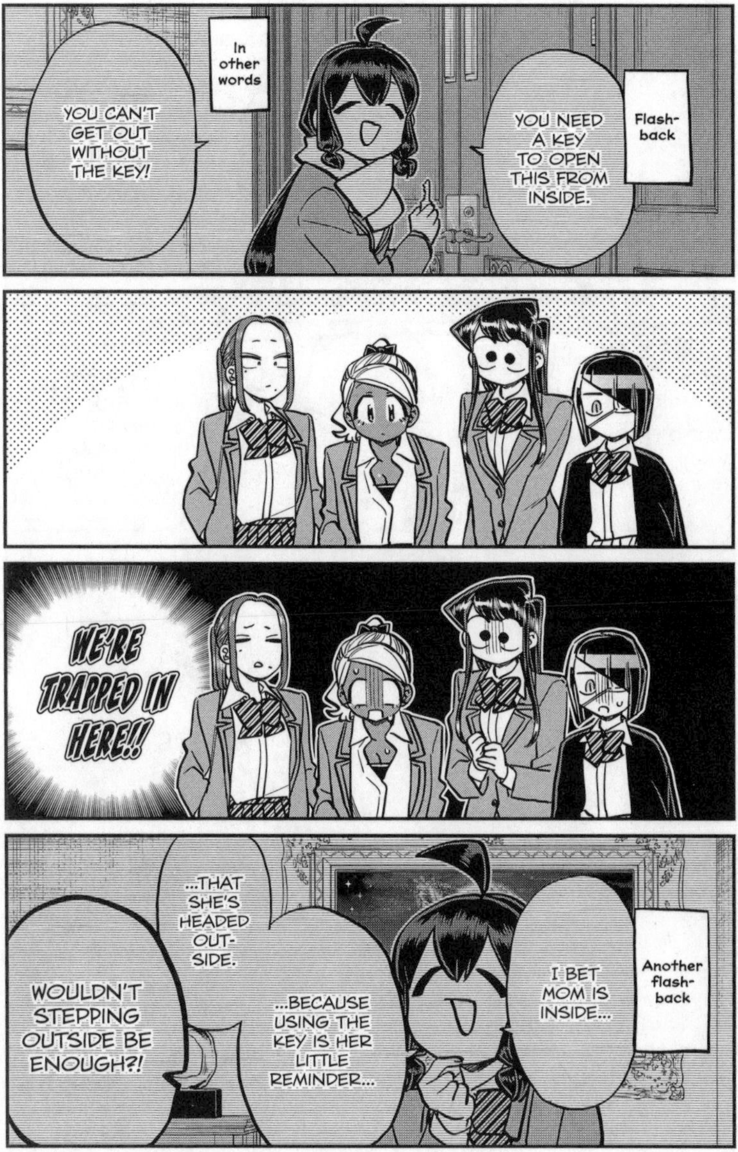
Flash-back
YOU NEED A KEY TO OPEN THIS FROM INSIDE.
In other words
YOU CAN'T GET OUT WITHOUT THE KEY!
WE'RE TRAPPED IN HERE!!
Another flash-back
I BET MOM IS INSIDE...
...BECAUSE USING THE KEY IS HER LITTLE REMINDER...
...THAT SHE'S HEADED OUT-SIDE.
WOULDN'T STEPPING OUTSIDE BE ENOUGH?!

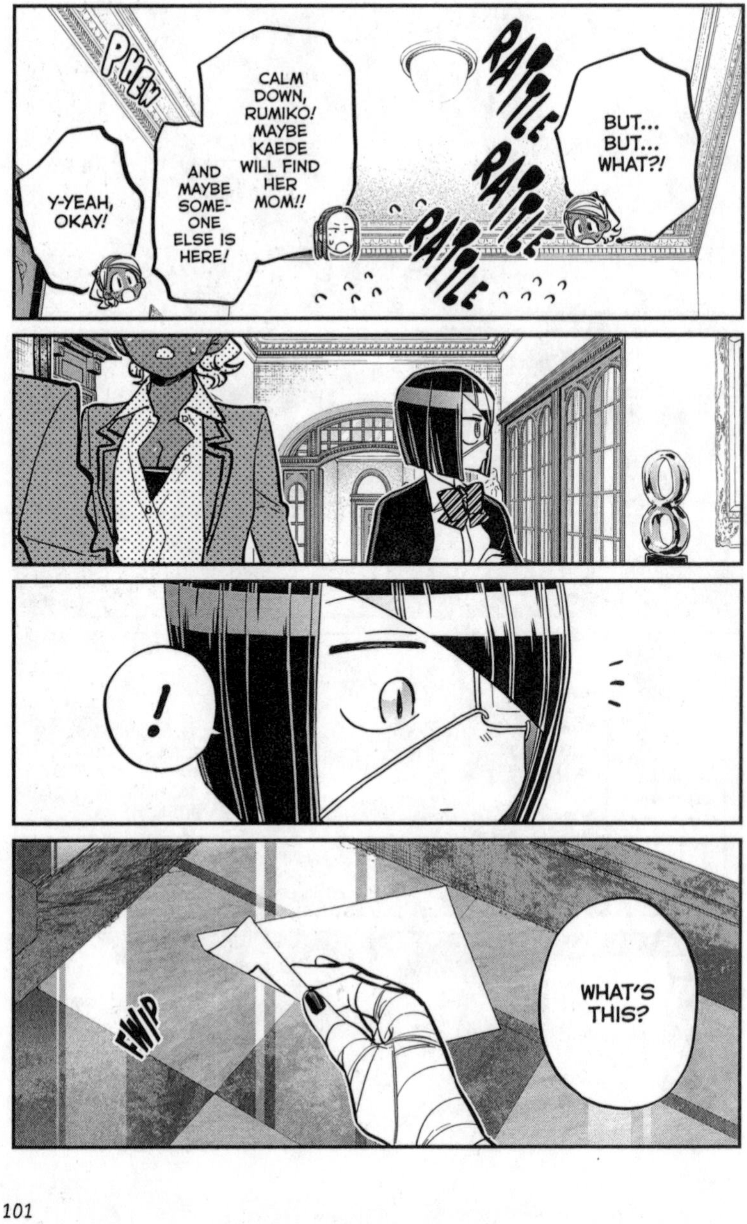
BUT... BUT... WHAT?!
RATTLE RATTLE RATTLE RATTLE
CALM DOWN, RUMIKO! MAYBE KAEDE WILL FIND HER MOM!!
AND MAYBE SOME-ONE ELSE IS HERE!
PHEW
Y-YEAH, OKAY!
!
WHAT'S THIS?
FWIP

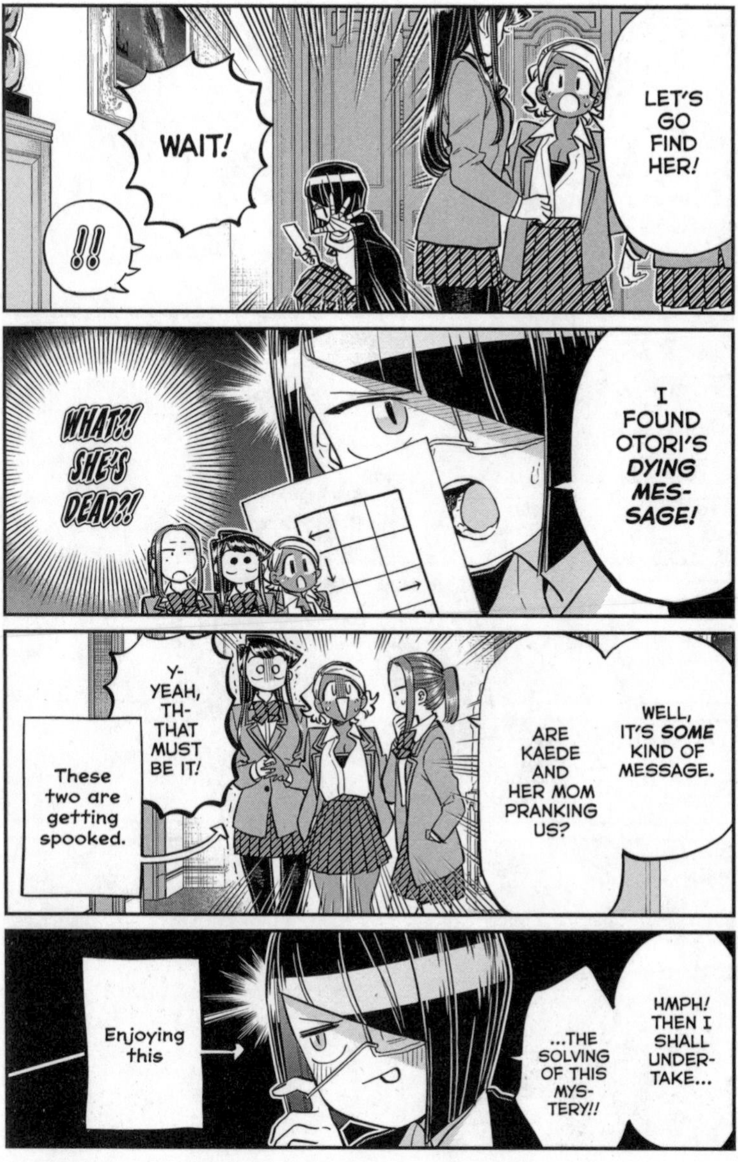
LET'S GO FIND HER!
WAIT!
!!
I FOUND OTORI'S *DYING MESSAGE!*
WHAT?! SHE'S DEAD?!
WELL, IT'S *SOME* KIND OF MESSAGE.
ARE KAEDE AND HER MOM PRANKING US?
Y-YEAH, TH-THAT MUST BE IT!
These two are getting spooked.
HMPH! THEN I SHALL UNDERTAKE...
...THE SOLVING OF THIS MYSTERY!!
Enjoying this

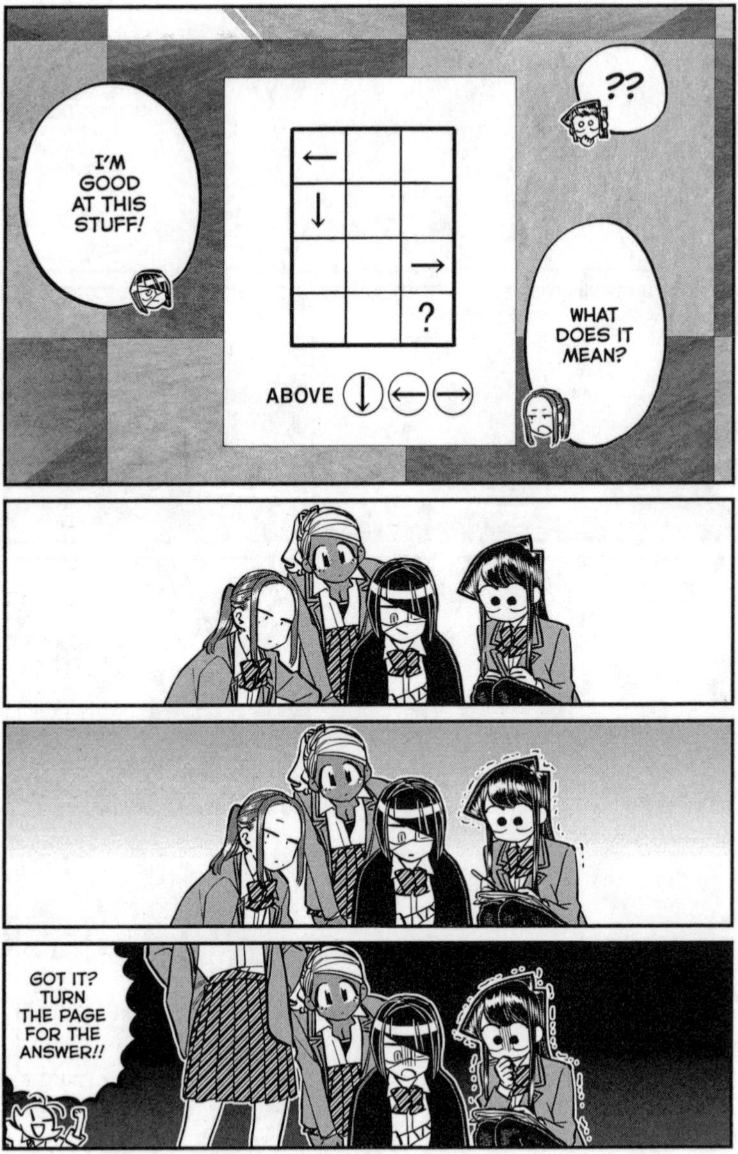
??
WHAT DOES IT MEAN?
I'M GOOD AT THIS STUFF!
?
ABOVE
GOT IT? TURN THE PAGE FOR THE ANSWER!!

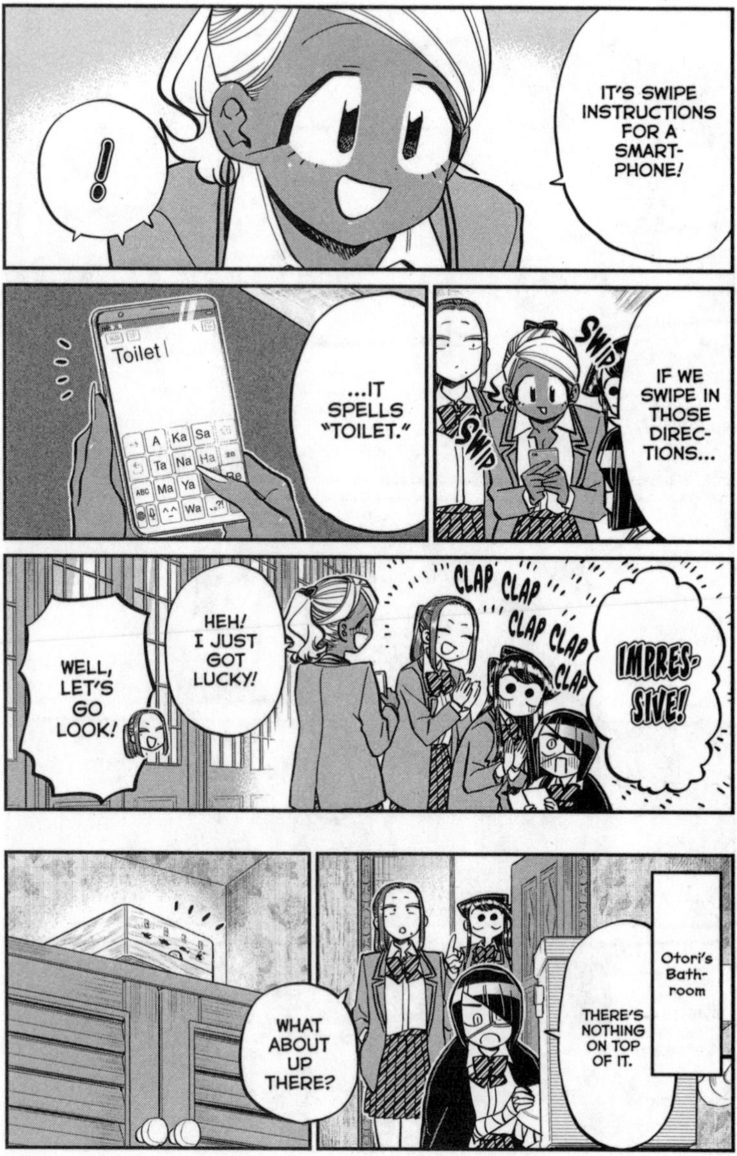
IT'S SWIPE INSTRUCTIONS FOR A SMART-PHONE!
!
SWIP
SWIP
IF WE SWIPE IN THOSE DIREC-TIONS...
...IT SPELLS "TOILET."
Toilet
A Ka Sa Ta Na Ha Ma Ya Wa
IMPRES-SIVE!
CLAP CLAP CLAP CLAP CLAP
HEH! I JUST GOT LUCKY!
WELL, LET'S GO LOOK!
Otori's Bath-room
THERE'S NOTHING ON TOP OF IT.
WHAT ABOUT UP THERE?

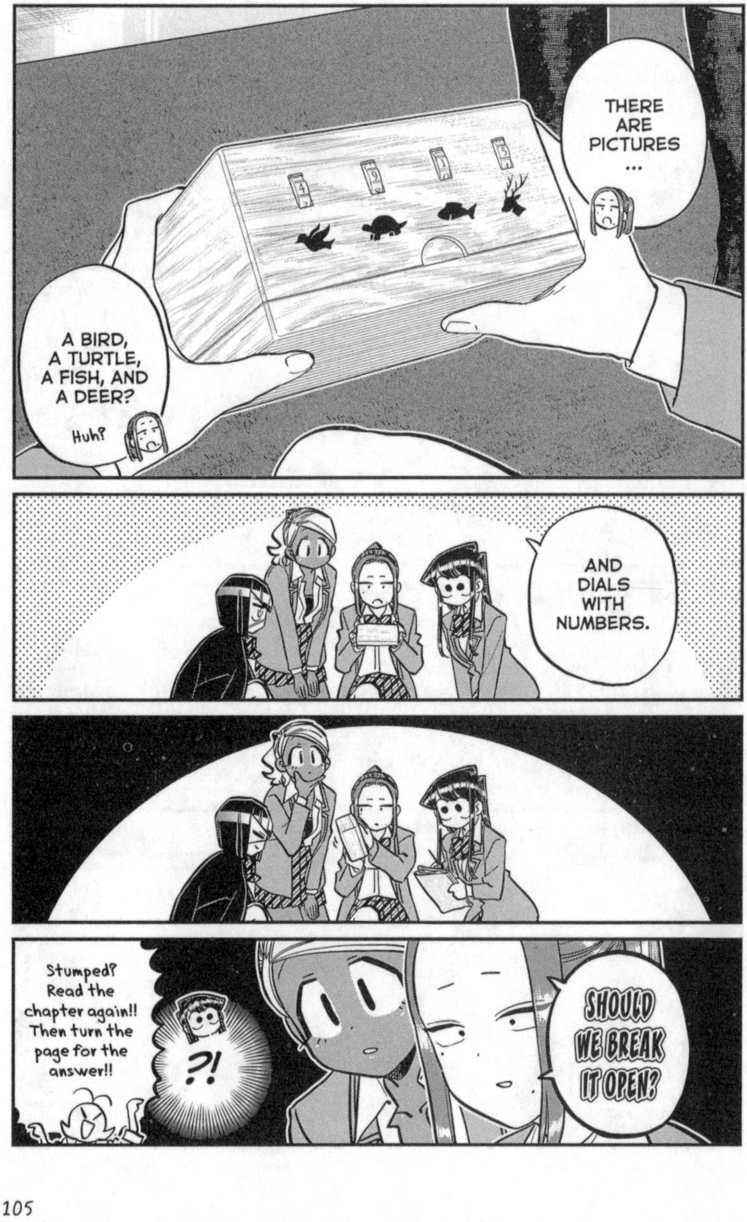
THERE ARE PICTURES ...
A BIRD, A TURTLE, A FISH, AND A DEER?
Huh?
AND DIALS WITH NUMBERS.
SHOULD WE BREAK IT OPEN?
?!
Stumped? Read the chapter again!! Then turn the page for the answer!!

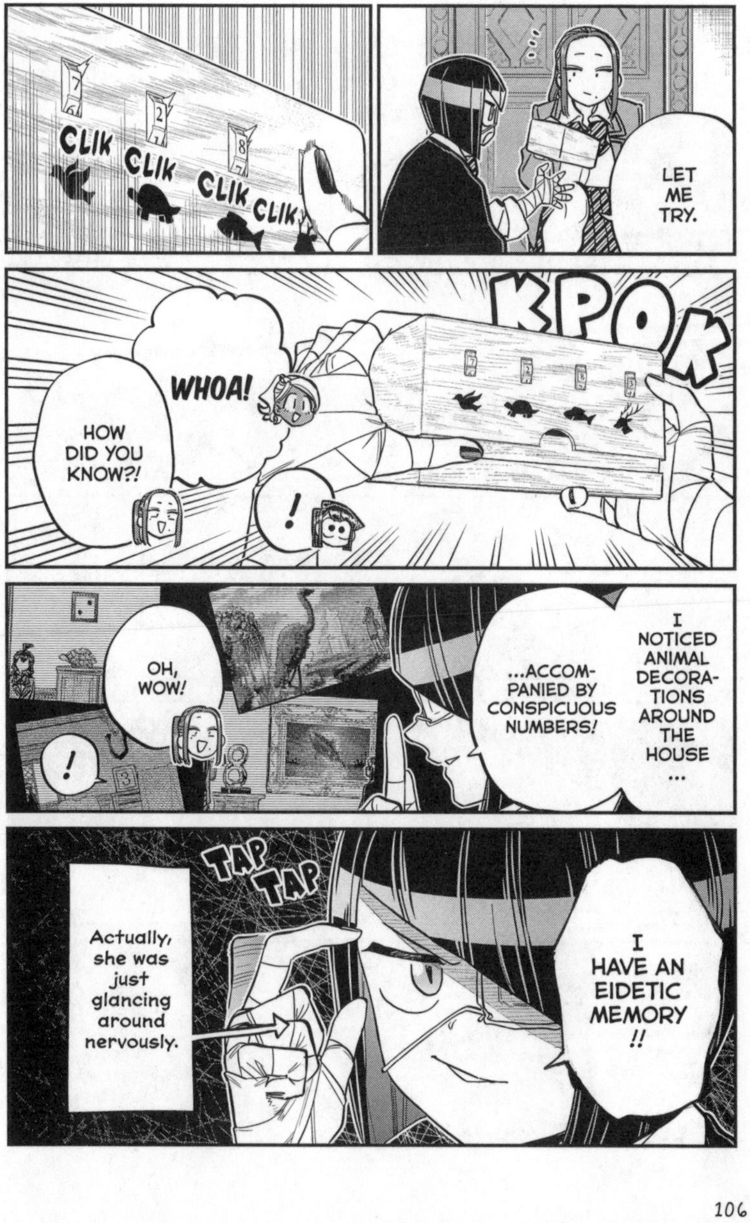
LET ME TRY.
CLIK
CLIK
CLIK
CLIK
KPOK
WHOA!
HOW DID YOU KNOW?!
!
I NOTICED ANIMAL DECORA-TIONS AROUND THE HOUSE...
...ACCOM-PANIED BY CONSPICUOUS NUMBERS!
OH, WOW!
!
TAP TAP
I HAVE AN EIDETIC MEMORY!!
Actually, she was just glancing around nervously.

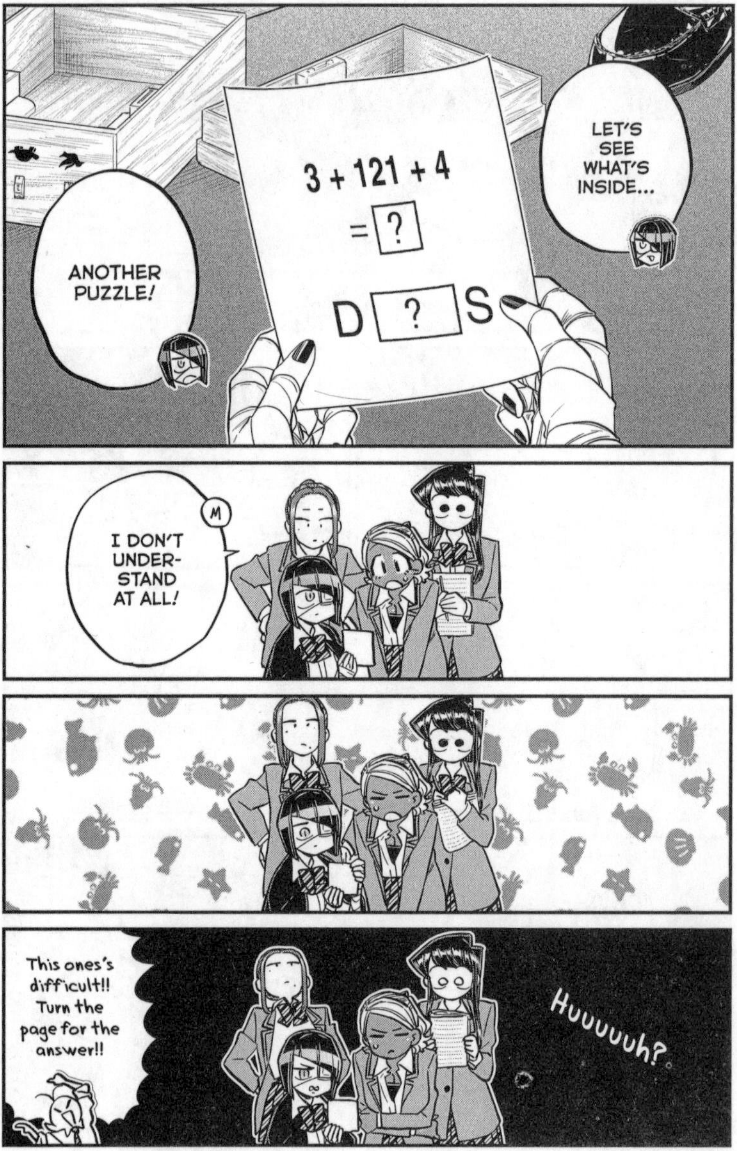
LET'S SEE WHAT'S INSIDE...
3 + 121 + 4
= ?
D ? S
ANOTHER PUZZLE!
M
I DON'T UNDER-STAND AT ALL!
Huuuuuh?
This ones's difficult!! Turn the page for the answer!!

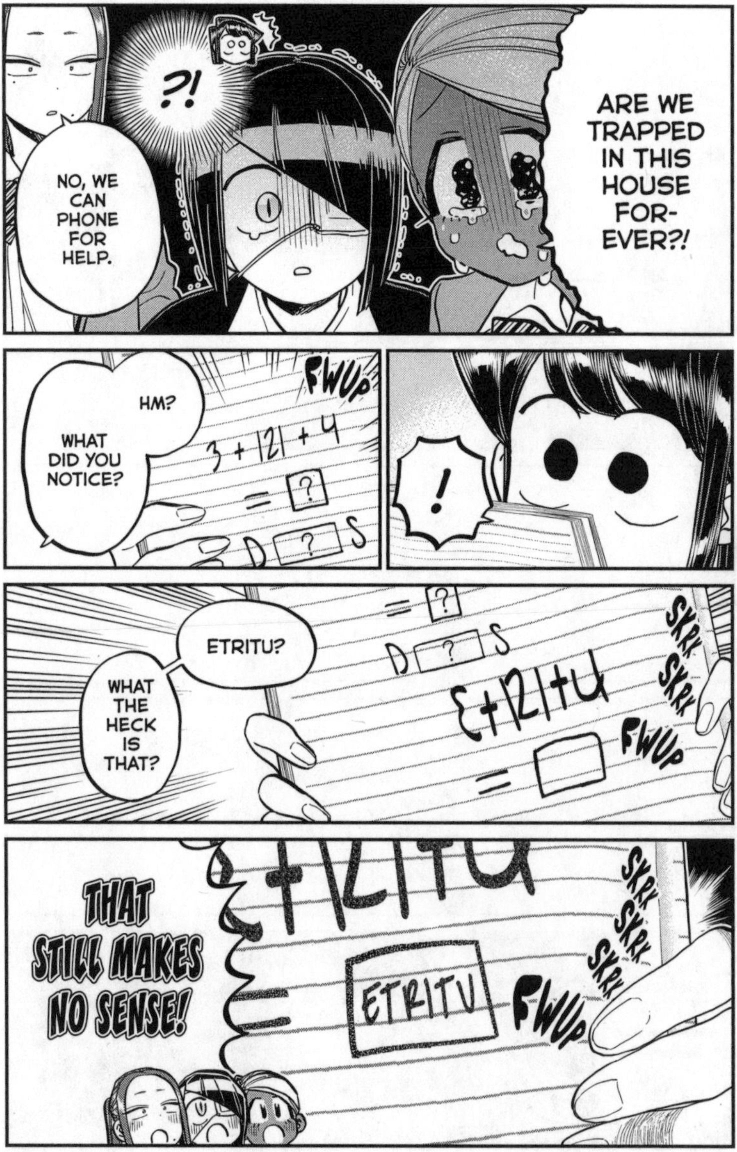
ARE WE TRAPPED IN THIS HOUSE FOR-EVER?!
?!
NO, WE CAN PHONE FOR HELP.
!
FWUP
HM?
WHAT DID YOU NOTICE?
3 + |2| + 4
= ?
D ? S
SKRK SKRK
FWUP
ETRITU?
WHAT THE HECK IS THAT?
SKRK SKRK SKRK
FWUP
ETRITU
THAT STILL MAKES NO SENSE!

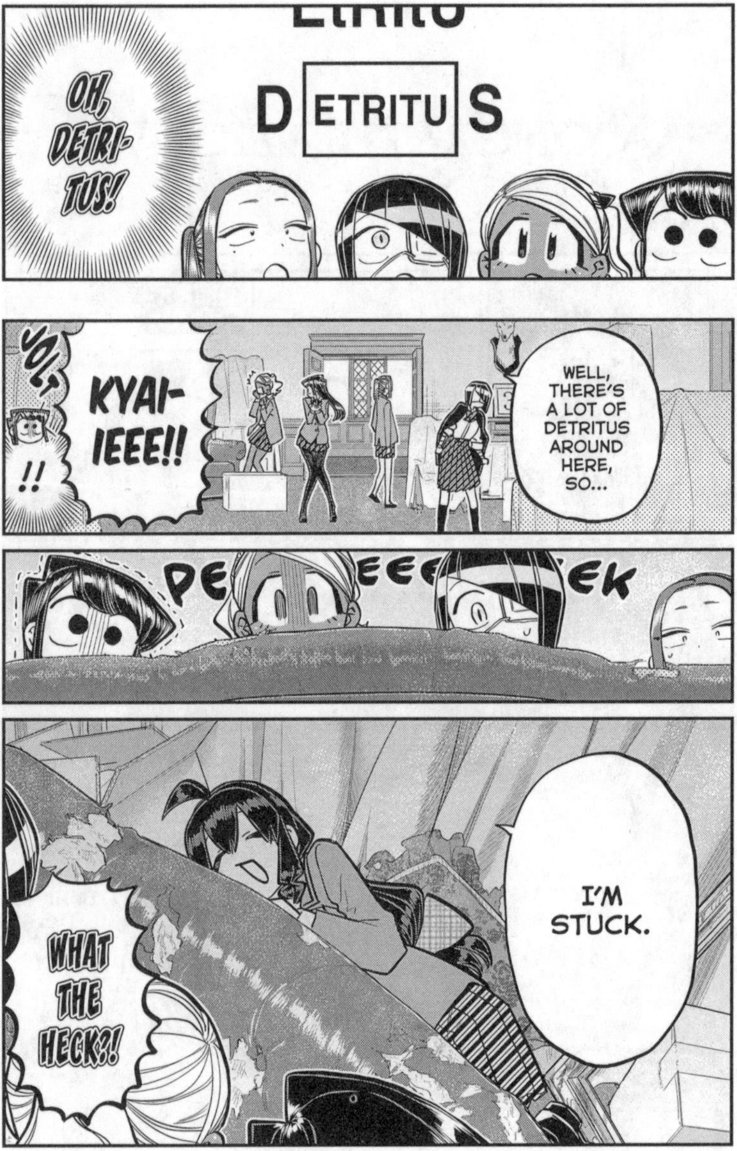
D ETRITU S
OH, DETRI-TUS!
WELL, THERE'S A LOT OF DETRITUS AROUND HERE, SO...
KYAI-IEEE!!
JOLT !!
EEEEK
I'M STUCK.
WHAT THE HECK?!

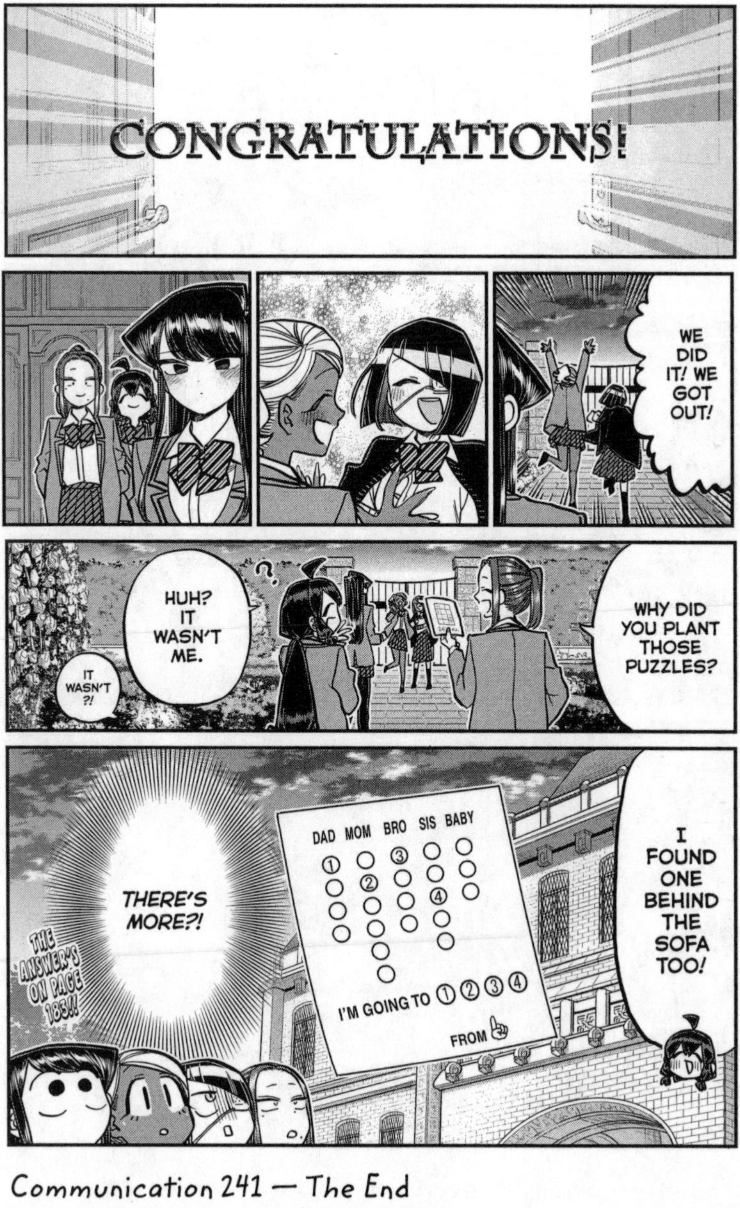
CONGRATULATIONS!
WE DID IT! WE GOT OUT!
WHY DID YOU PLANT THOSE PUZZLES?
HUH? IT WASN'T ME.
IT WASN'T ?!
I FOUND ONE BEHIND THE SOFA TOO!
DAD MOM BRO SIS BABY
I'M GOING TO ①②③④
FROM
THERE'S MORE?!
THE ANSWER'S ON PAGE 183!!

Communication 241 — The End

Komi Can't Communicate

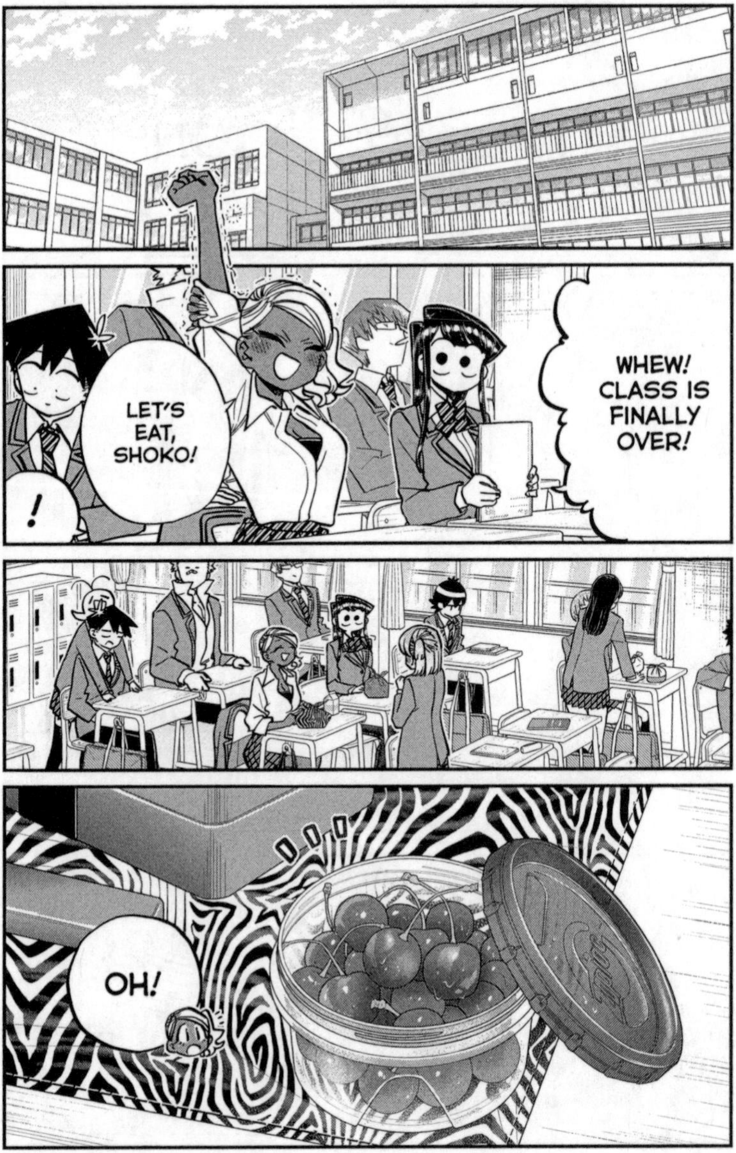
WHEW! CLASS IS FINALLY OVER!
LET'S EAT, SHOKO!
!
OH!

Communication 242: No Good

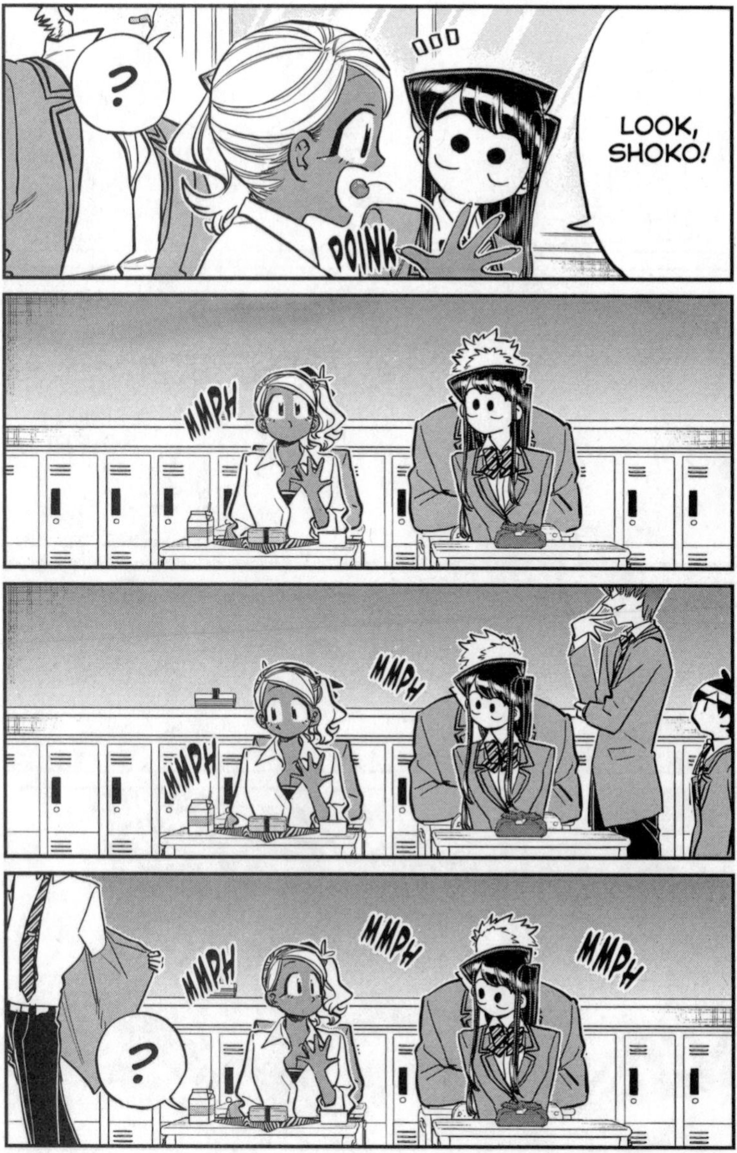
LOOK, SHOKO!
POINK
?
MMPH
MMPH
MMPH
MMPH
MMPH
MMPH
?

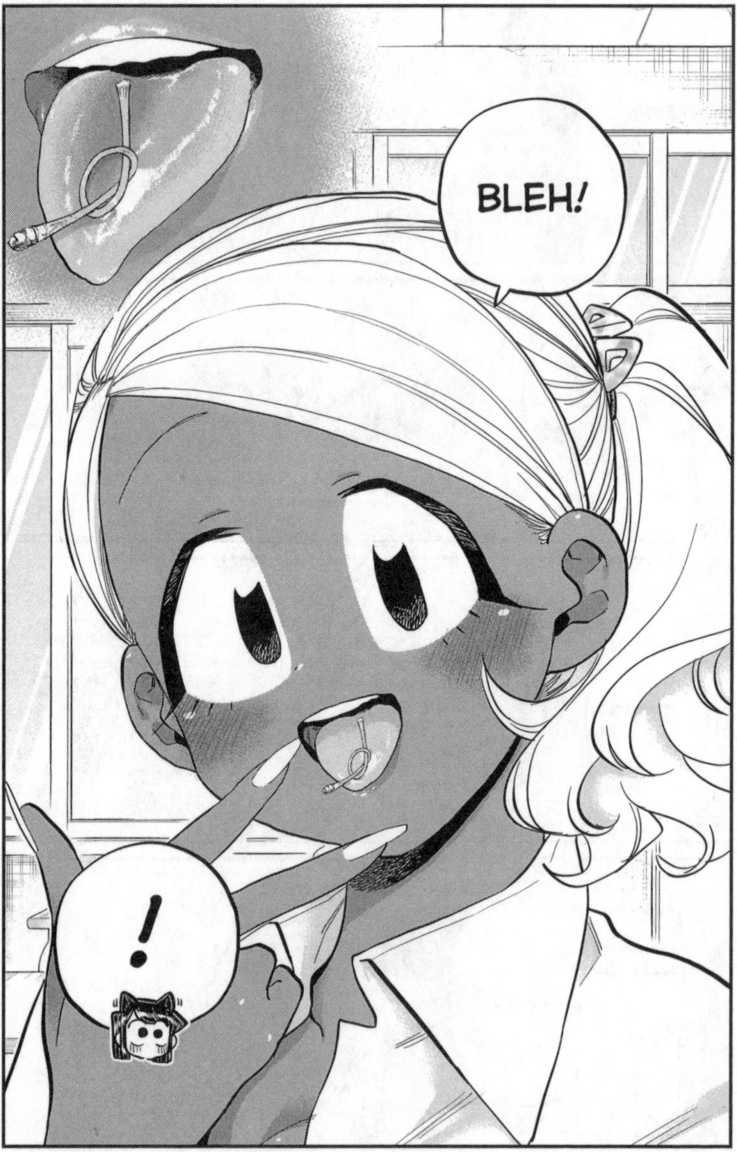
BLEH!
!

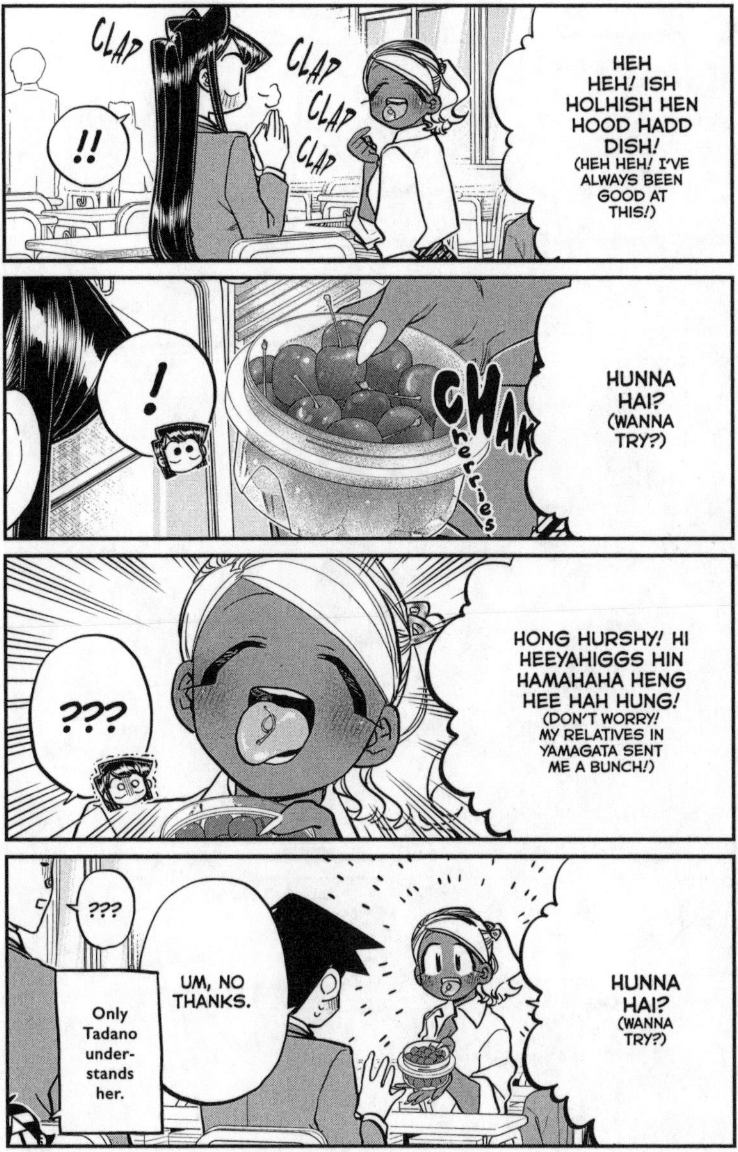
HEH HEH! ISH HOLHISH HEN HOOD HADD DISH!
(HEH HEH! I'VE ALWAYS BEEN GOOD AT THIS!)
CLAP
CLAP
CLAP
CLAP
!!
HUNNA HAI?
(WANNA TRY?)
CHAK
cherries
!
HONG HURSHY! HI HEEYAHIGGS HIN HAMAHAHA HENG HEE HAH HUNG!
(DON'T WORRY! MY RELATIVES IN YAMAGATA SENT ME A BUNCH!)
???
HUNNA HAI?
(WANNA TRY?)
UM, NO THANKS.
???
Only Tadano under-stands her.

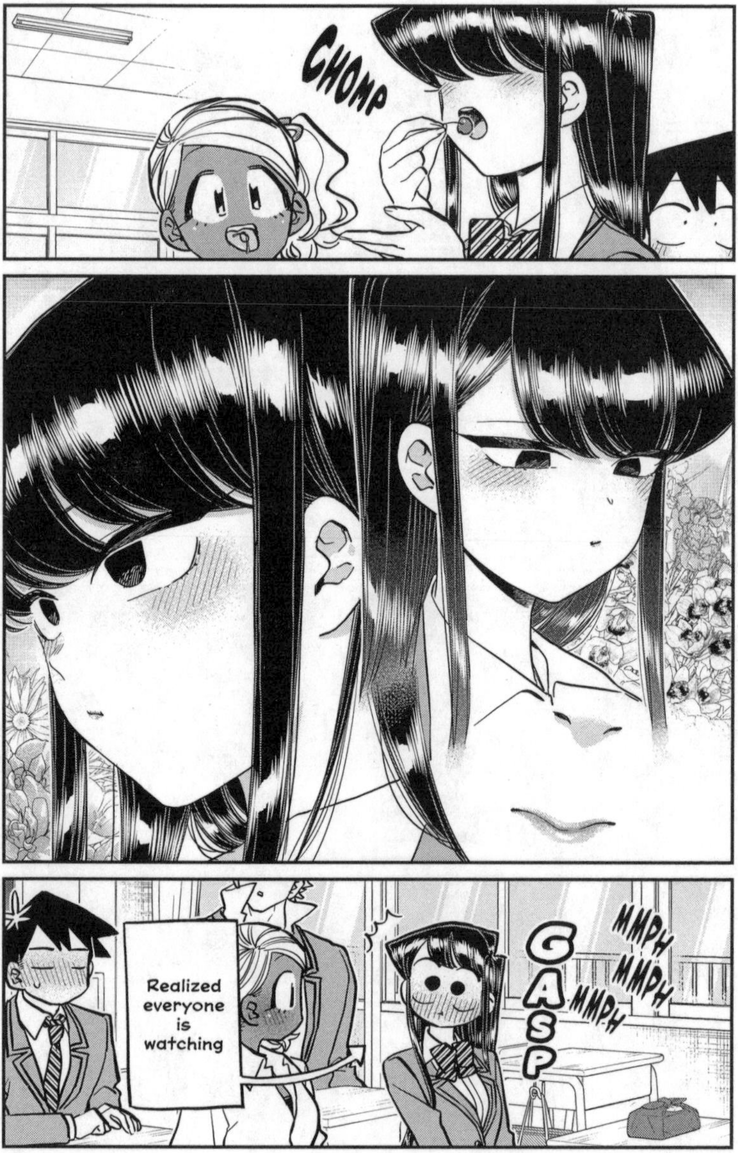
CHOMP
MMPH MMPH MMPH
GASP
Realized everyone is watching

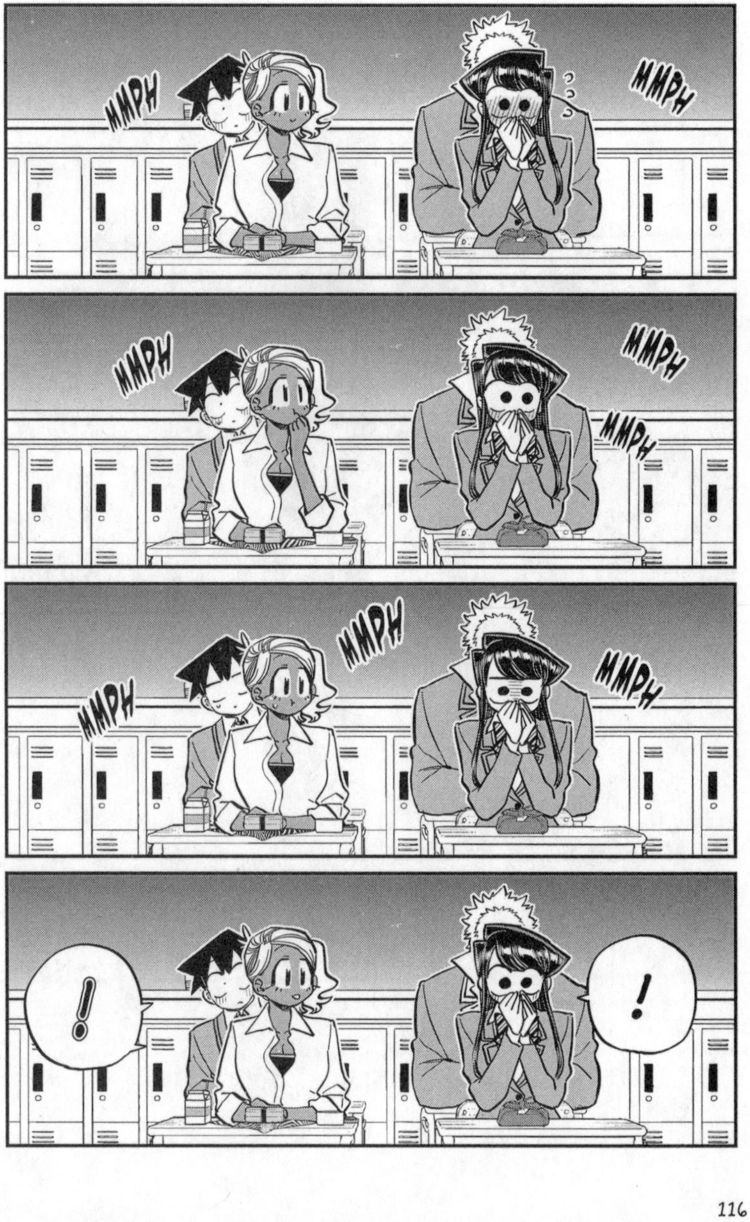
MMPH
MMPH
MMPH
MMPH
MMPH
MMPH
MMPH
MMPH
!
!

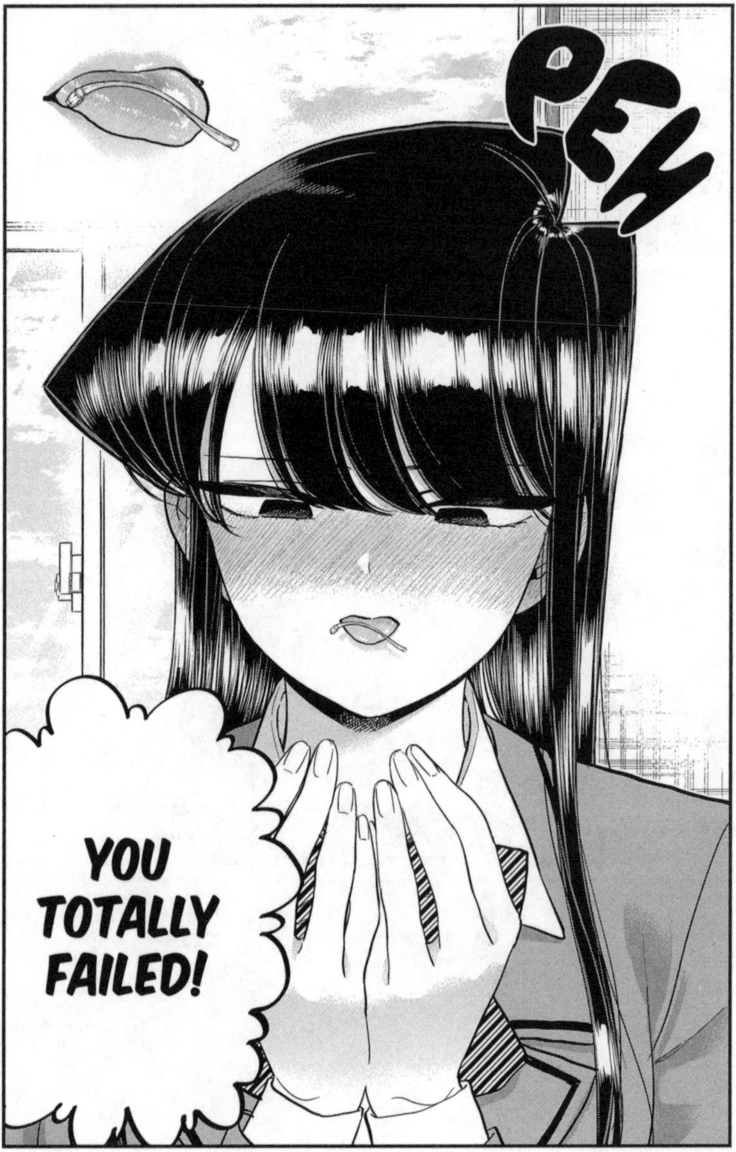
PEH
YOU TOTALLY FAILED!

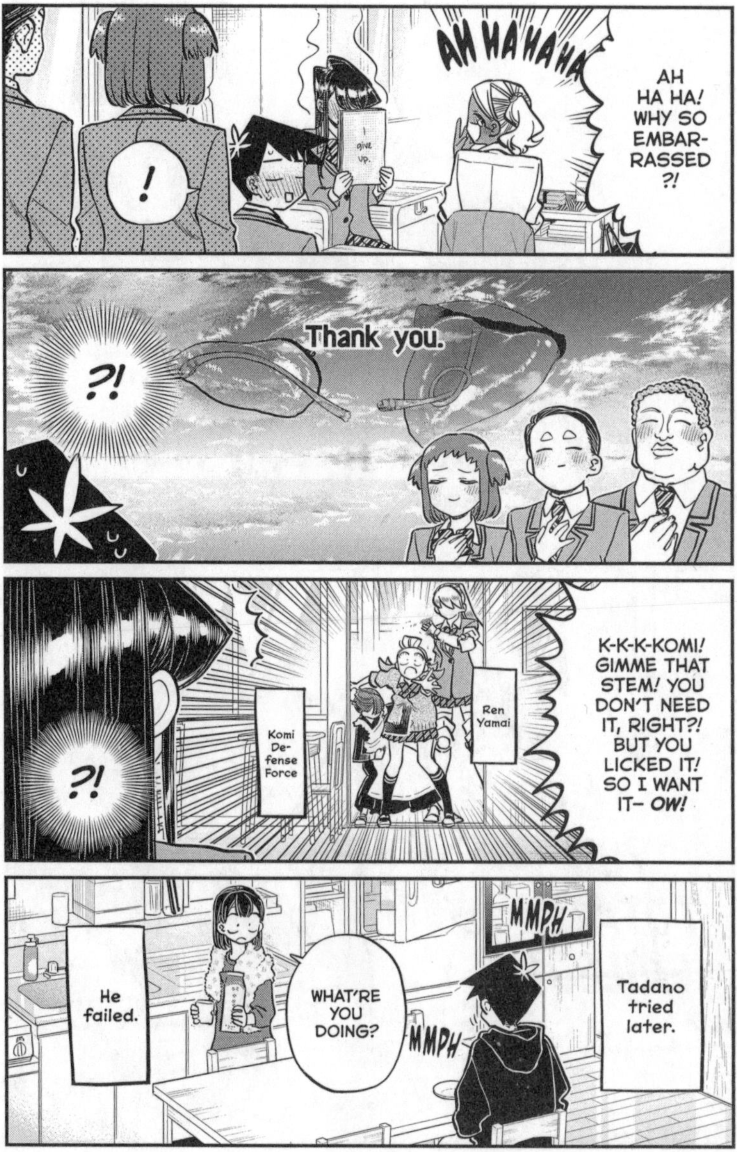
AH HA HA! WHY SO EMBARRASSED ?!
AH HA HA HA HA
I give up.
!
Thank you.
?!
K-K-K-KOMI! GIMME THAT STEM! YOU DON'T NEED IT, RIGHT?! BUT YOU LICKED IT! SO I WANT IT– *OW!*
Ren Yamai
Komi Defense Force
?!
Tadano tried later.
MMPH
WHAT'RE YOU DOING?
MMPH
He failed.

Communication 242 — The End

Komi Can't Communicate

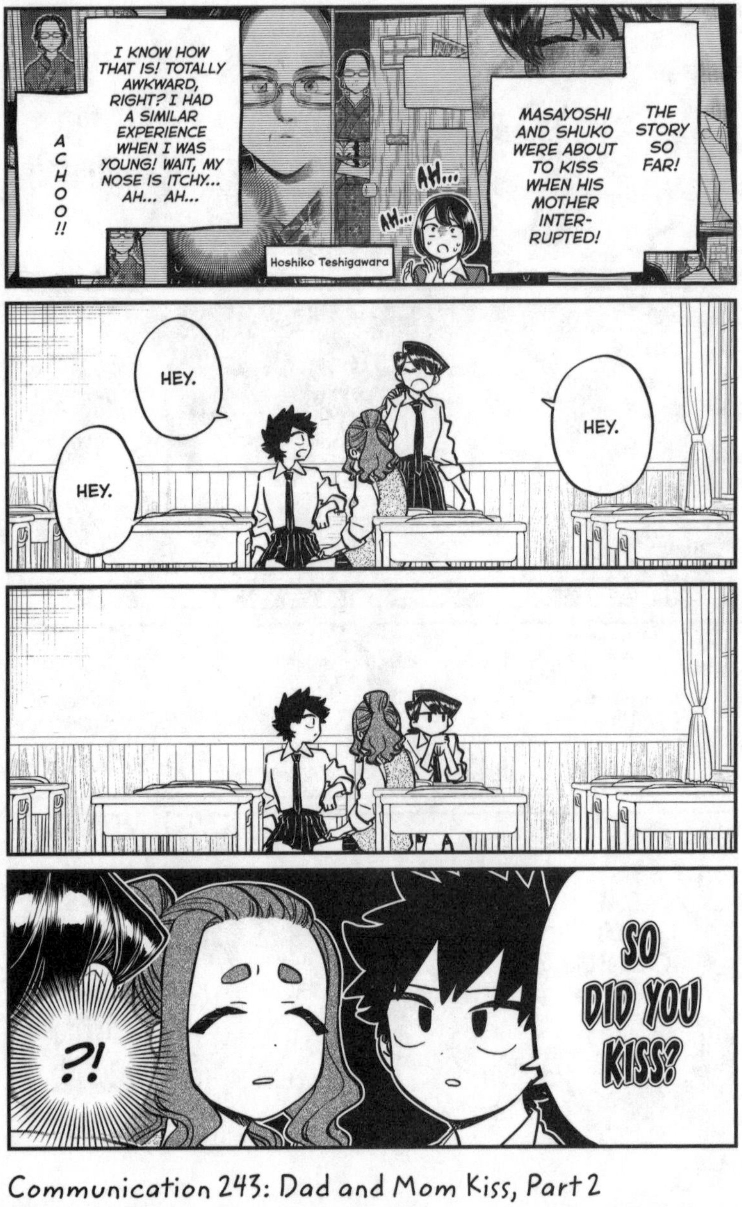
THE STORY SO FAR!
MASAYOSHI AND SHUKO WERE ABOUT TO KISS WHEN HIS MOTHER INTER-RUPTED!
AH...
AH...
Hoshiko Teshigawara
I KNOW HOW THAT IS! TOTALLY AWKWARD, RIGHT? I HAD A SIMILAR EXPERIENCE WHEN I WAS YOUNG! WAIT, MY NOSE IS ITCHY... AH... AH...
ACHOO!!
HEY.
HEY.
HEY.
SO DID YOU KISS?
?!

Communication 243: Dad and Mom Kiss, Part 2

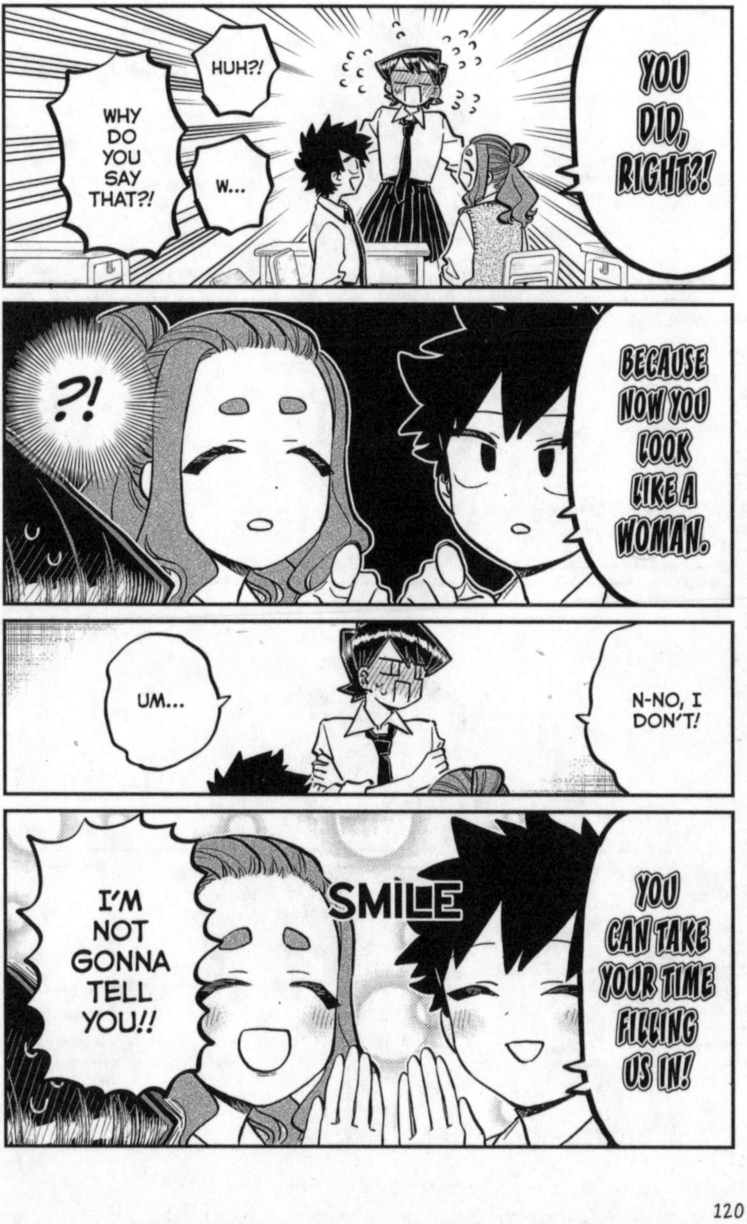
YOU DID, RIGHT?!
HUH?!
W...
WHY DO YOU SAY THAT?!
BECAUSE NOW YOU LOOK LIKE A WOMAN.
?!
N-NO, I DON'T!
UM...
YOU CAN TAKE YOUR TIME FILLING US IN!
SMILE
I'M NOT GONNA TELL YOU!!

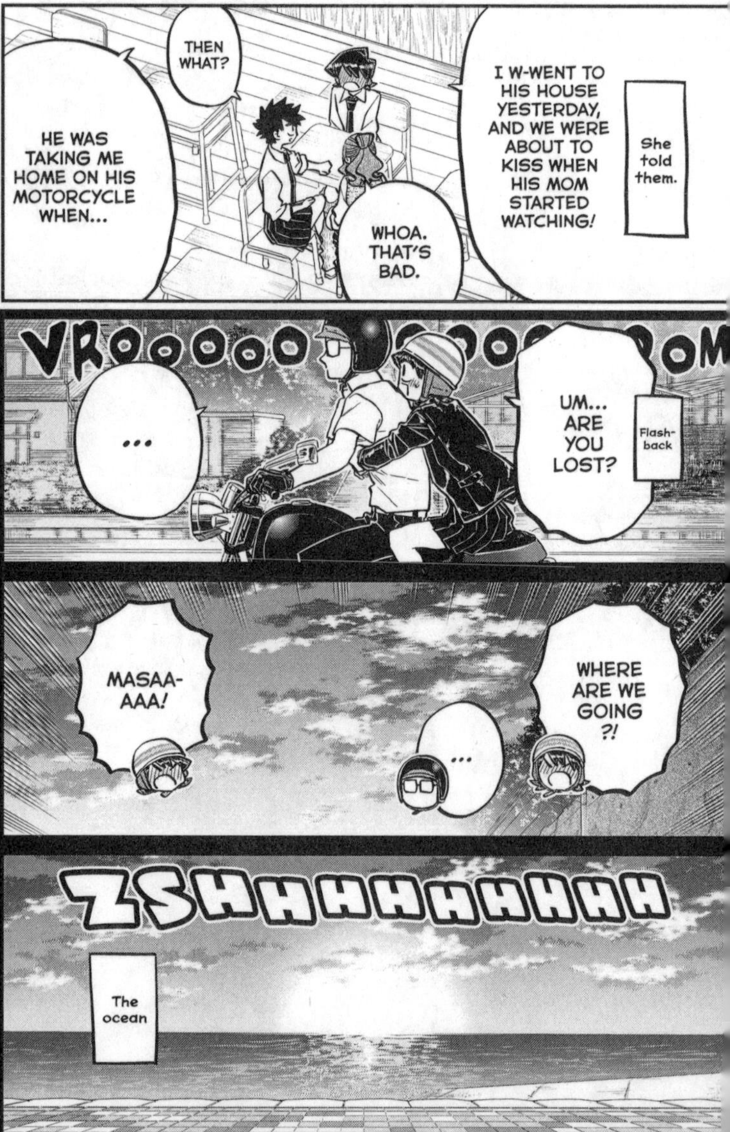
She told them.
I W-WENT TO HIS HOUSE YESTERDAY, AND WE WERE ABOUT TO KISS WHEN HIS MOM STARTED WATCHING!
WHOA. THAT'S BAD.
THEN WHAT?
HE WAS TAKING ME HOME ON HIS MOTORCYCLE WHEN...
VROOOOOO OOOO OOM
Flash-back
UM... ARE YOU LOST?
...
WHERE ARE WE GOING?!
...
MASAA-AAA!
ZSHHHHHHHHHH
The ocean

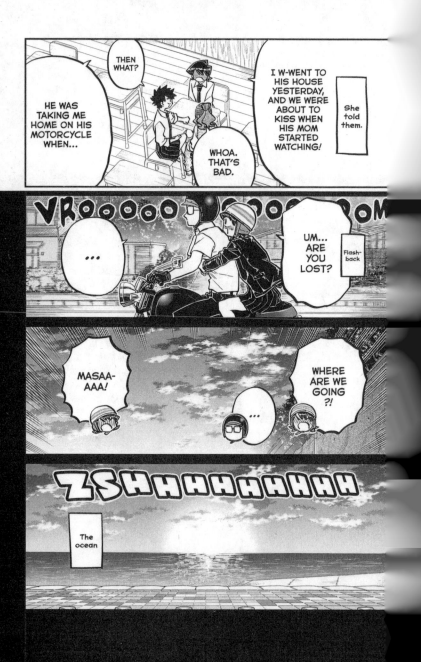

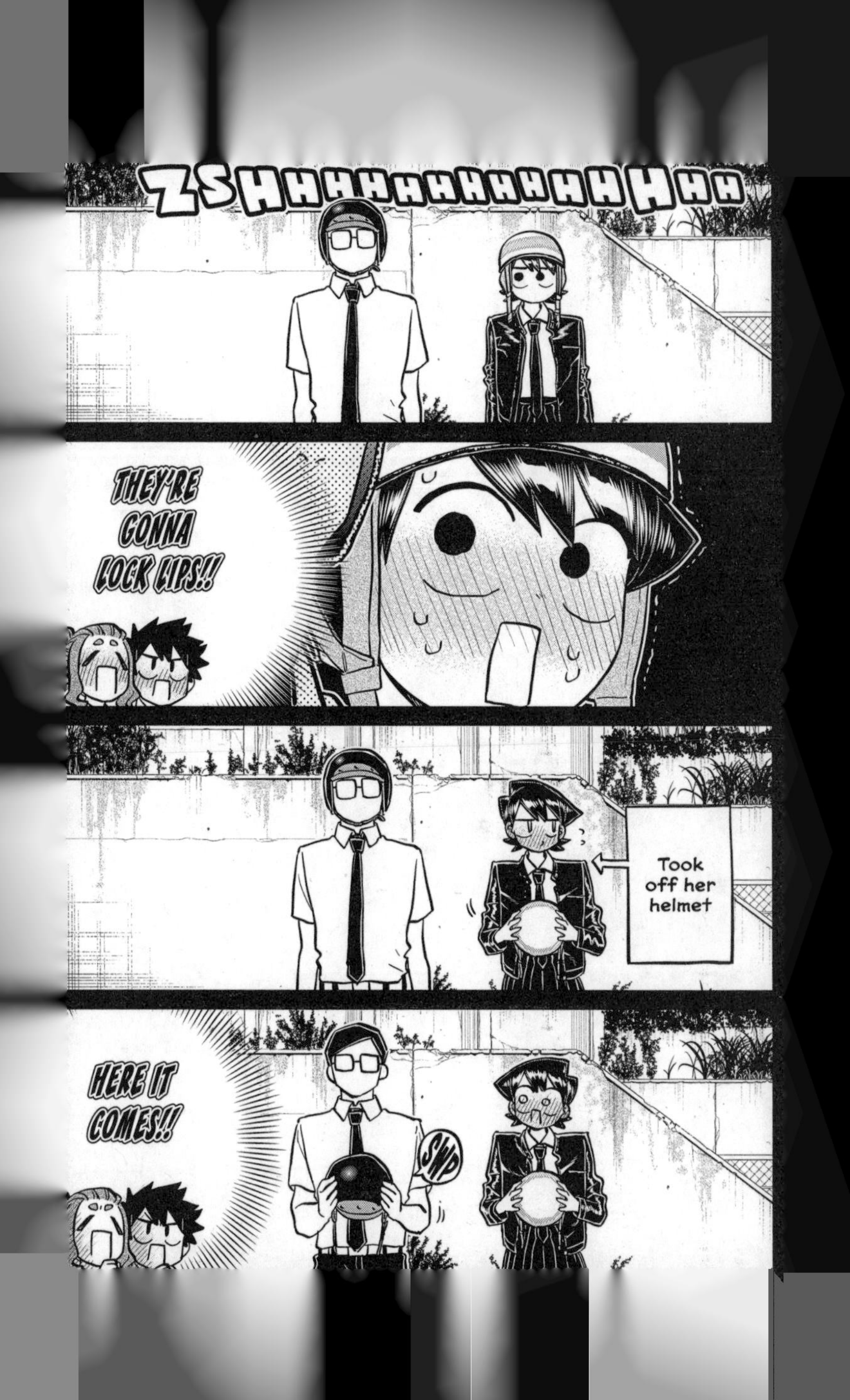
ZSHHHHHHHHHHHHHHH
THEY'RE GONNA LOCK LIPS!!
Took off her helmet
HERE IT COMES!!
SWP

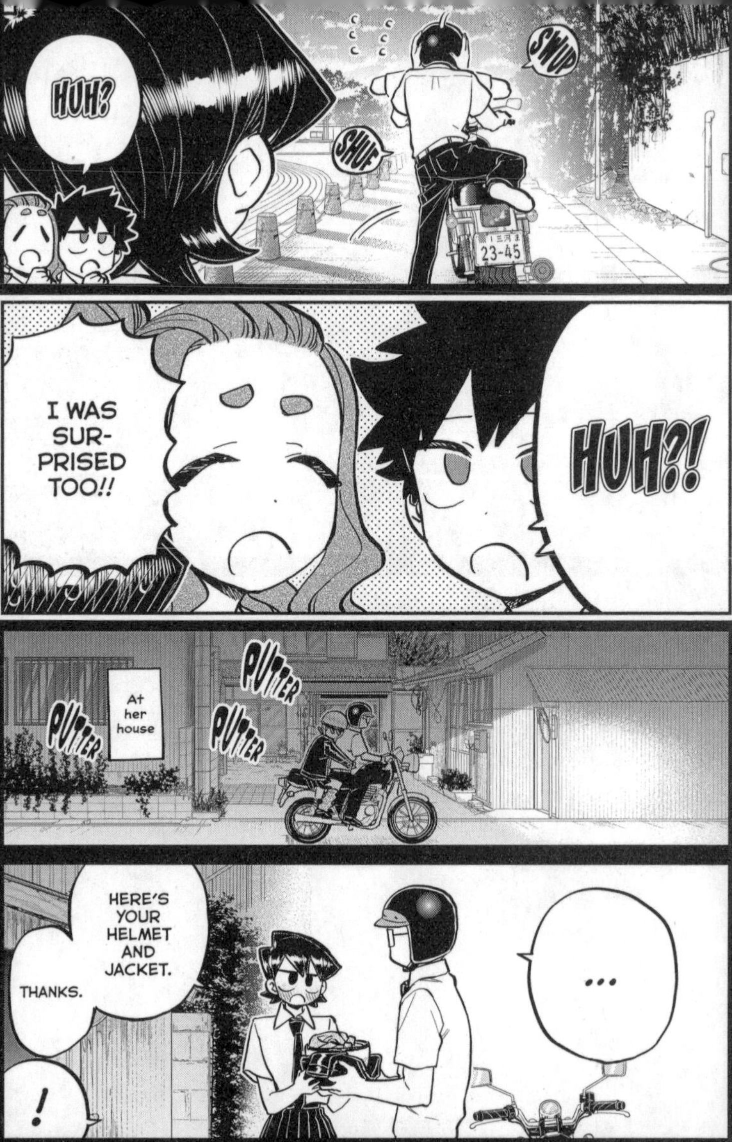
SWUP
SHUF
HUH?
HUH?!
I WAS SURPRISED TOO!!
PUTTER
PUTTER
At her house
PUTTER
...
HERE'S YOUR HELMET AND JACKET.
THANKS.
!

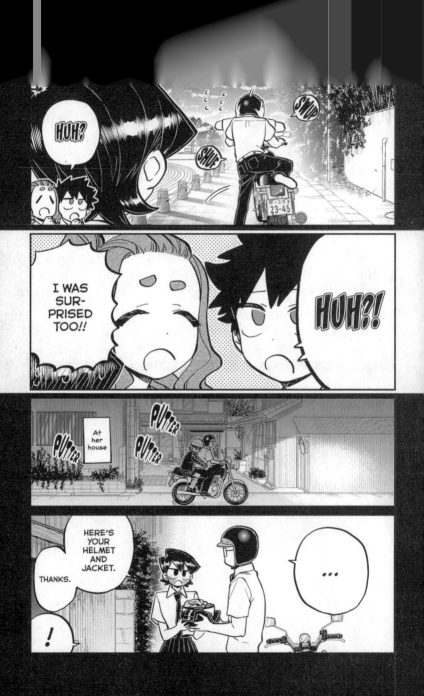

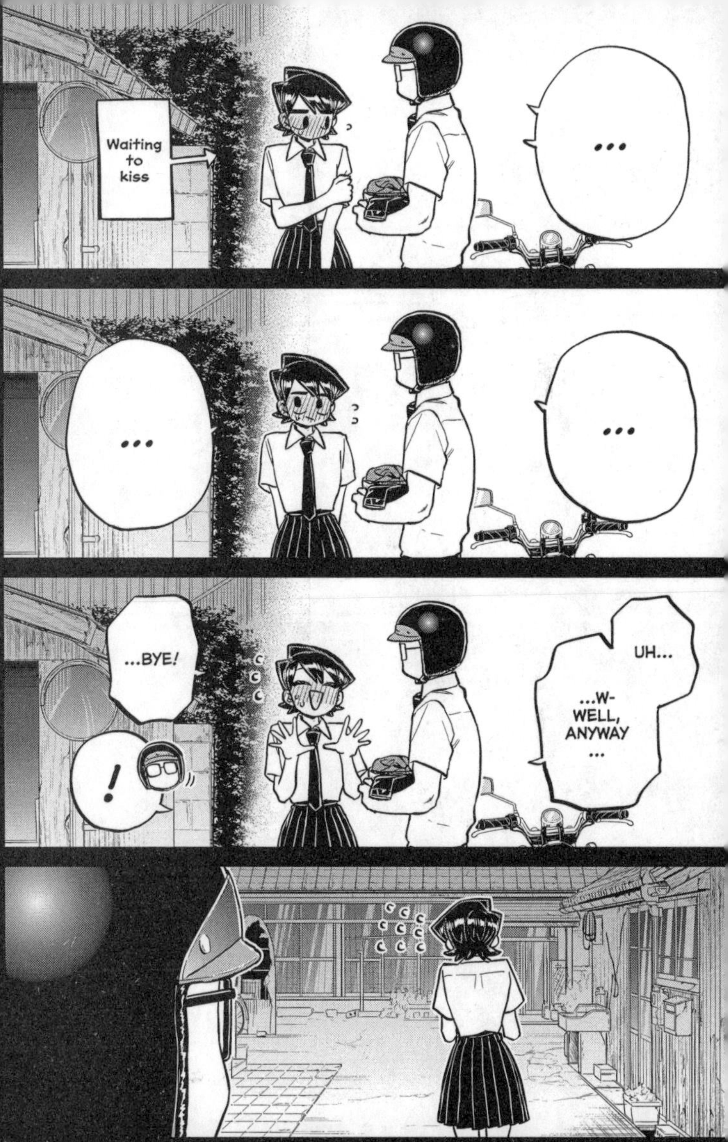
...
Waiting to kiss
...
...
UH... ...W-WELL, ANYWAY...
...BYE!
!

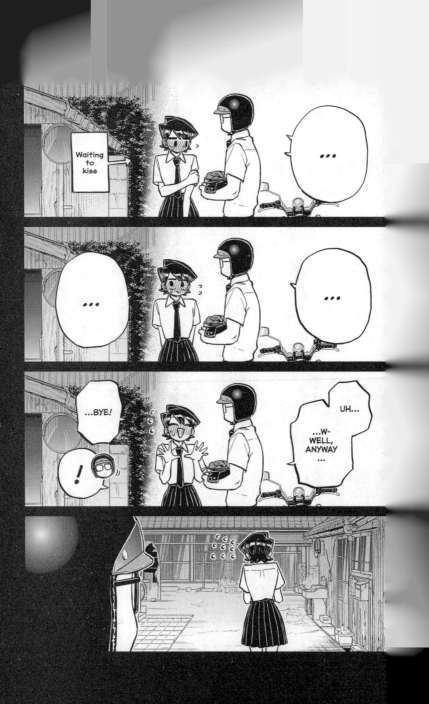

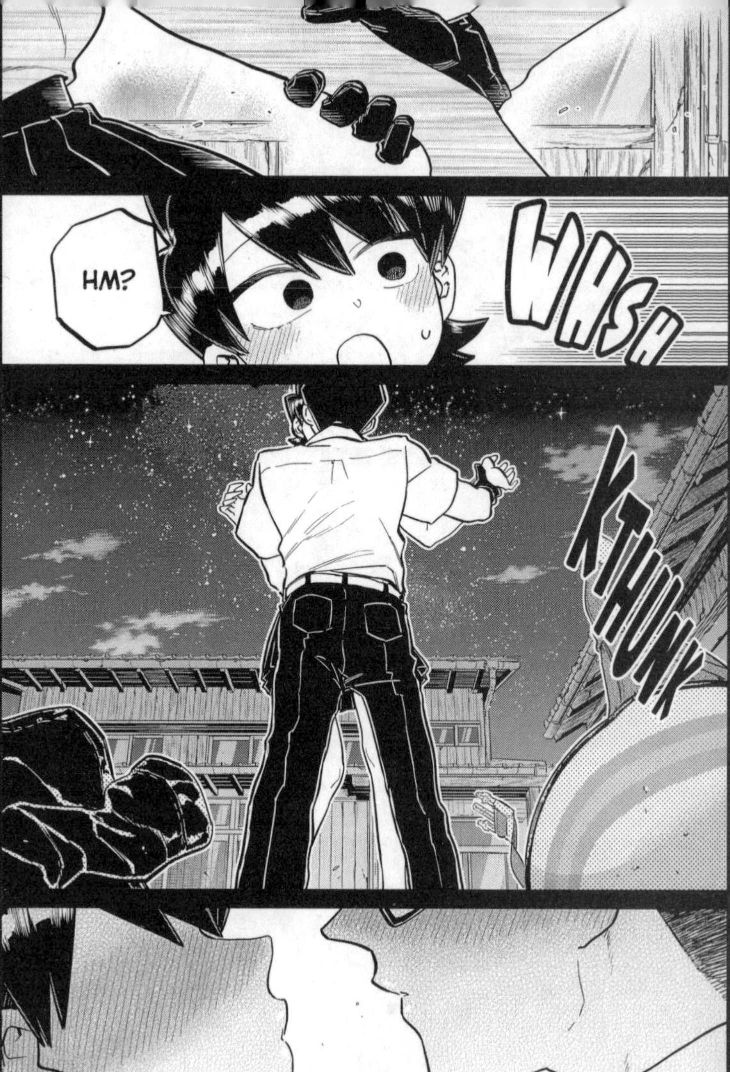
WHSH
HM?
KTHUNK
GASP

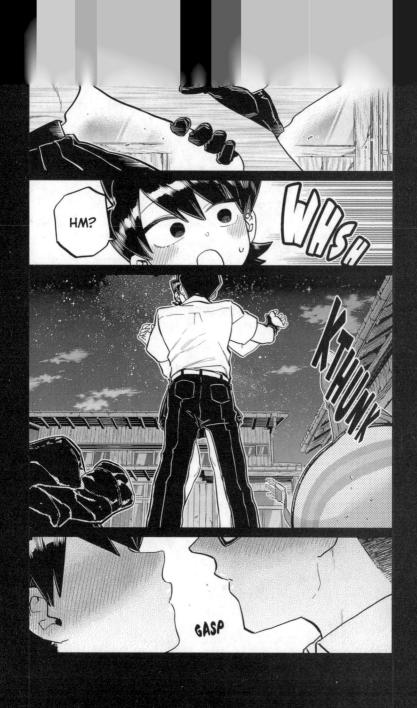

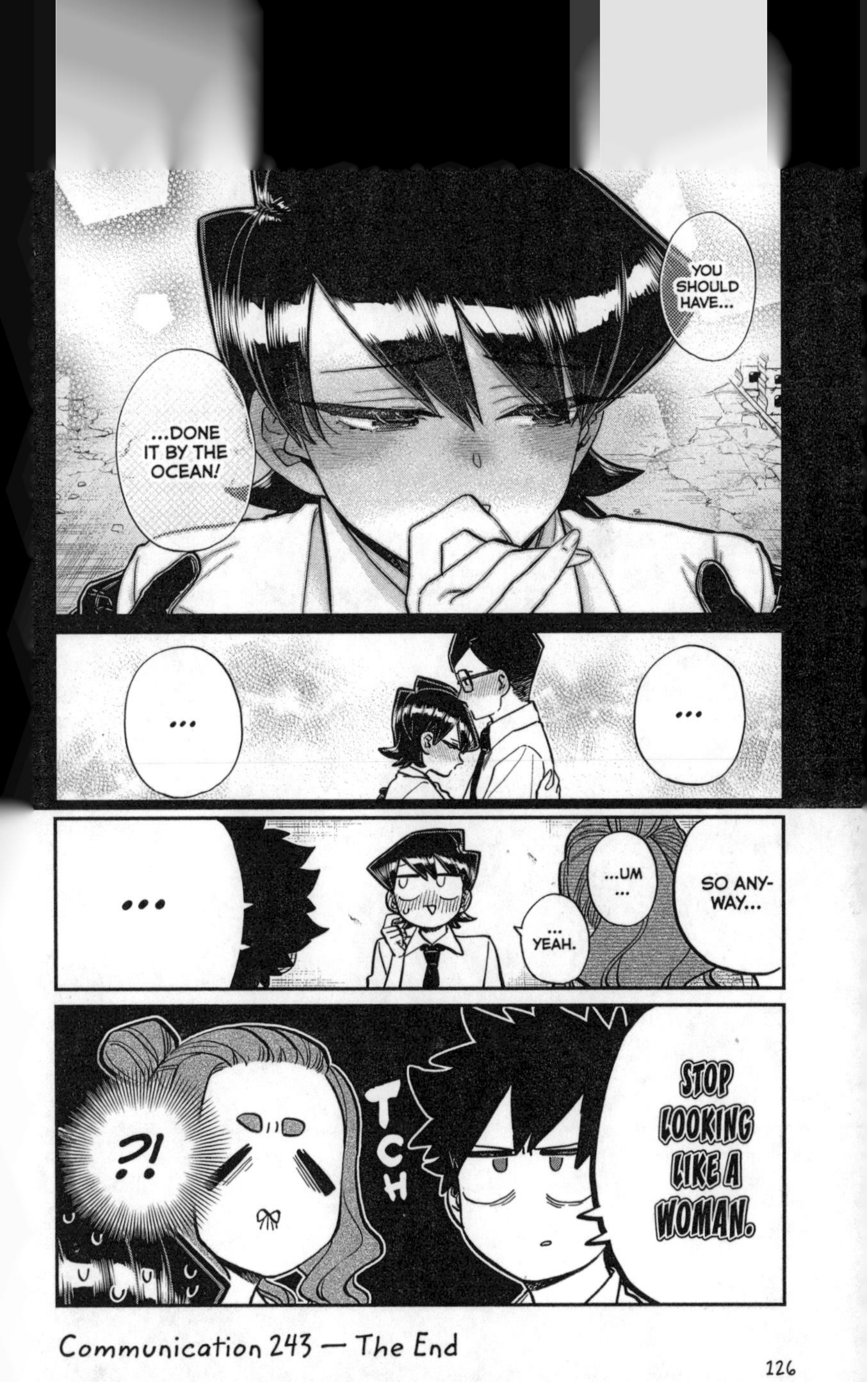
YOU SHOULD HAVE...
...DONE IT BY THE OCEAN!
...
...
SO ANY-WAY...
...UM ...
... YEAH.
...
STOP LOOKING LIKE A WOMAN.
TCH
?!

Communication 243 — The End

Komi Can't Communicate

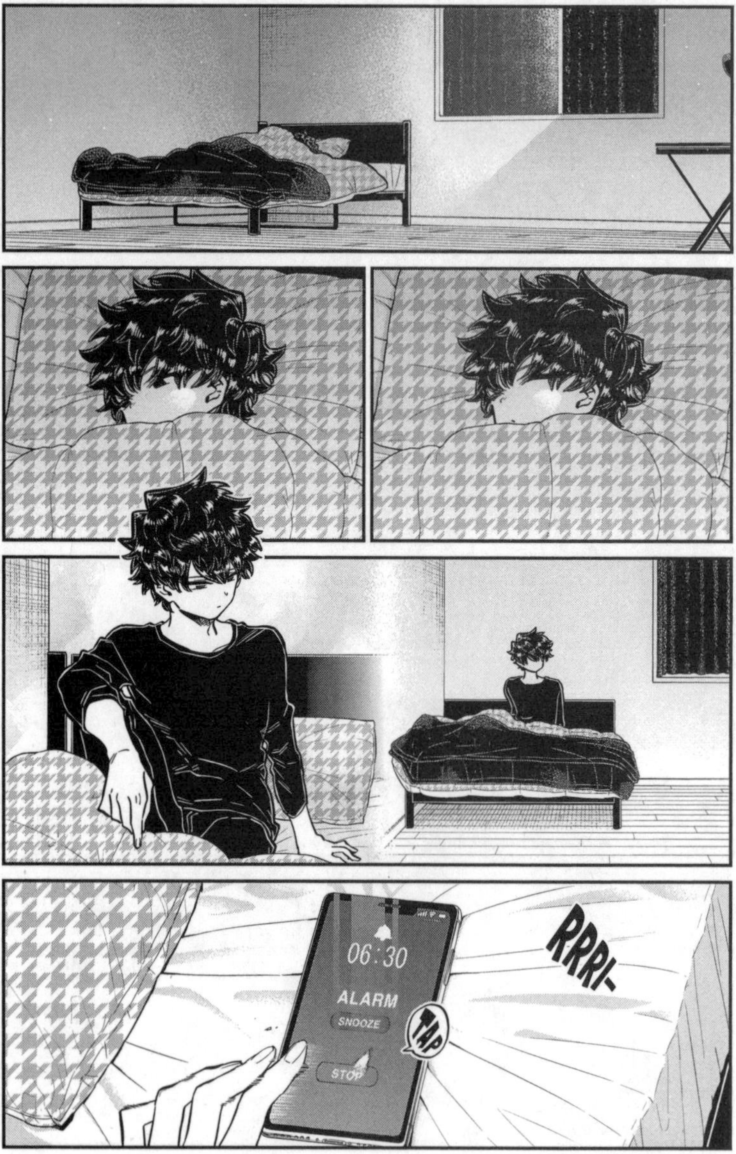
RRRI-
06:30
ALARM
SNOOZE
STOP
TAP

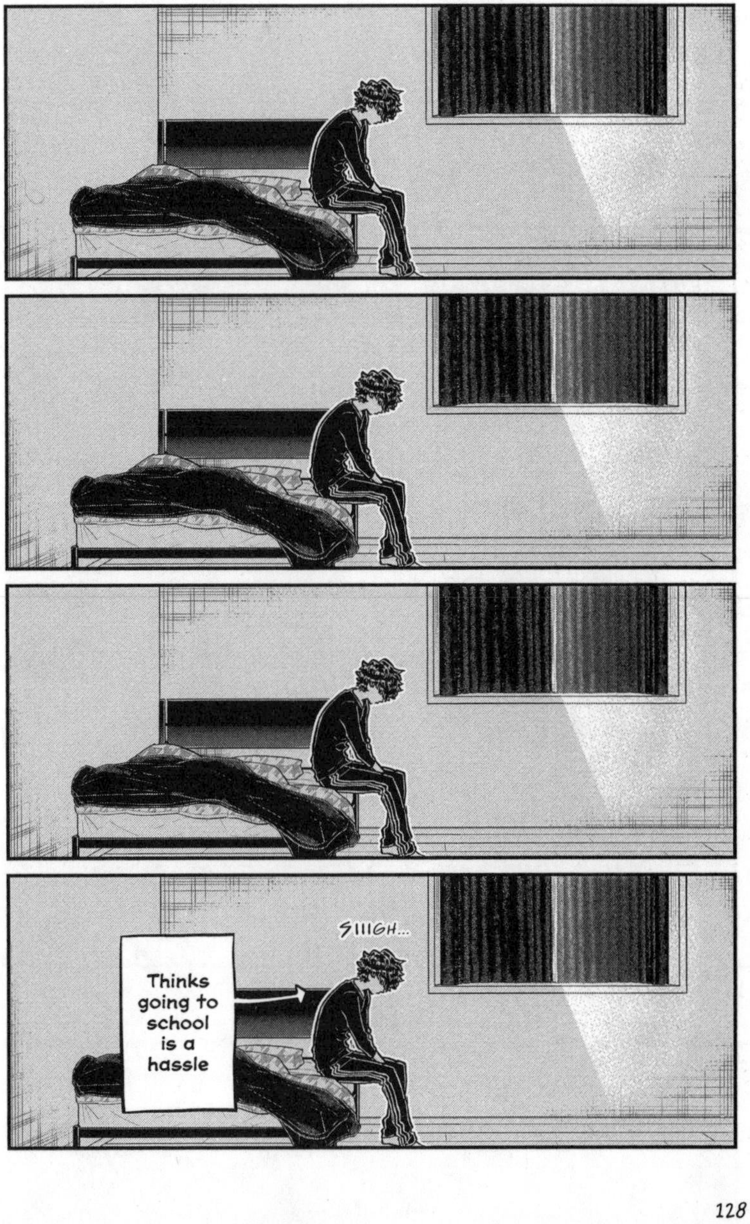
SIIIGH...
Thinks going to school is a hassle

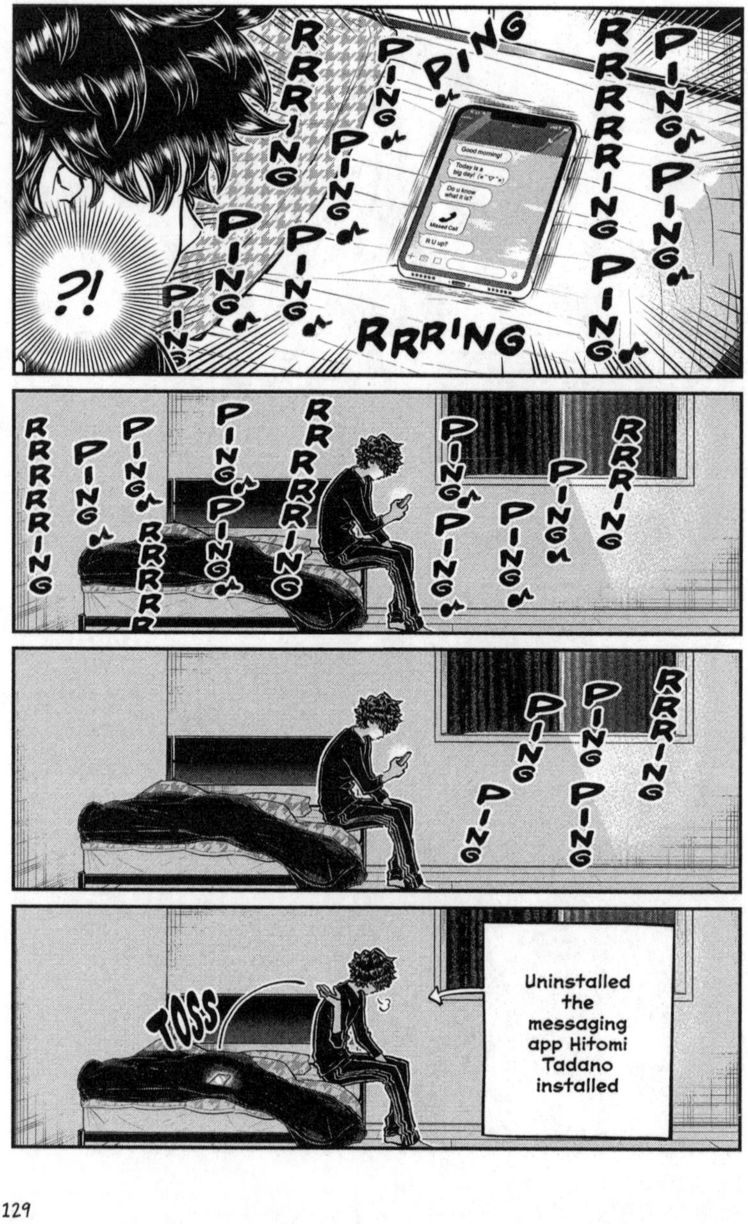
PING PING
RRRRRRING PING
PING
Good morning!
Today is a big day! (๑˘▽˘๑)
Do u know what it is?
Missed Call
R U up?
PING
PING
RRRRING
PING
PING
RRRING
PING
PING
PIN
?!
RRRING
PING
PING
PING PING
RRRRRRRING
PING PING
PING
RRRRR
PING
RRRRRING
RRRING
PING PING
PING
PING
PING
TOSS
Uninstalled the messaging app Hitomi Tadano installed

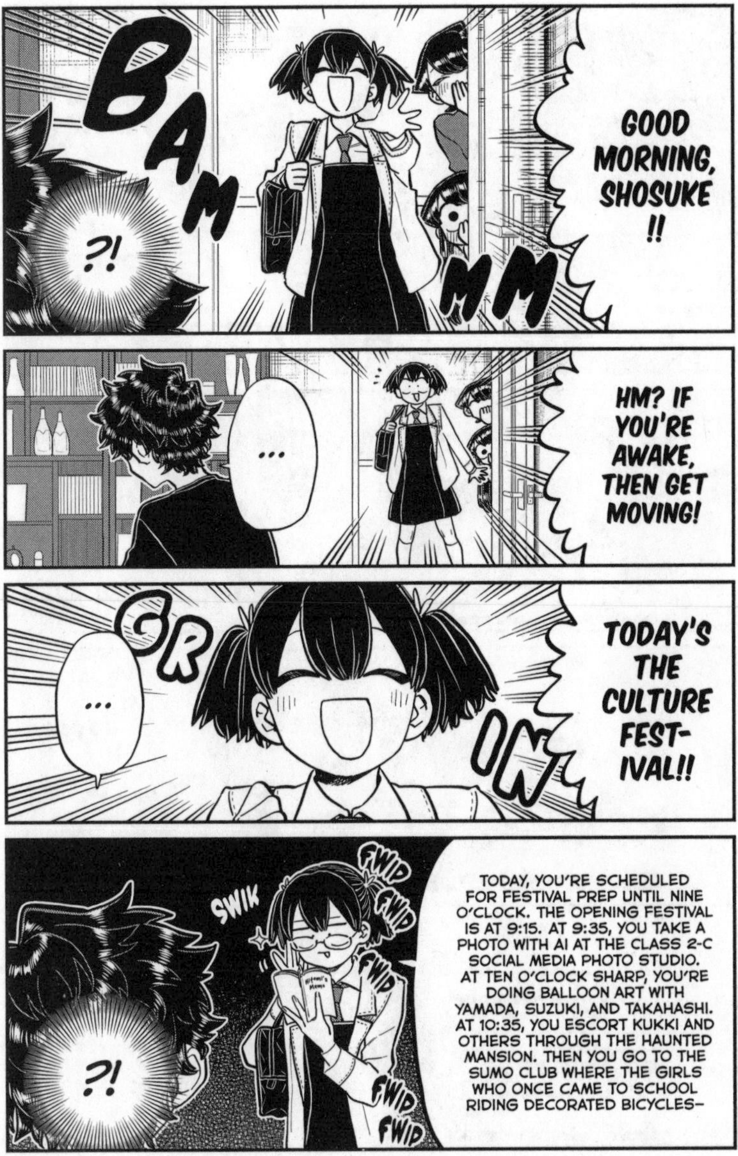
GOOD MORNING, SHOSUKE !!
MM
BAM
?!
HM? IF YOU'RE AWAKE, THEN GET MOVING!
...
TODAY'S THE CULTURE FEST-IVAL!!
ON
CR
...
TODAY, YOU'RE SCHEDULED FOR FESTIVAL PREP UNTIL NINE O'CLOCK. THE OPENING FESTIVAL IS AT 9:15. AT 9:35, YOU TAKE A PHOTO WITH AI AT THE CLASS 2-C SOCIAL MEDIA PHOTO STUDIO. AT TEN O'CLOCK SHARP, YOU'RE DOING BALLOON ART WITH YAMADA, SUZUKI, AND TAKAHASHI. AT 10:35, YOU ESCORT KUKKI AND OTHERS THROUGH THE HAUNTED MANSION. THEN YOU GO TO THE SUMO CLUB WHERE THE GIRLS WHO ONCE CAME TO SCHOOL RIDING DECORATED BICYCLES–
FWIP
FWIP
FWIP
FWIP
FWIP
SWIK
?!

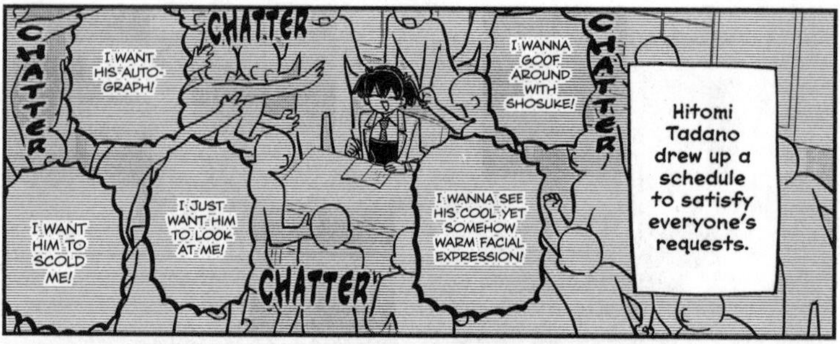
Hitomi Tadano drew up a schedule to satisfy everyone's requests.
CHATTER
I WANNA GOOF AROUND WITH SHOSUKE!
CHATTER
I WANT HIS AUTO-GRAPH!
CHATTER
I WANNA SEE HIS COOL YET SOMEHOW WARM FACIAL EXPRESSION!
I JUST WANT HIM TO LOOK AT ME!
CHATTER
I WANT HIM TO SCOLD ME!

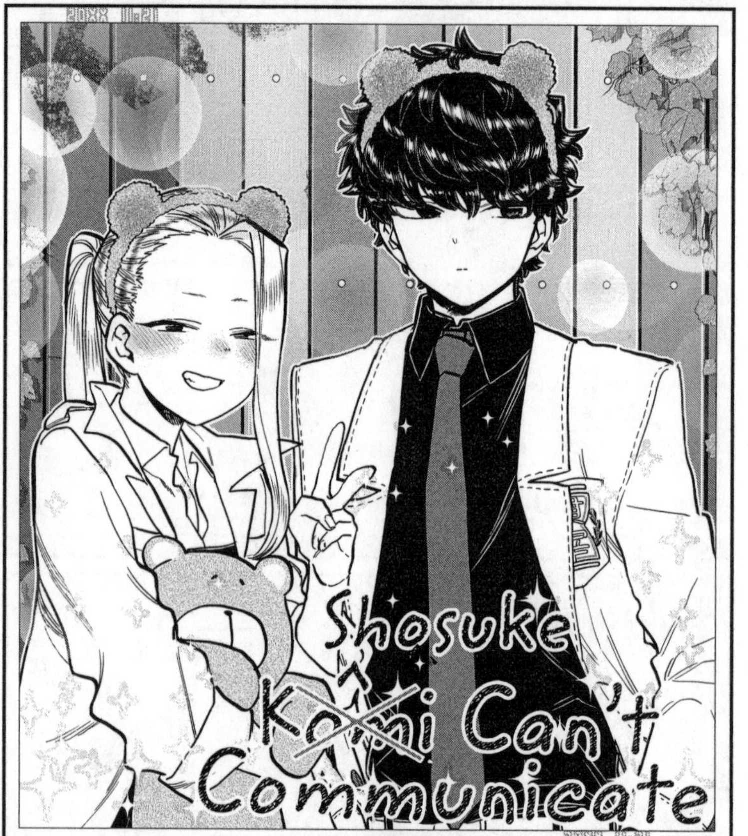
Shosuke
Komi Can't Communicate

Communication 244: Younger Brother's Culture Festival

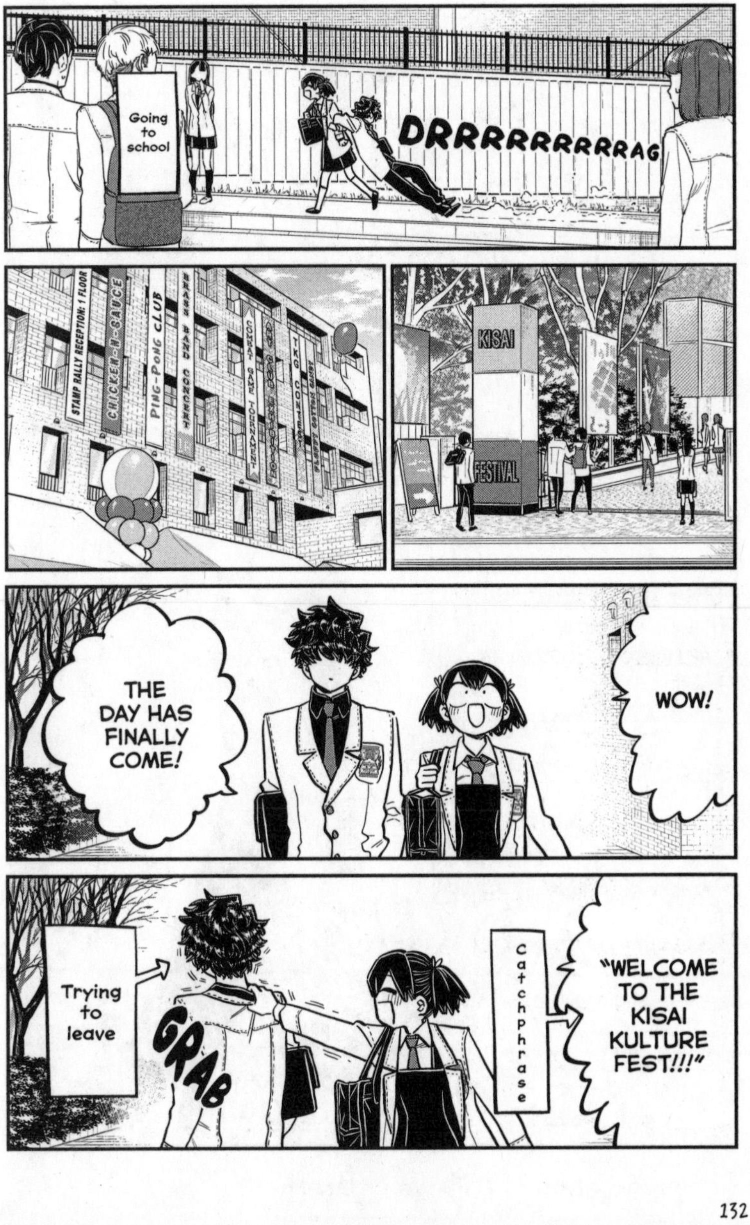
Going to school
DRRRRRRRRRRAG
KISAI
FESTIVAL
STAMP RALLY RECEPTION: 1 FLOOR
CHICKEN-N-SAUCE
PING-PONG CLUB
BRASS BAND CONCERT
COMBAT GAME TOURNAMENT
TKG CONTEST
WOW!
THE DAY HAS FINALLY COME!
“WELCOME TO THE KISAI KULTURE FEST!!!”
Catchphrase
GRAB
Trying to leave

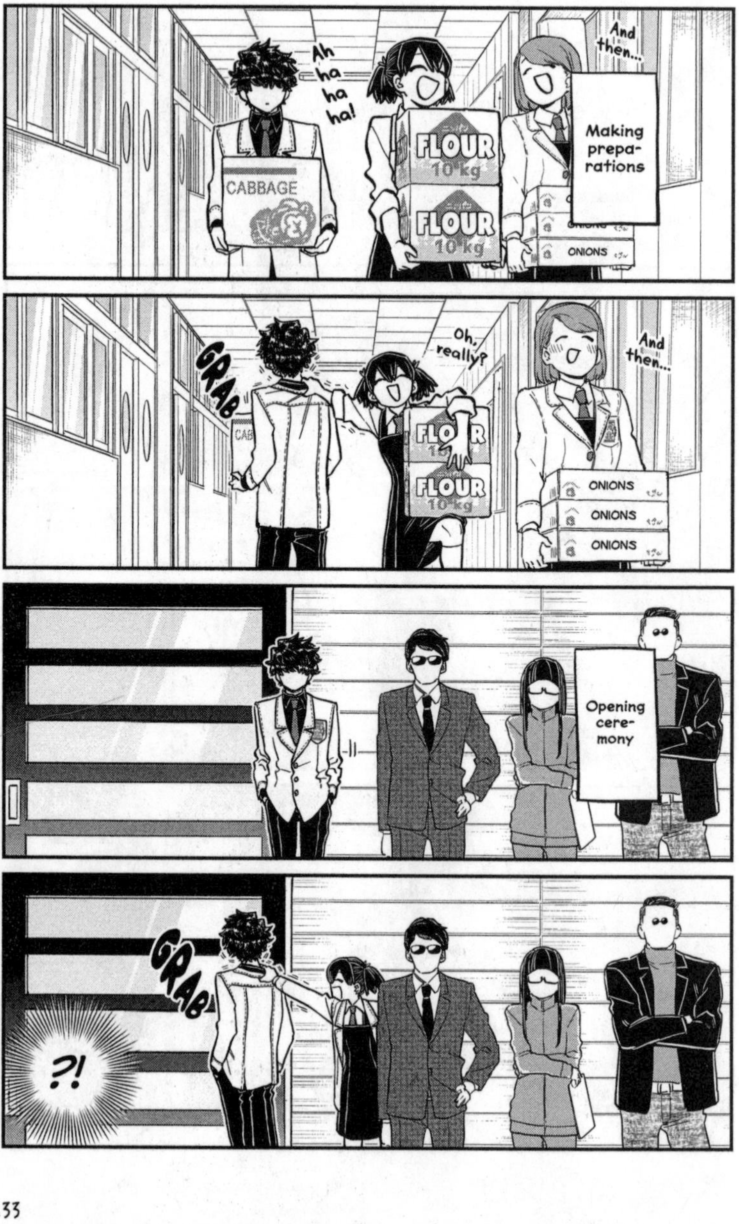
And then...
Making prepa-rations
ONIONS
ONIONS
FLOUR 10 kg
FLOUR 10 kg
Ah ha ha ha!
CABBAGE
And then...
ONIONS
ONIONS
ONIONS
Oh, really?
FLOUR 10 kg
GRAB
Opening cere-mony
GRAB
?!

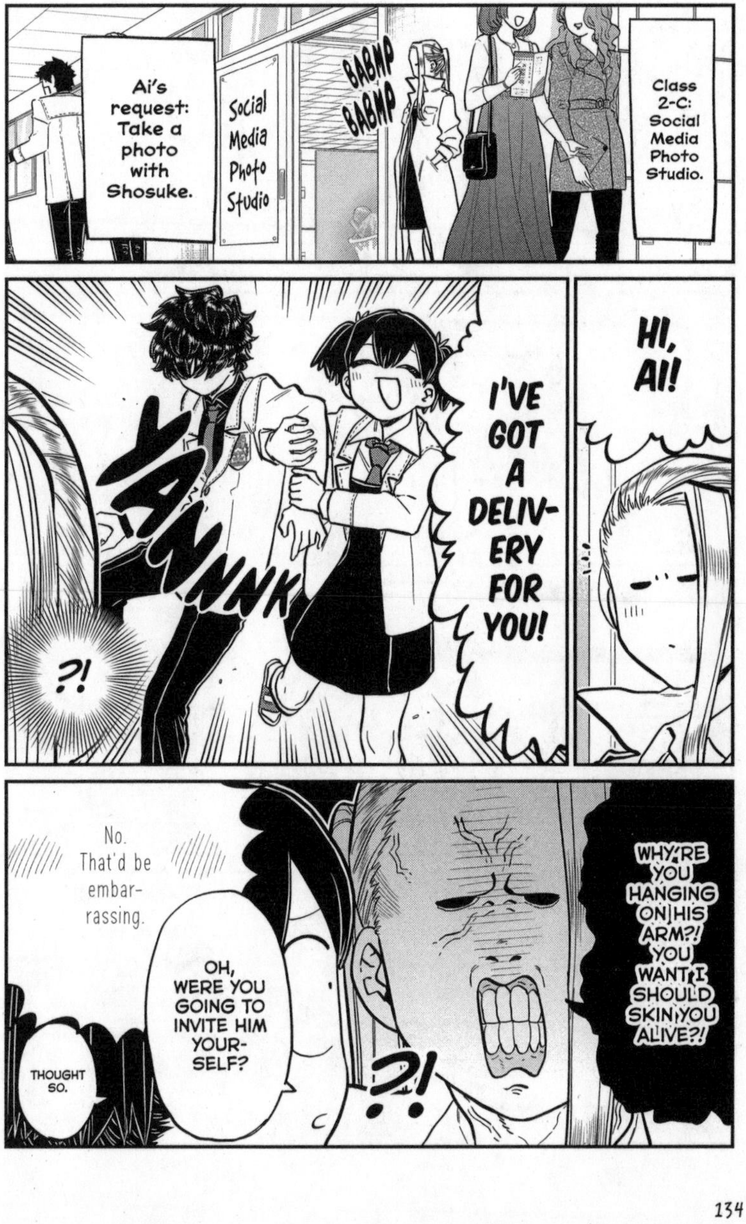
Class 2-C: Social Media Photo Studio.
BABMP BABMP
Social Media Photo Studio
Ai's request: Take a photo with Shosuke.
HI, AI!
I'VE GOT A DELIVERY FOR YOU!
YANNNK
?!
WHY'RE YOU HANGING ON HIS ARM?! YOU WANT I SHOULD SKIN YOU ALIVE?!
?!
OH, WERE YOU GOING TO INVITE HIM YOURSELF?
No. That'd be embarrassing.
THOUGHT SO.

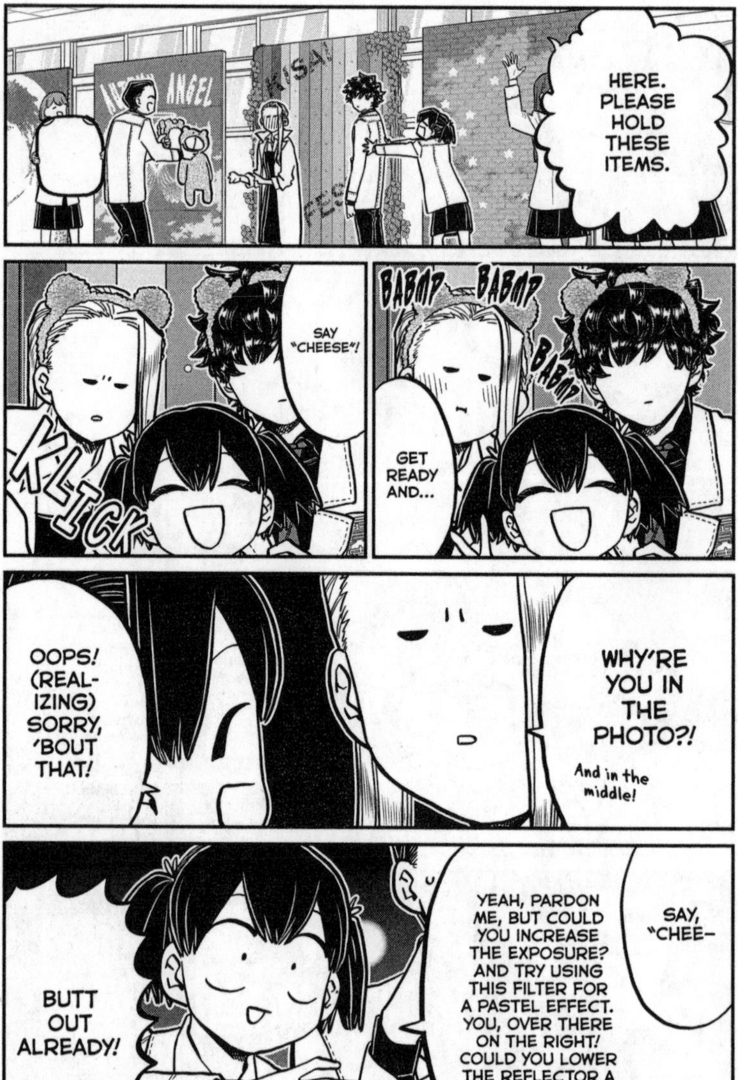
HERE. PLEASE HOLD THESE ITEMS.
ANGEL
BABMP BABMP BABMP
GET READY AND...
SAY "CHEESE"!
KLICK
WHY'RE YOU IN THE PHOTO?!
And in the middle!
OOPS! (REALIZING) SORRY, 'BOUT THAT!
SAY, "CHEE–
YEAH, PARDON ME, BUT COULD YOU INCREASE THE EXPOSURE? AND TRY USING THIS FILTER FOR A PASTEL EFFECT. YOU, OVER THERE ON THE RIGHT! COULD YOU LOWER THE REFLECTOR A LITTLE? THANKS!
BUTT OUT ALREADY!

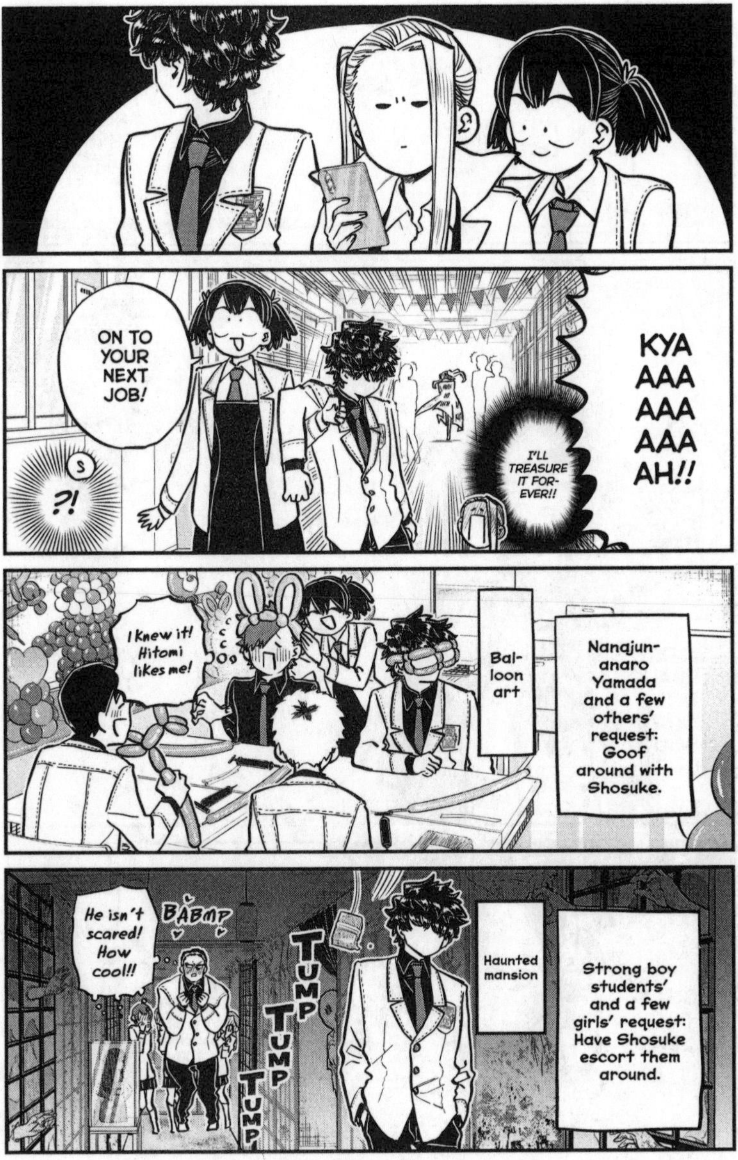

KYA AAA AAA AAA AH!!
I'LL TREASURE IT FOREVER!!
ON TO YOUR NEXT JOB!
?!
Nanajunanaro Yamada and a few others' request: Goof around with Shosuke.
Balloon art
I knew it! Hitomi likes me!
Strong boy students' and a few girls' request: Have Shosuke escort them around.
Haunted mansion
TUMP TUMP TUMP
BABMP
He isn't scared! How cool!!

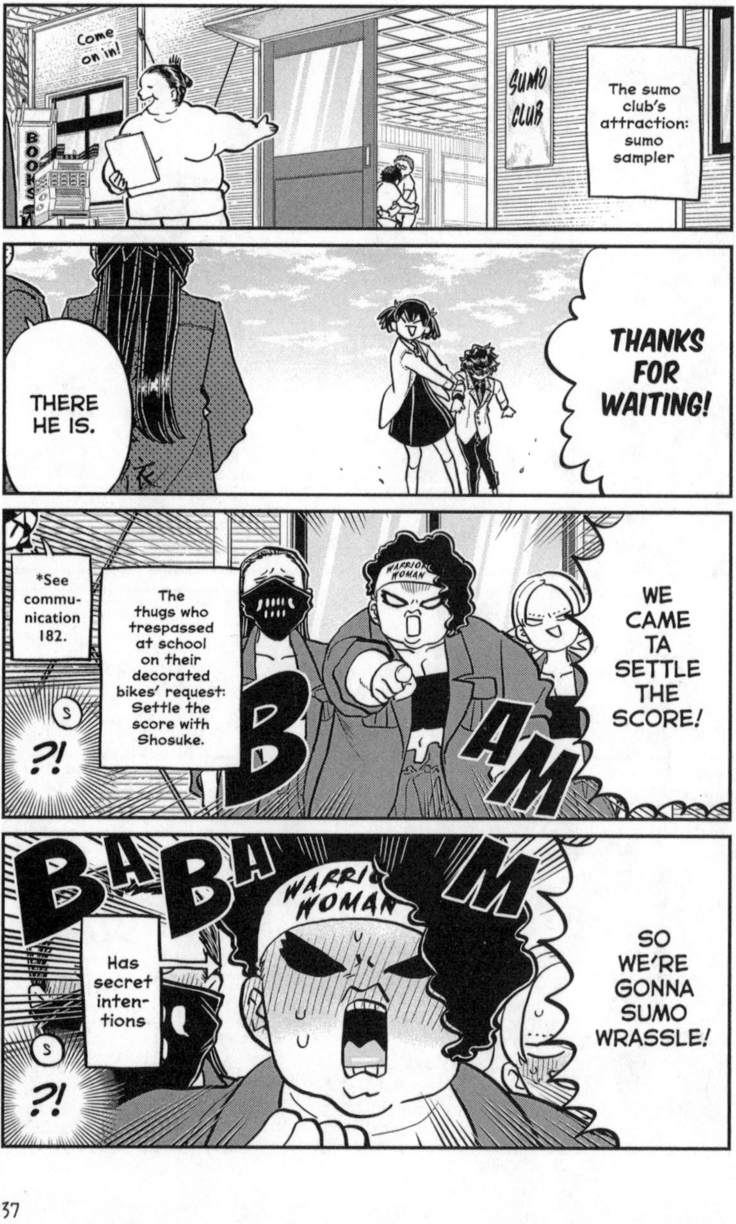
The sumo club's attraction: sumo sampler
SUMO CLUB
Come on in!
BOOKS
THANKS FOR WAITING!
THERE HE IS.
WE CAME TA SETTLE THE SCORE!
WARRIOR WOMAN
BAM
The thugs who trespassed at school on their decorated bikes' request: Settle the score with Shosuke.
*See communication 182.
?!
SO WE'RE GONNA SUMO WRASSLE!
BABAM
WARRIOR WOMAN
Has secret intentions
?!

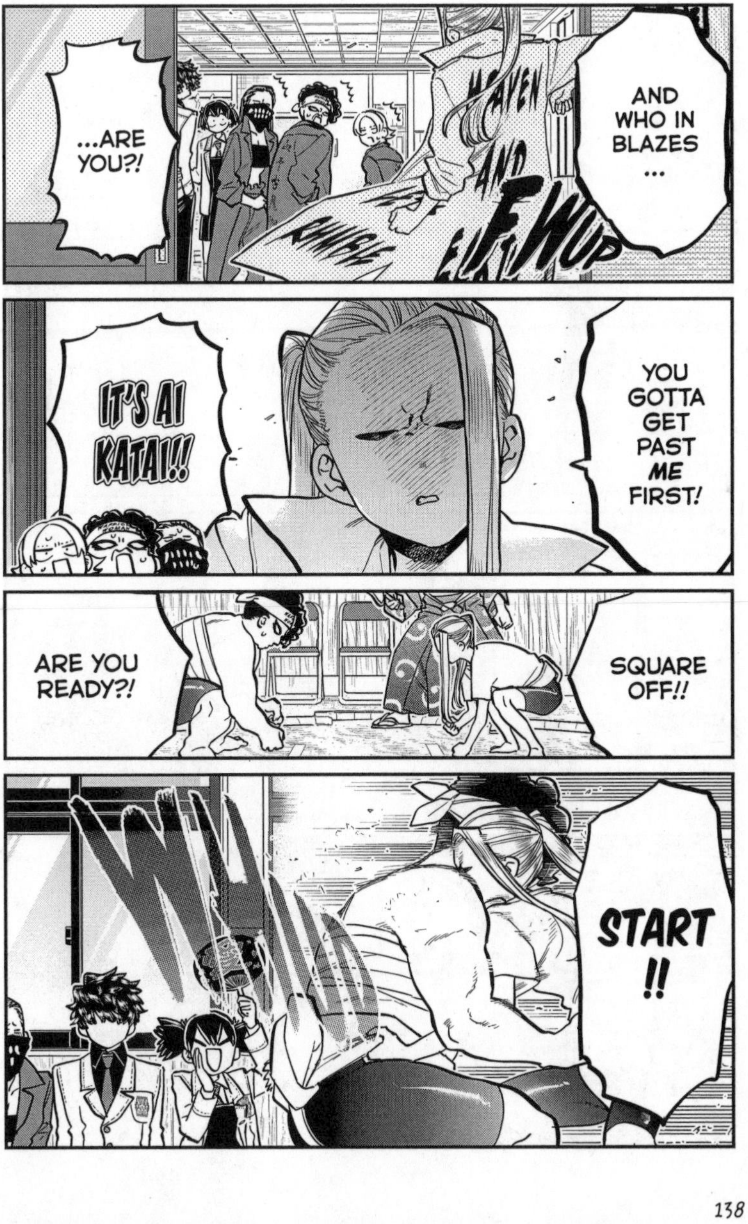
AND WHO IN BLAZES ...
FWUP
...ARE YOU?!
YOU GOTTA GET PAST *ME* FIRST!
IT'S AI KATAI!!
SQUARE OFF!!
ARE YOU READY?!
START !!

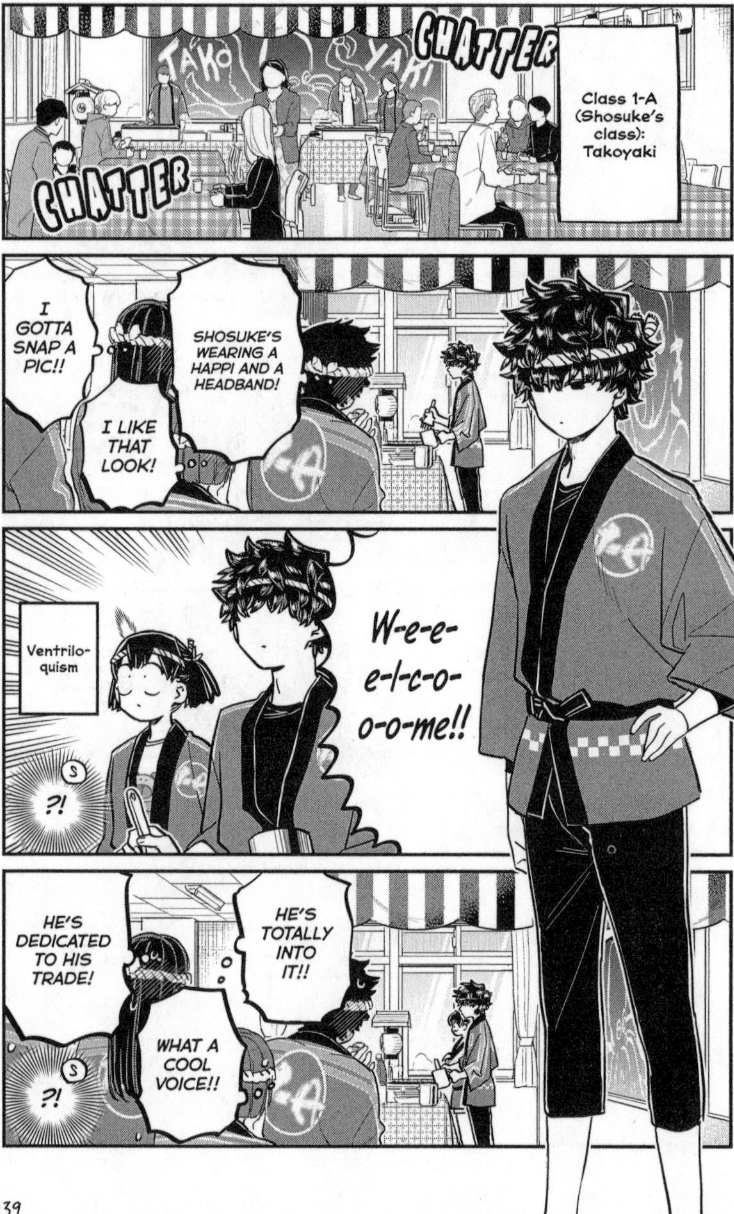
Class 1-A (Shosuke's class): Takoyaki
CHATTER
TAKO I YAKI
CHATTER
SHOSUKE'S WEARING A HAPPI AND A HEADBAND!
I LIKE THAT LOOK!
I GOTTA SNAP A PIC!!
W-e-e-e-l-c-o-o-o-me!!
Ventrilo-quism
S
?!
HE'S TOTALLY INTO IT!!
WHAT A COOL VOICE!!
HE'S DEDICATED TO HIS TRADE!
S
?!

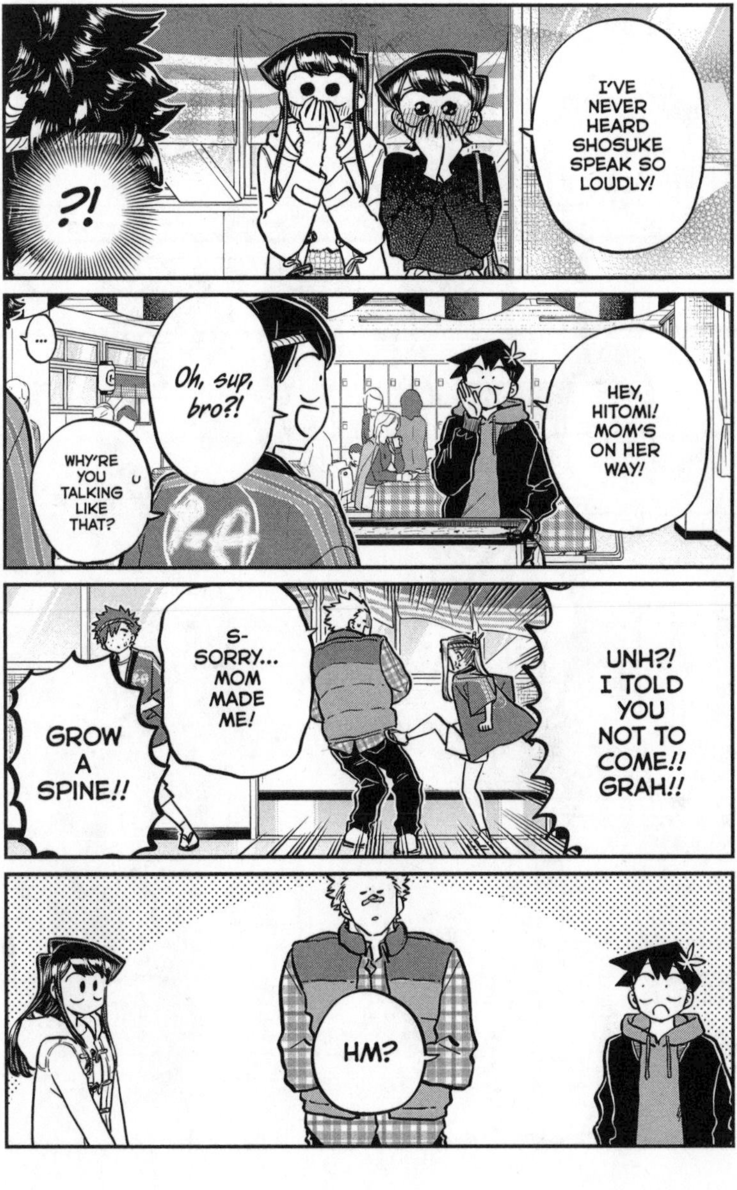
I'VE NEVER HEARD SHOSUKE SPEAK SO LOUDLY!
?!
HEY, HITOMI! MOM'S ON HER WAY!
Oh, sup, bro?!
WHY'RE YOU TALKING LIKE THAT?
...
UNH?! I TOLD YOU NOT TO COME!! GRAH!!
S-SORRY... MOM MADE ME!
GROW A SPINE!!
HM?

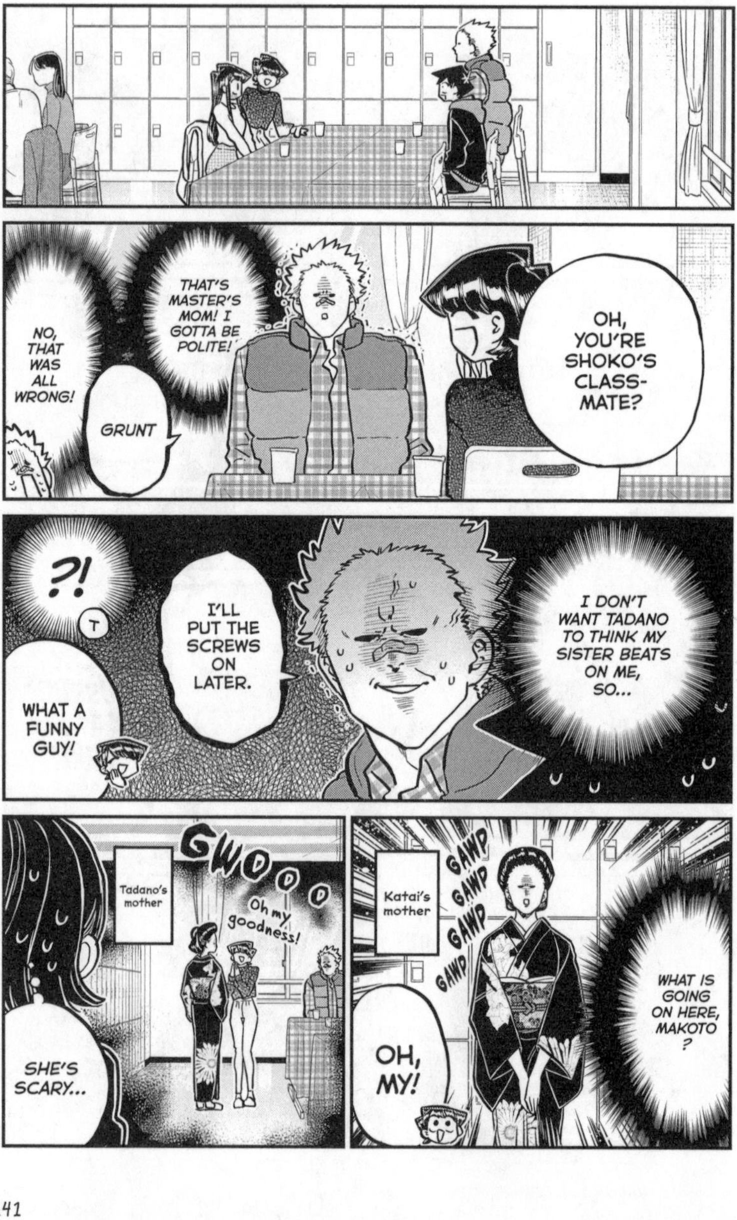
OH, YOU'RE SHOKO'S CLASSMATE?
THAT'S MASTER'S MOM! I GOTTA BE POLITE!
GRUNT
NO, THAT WAS ALL WRONG!
I DON'T WANT TADANO TO THINK MY SISTER BEATS ON ME, SO...
I'LL PUT THE SCREWS ON LATER.
?!
T
WHAT A FUNNY GUY!
Katai's mother
GAWP GAWP GAWP GAWP
WHAT IS GOING ON HERE, MAKOTO?
OH, MY!
Tadano's mother
GWOOOO
Oh my goodness!
SHE'S SCARY...

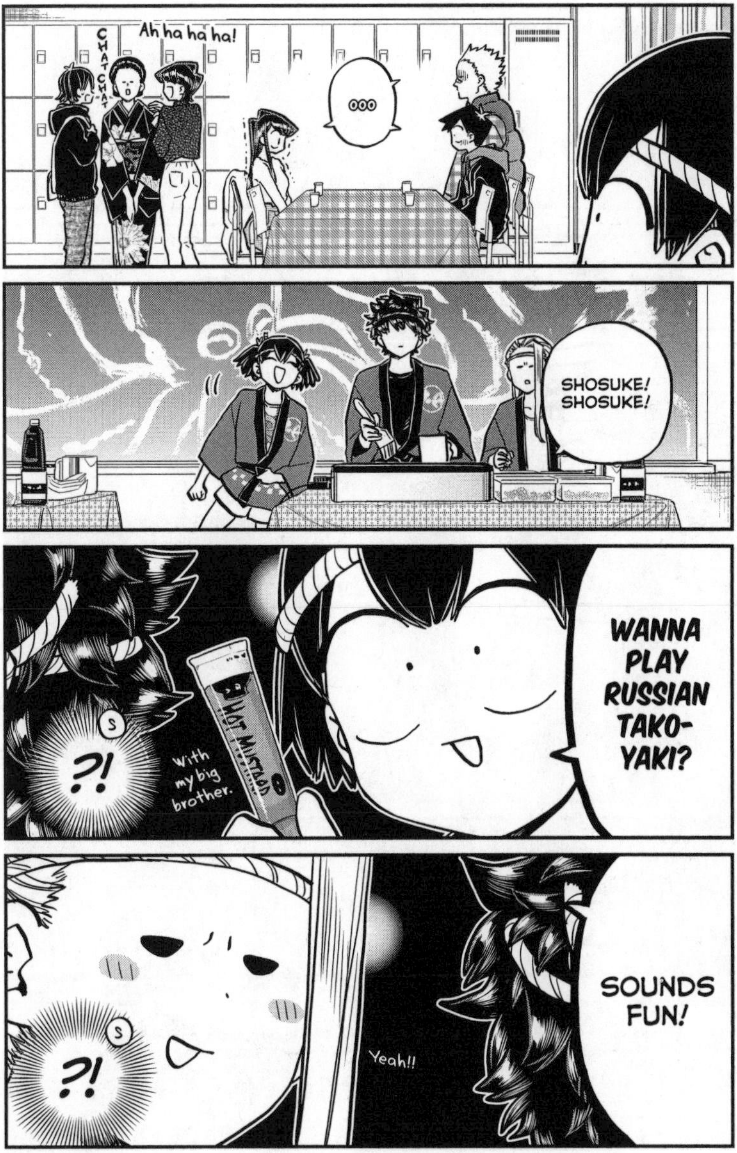
...
Ah ha ha ha!
CHAT CHAT
SHOSUKE! SHOSUKE!
WANNA PLAY RUSSIAN TAKO-YAKI?
With my big brother.
HOT MUSTARD
S
?!
SOUNDS FUN!
Yeah!!
S
?!

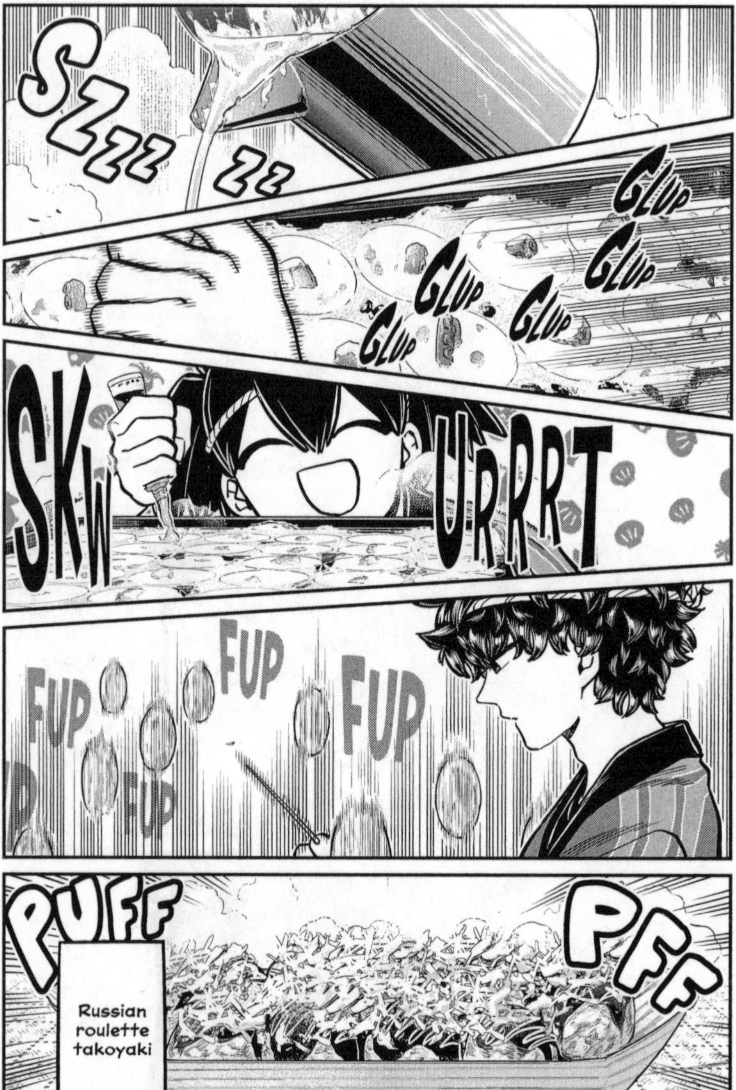
SZZZ ZZ
GLUP GLUP
GLUP GLUP
GLUP GLUP
SKWURRRT
FUP
FUP
FUP
FUP
PUFF
PFF
Russian roulette takoyaki

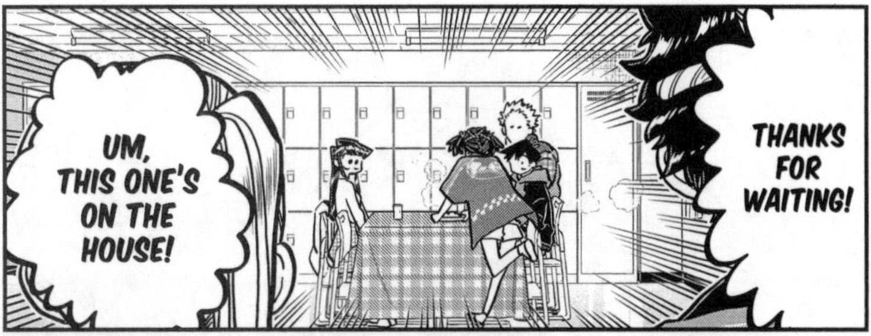
THANKS FOR WAITING!
UM, THIS ONE'S ON THE HOUSE!

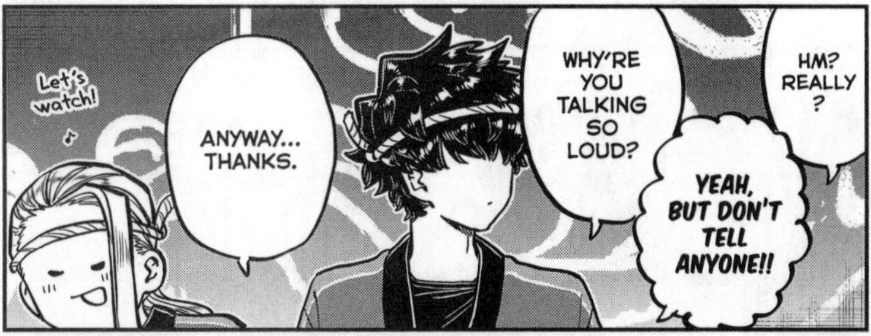
HM? REALLY ?
YEAH, BUT DON'T TELL ANYONE!!
WHY'RE YOU TALKING SO LOUD?
ANYWAY... THANKS.
Let's watch!

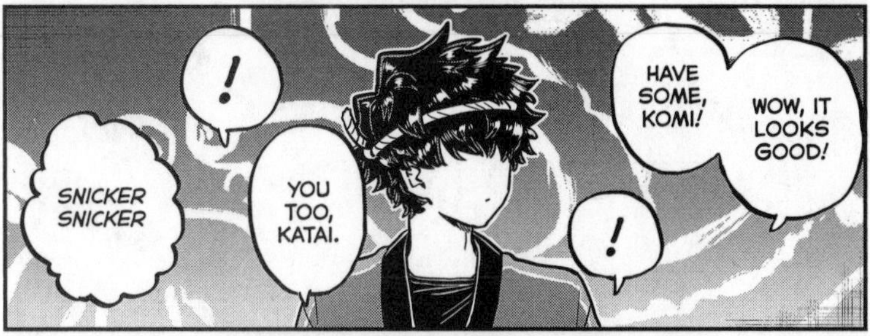
HAVE SOME, KOMI!
WOW, IT LOOKS GOOD!
!
YOU TOO, KATAI.
!
SNICKER SNICKER

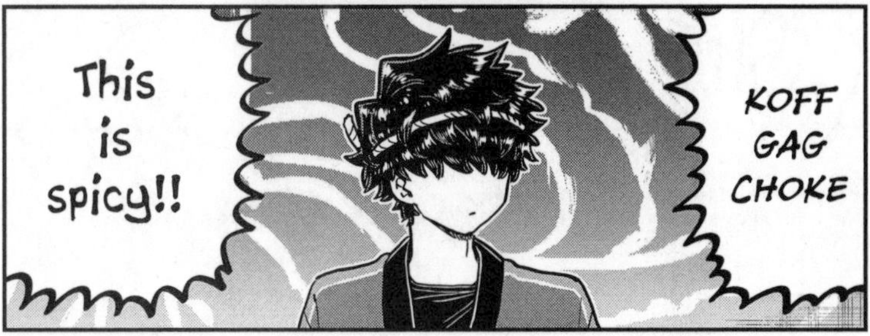
KOFF GAG CHOKE
This is spicy!!

Communication 244 — The End

HM? YOU WEREN'T WATCHING?
WANNA KNOW WHO GOT THE HOT MUSTARD?
WELL, DO YA?

It was him.
That's spicy!!

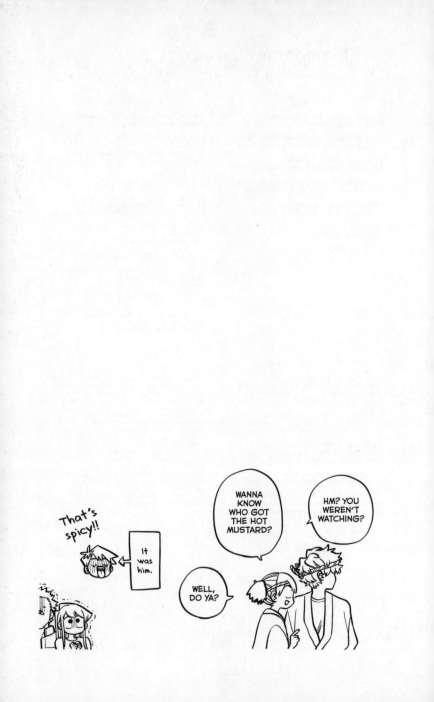

✝ NAKANAKA'S ULTIMATE LYRICS ✝

† fanatic †

The beginning of the apocalypse/
can't go back forever/

Ends of madness, Sparkle of scarlet life
Stone of sages, Ancient ruler, Ghoul-demon

Pandora, forbidden to touch
Mirages bloom at twilight, Afterimage

Marionette trapped in a warped labyrinth
Purified nothingness, Form of the future

Shimmer in the abyss, Infinite past
No ear for voices calling for a messiah

Uroboros…
…needs no requiem.

—The apocalypse has begun—

Enemy-nemee

The enemy! The enemy! The enemy!
(enemy! enemy! enemy!)

With firearm and freedom and the sign of
the cross!
Attack! Annihilate! Who will bitter words
save?

Mee! Mee! Mee!
(enemy! enemy! enemy!)

Puddles in the armored car's tracks
Ill feeling as we're doing this and that
Bribery runs rampant! Huh?! Interest?!

Aah… Obstruction! Obstruction!
Obstruction!
(enemy! enemy! enemy!)

Spin, spin, spinning wheels come spin,
spin
And snap multiplication table repeating
controlling nutcracking!
(Doll!)
It's only raucous reality! Cao Cao is great!
All who agree will fall to ruin!

Who is the enemy we must defeat?!!
Aah-nemee!!!
(enemy! enemy! enemy!)

Perro Rabioso ~Mad Dog~

I was mad? I am mad even now?
You say this unpleasant world is pretty but
How can I bless under the blue moon?
I do not want to see or feel

Lukewarm wind strokes my cheek
I want to sleep like a princess in a box
Even so I will fight in my chains

Smiles and laughs admire me
I want to see the blue sky in a faraway land
Even so I will rise with my sword

The melancholy when I smile
You should have cut it with your blade

I was mad? I am mad even now?
You say this unpleasant world is pretty but
How can I bless under the blue moon?
I do not want to see or feel

Duet

Who understands this world?
A duet shakes the heavens, I want in
Casual blackmail, Blithe retribution
Love, wisdom shot from the east capital
Our unexpiring soul is here
Dedicating ourselves to each sound
Foreshadowing behavior holds the key
None understand my aim

What rotted and when?
End everything, Annoying shutter
Don't whine, Take a chance and get alive
Do not trust the hollow data lineup
Did you hallucinate in exhaustion?
Compromise upon compromise the
mille-feuille
Battle is luck, Yeah, this is the peak
For meandering excuses, a beer in one hand

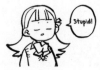

Stupid!

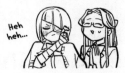

Heh
heh…

Komi Can't Communicate

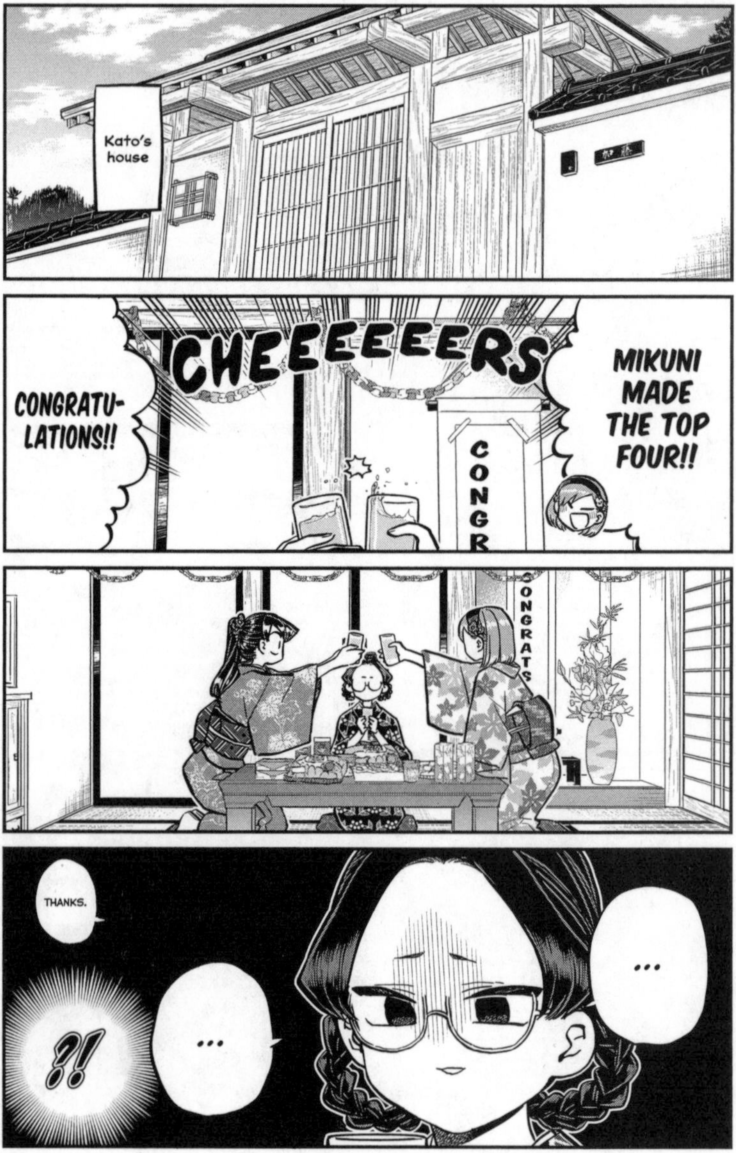

Kato's house
MIKUNI MADE THE TOP FOUR!!
CHEEEEEERS
CONGRATU-
LATIONS!!
CONGR
CONGRATS
...
THANKS.
...
?!

Communication 245: Lateral Thinking in Love Talk

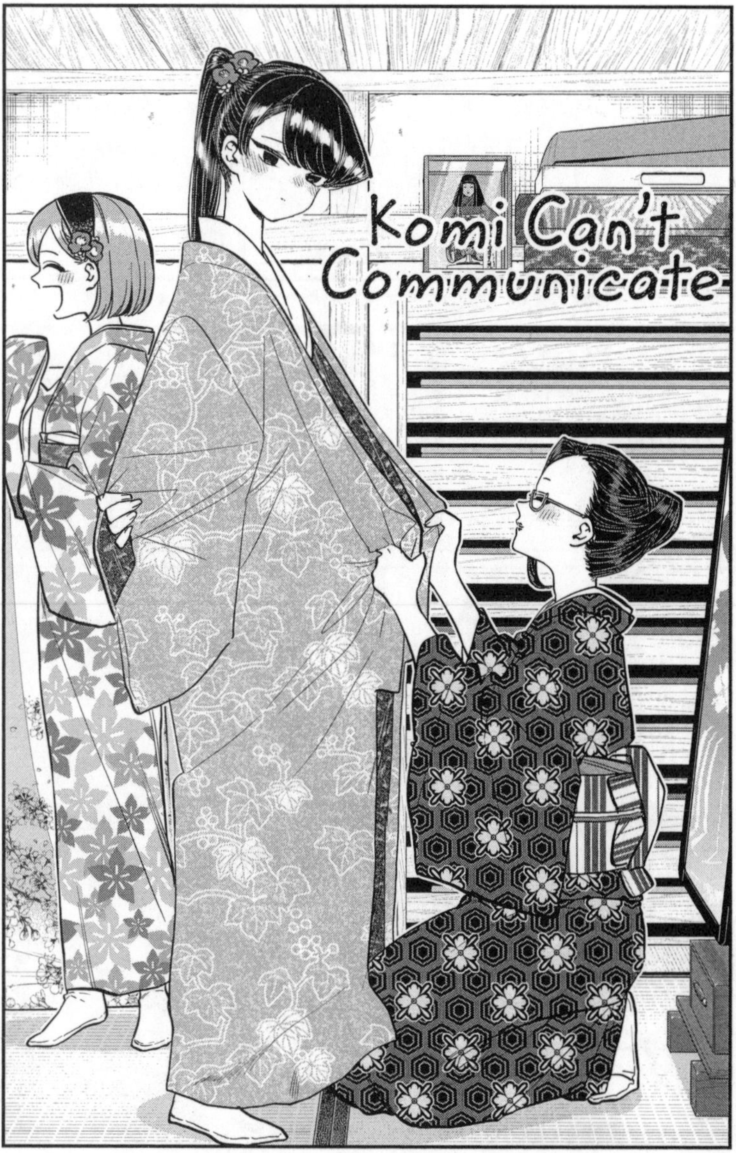
Komi Can't Communicate

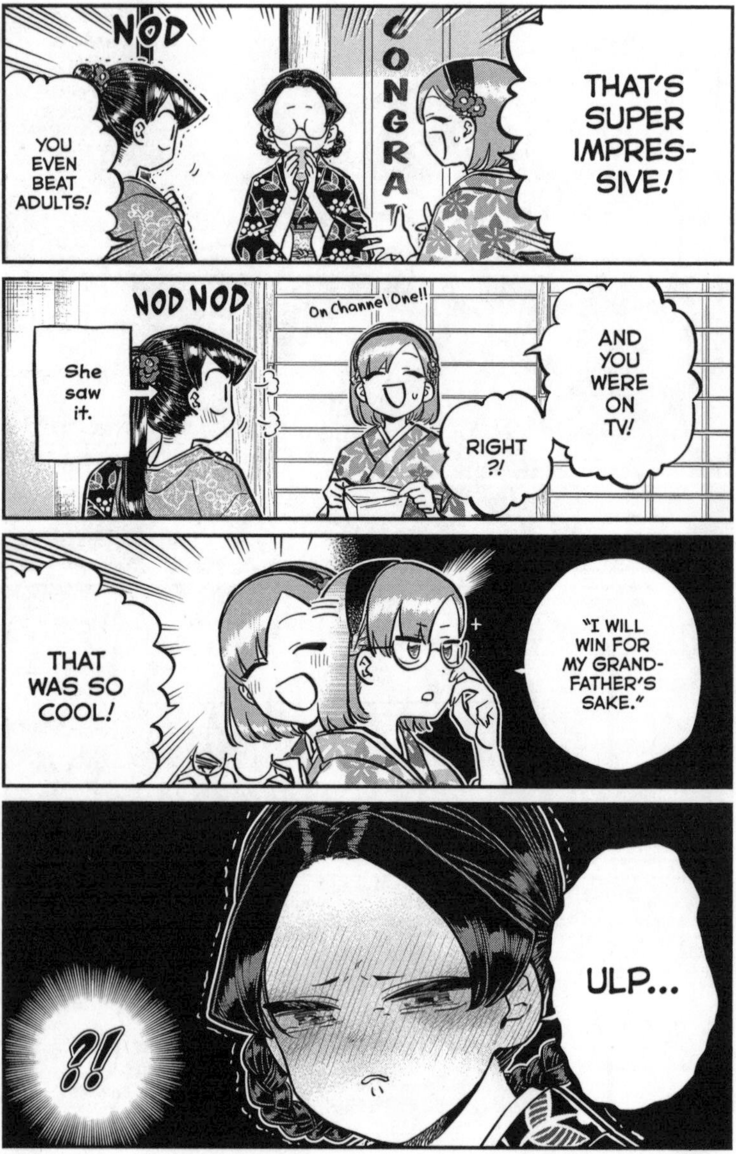
THAT'S SUPER IMPRESSIVE!
CONGRAT
NOD
YOU EVEN BEAT ADULTS!
AND YOU WERE ON TV!
RIGHT?!
On Channel One!!
NOD NOD
She saw it.
"I WILL WIN FOR MY GRAND-FATHER'S SAKE."
THAT WAS SO COOL!
ULP...
?!

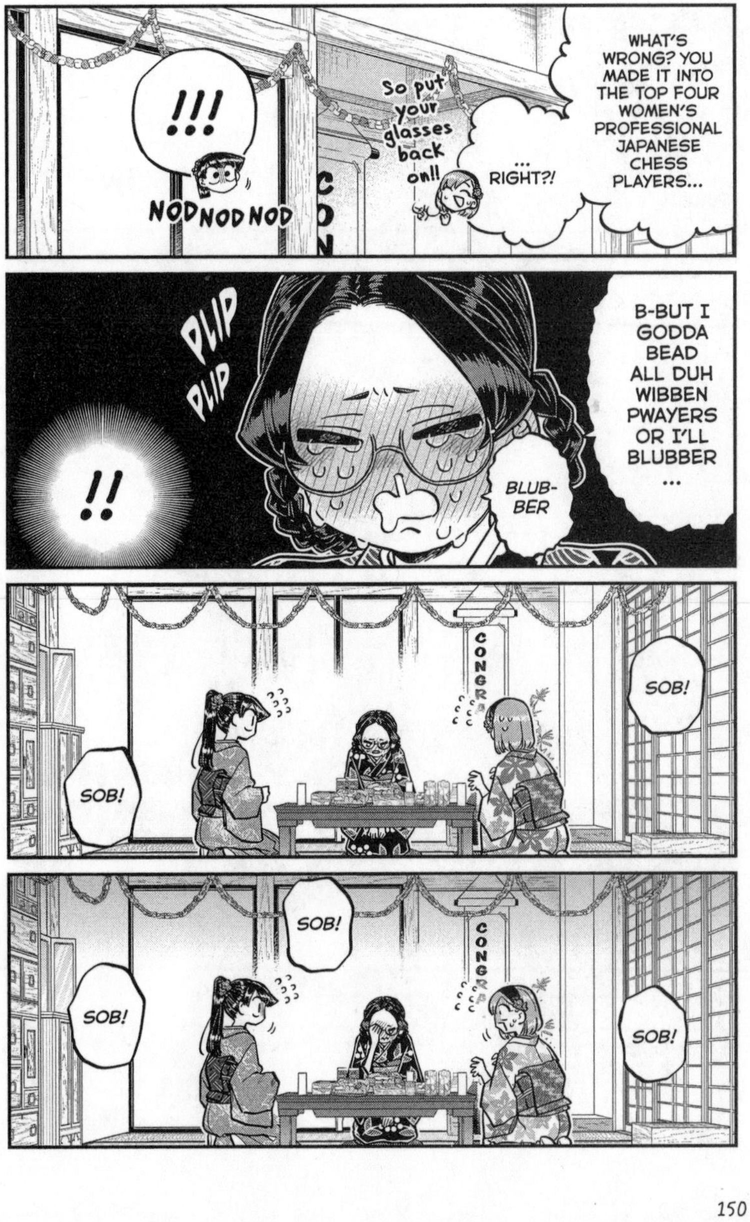
WHAT'S WRONG? YOU MADE IT INTO THE TOP FOUR WOMEN'S PROFESSIONAL JAPANESE CHESS PLAYERS...
... RIGHT?!
So put your glasses back on!!
!!!
NODNODNOD
B-BUT I GODDA BEAD ALL DUH WIBBEN PWAYERS OR I'LL BLUBBER ...
BLUB-BER
PLIP PLIP
!!
SOB!
SOB!
SOB!
SOB!
SOB!

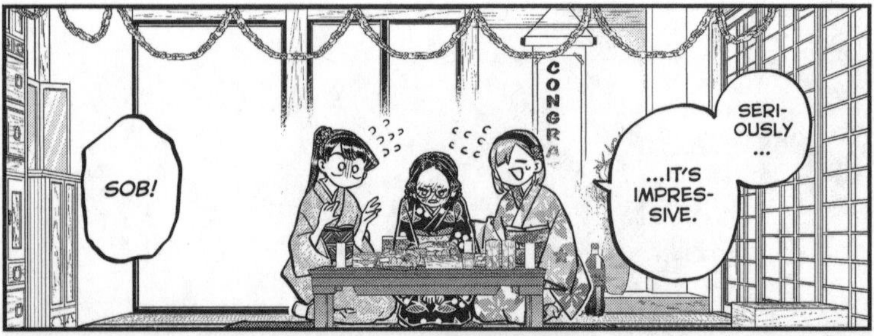
SERIOUSLY... ...IT'S IMPRESSIVE.
CONGRA
SOB!

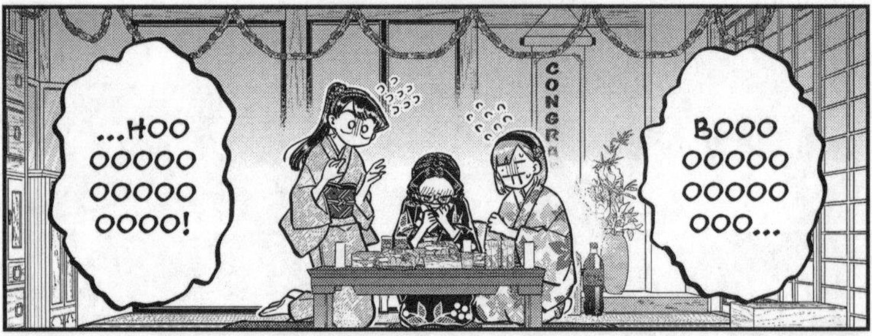
BOOO00000OOOOOOOO...
CONGRA
...HOOOOOOOOOOOOOOOOOO!

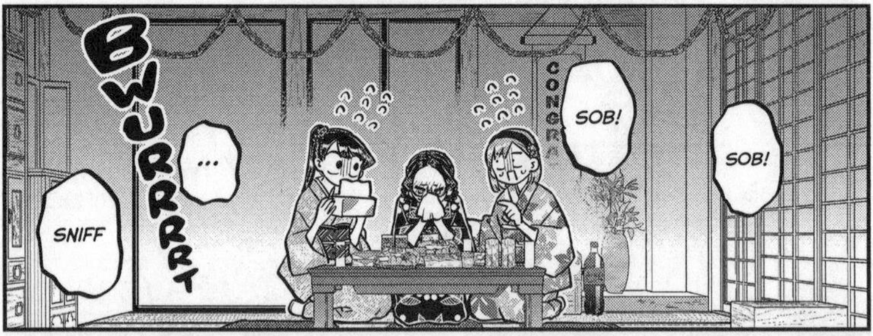
SOB!
SOB!
CONGRA
...
BWURRRRT
SNIFF

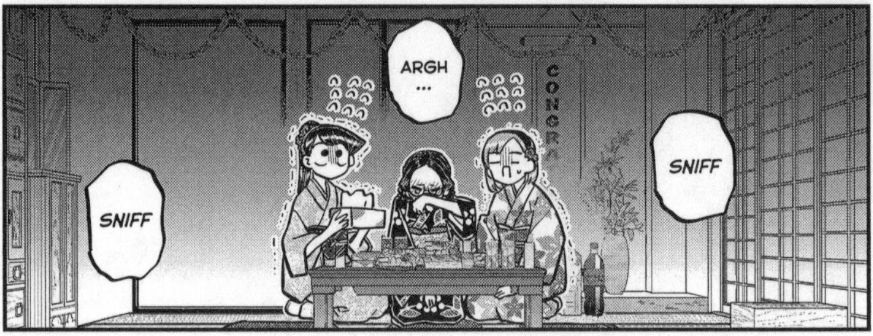
SNIFF
CONGRA
ARGH...
SNIFF

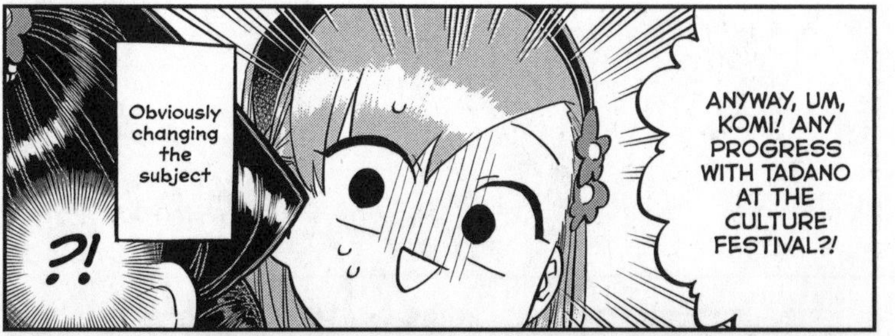
ANYWAY, UM, KOMI! ANY PROGRESS WITH TADANO AT THE CULTURE FESTIVAL?!
Obviously changing the subject
?!
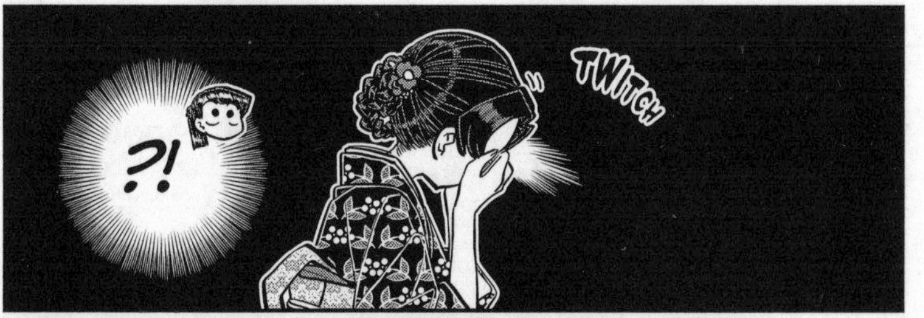
TWITCH
?!
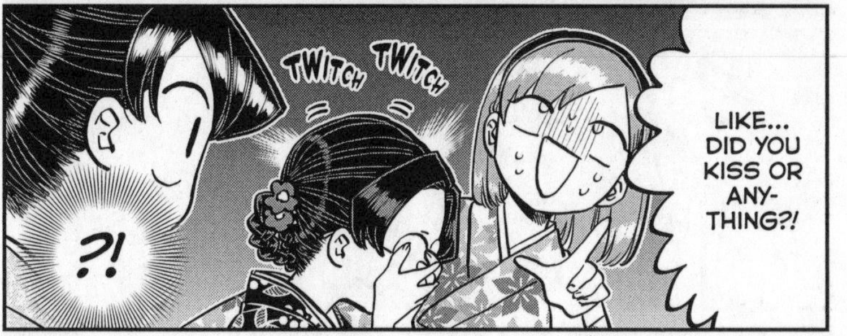
LIKE... DID YOU KISS OR ANY-THING?!
TWITCH
TWITCH
?!
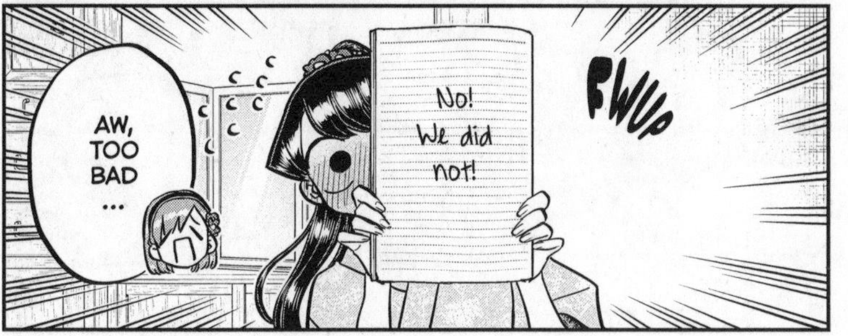
FWUP
No! We did not!
AW, TOO BAD ...

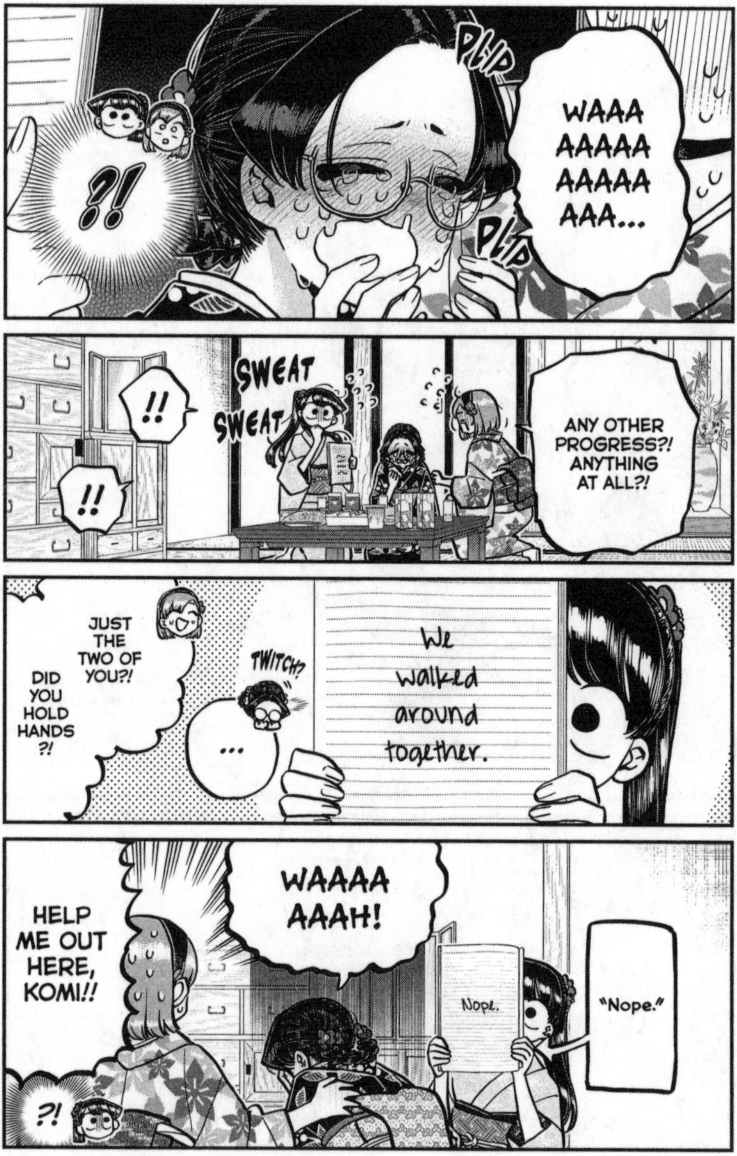
WAAA AAAAA AAAAA AAA...
PLIP
PLIP
?!
ANY OTHER PROGRESS?! ANYTHING AT ALL?!
SWEAT
SWEAT
!!
!!
We walked around together.
TWITCH?
...
JUST THE TWO OF YOU?!
DID YOU HOLD HANDS ?!
"Nope."
Nope.
WAAAA AAAH!
HELP ME OUT HERE, KOMI!!
?!

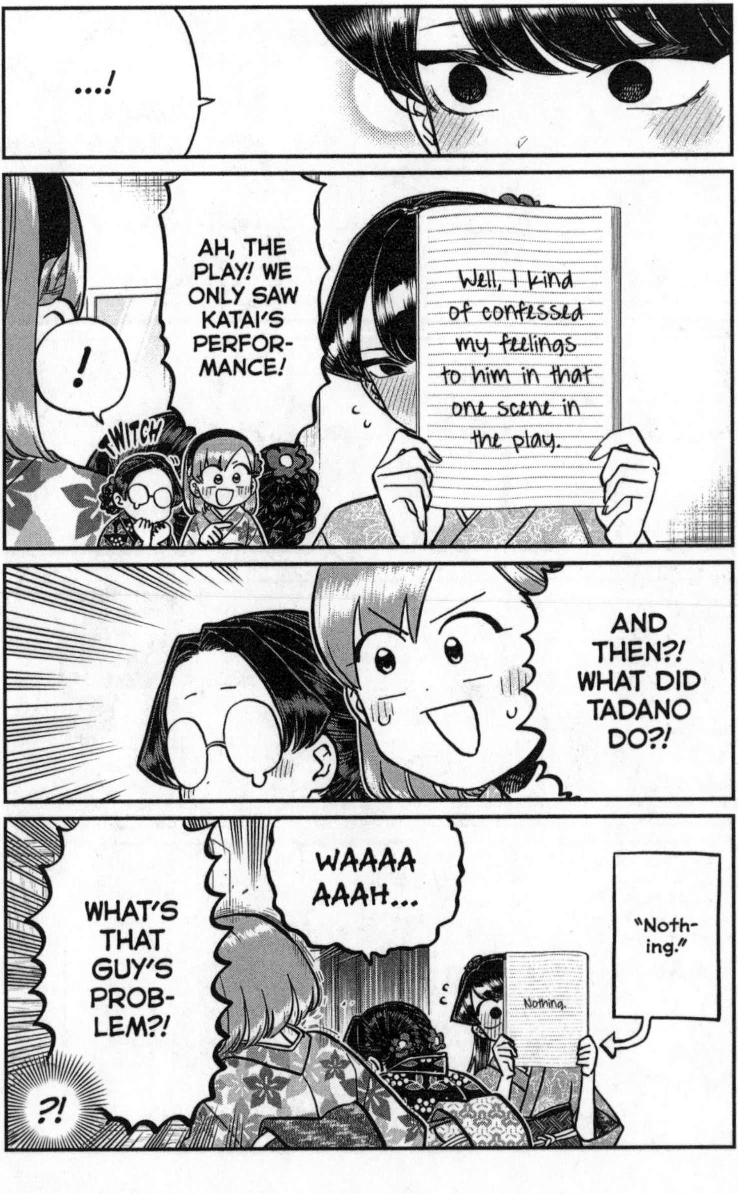
...!
Well, I kind of confessed my feelings to him in that one scene in the play.
AH, THE PLAY! WE ONLY SAW KATAI'S PERFORMANCE!
!
TWITCH
AND THEN?! WHAT DID TADANO DO?!
"Noth-ing."
Nothing.
WAAAA AAAH...
WHAT'S THAT GUY'S PROB-LEM?!
?!

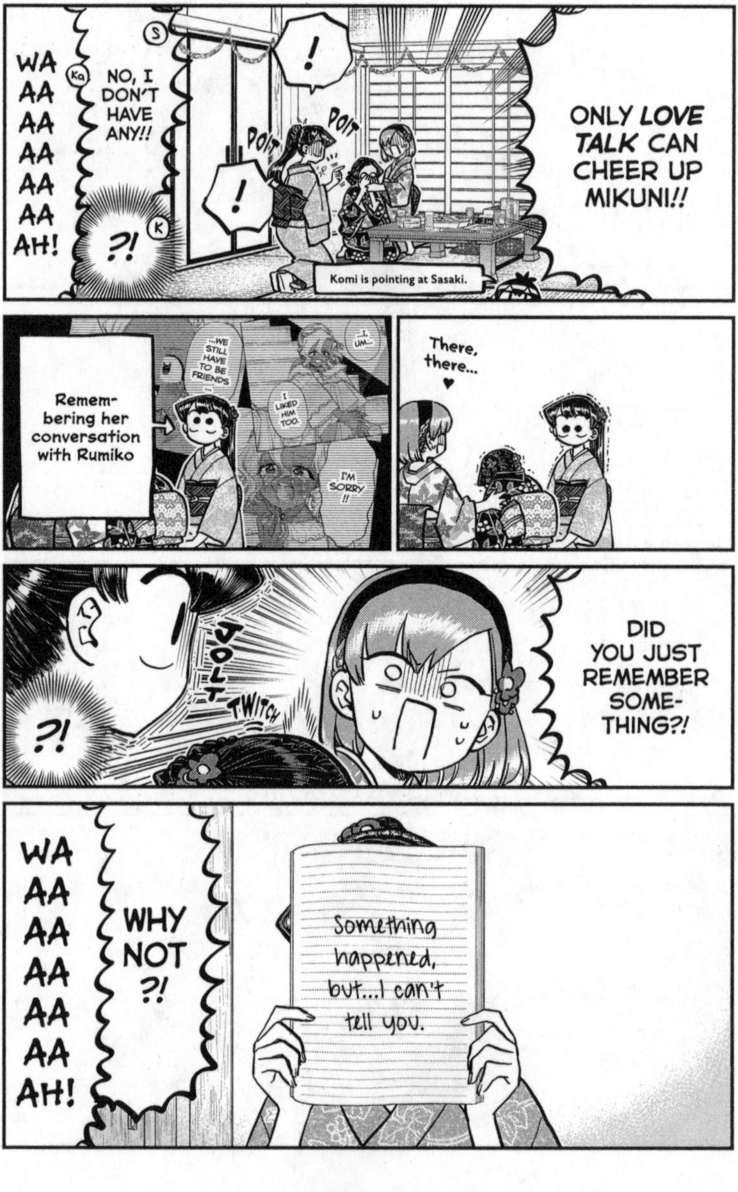

ONLY LOVE TALK CAN CHEER UP MIKUNI!!
!
POIT
POIT
!
NO, I DON'T HAVE ANY!!
?!
WAAAAAAAAAAAAH!
Komi is pointing at Sasaki.
There, there... ♥
...I, UM...
...WE STILL HAVE TO BE FRIENDS...
I LIKED HIM TOO.
I'M SORRY!!
Remembering her conversation with Rumiko
DID YOU JUST REMEMBER SOMETHING?!
JOLT
TWITCH
?!
Something happened, but...I can't tell you.
WHY NOT?!
WAAAAAAAAAAAAH!

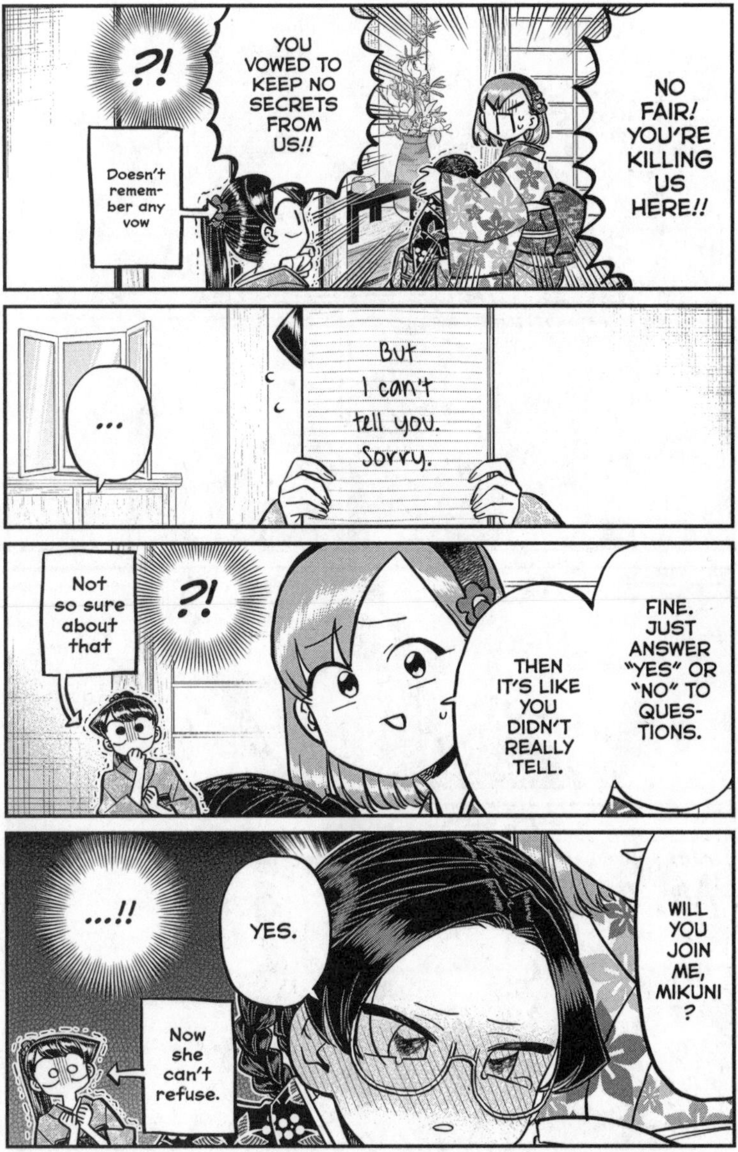
NO FAIR! YOU'RE KILLING US HERE!!
YOU VOWED TO KEEP NO SECRETS FROM US!!
?!
Doesn't remember any vow
But I can't tell you. Sorry.
...
FINE. JUST ANSWER "YES" OR "NO" TO QUESTIONS.
THEN IT'S LIKE YOU DIDN'T REALLY TELL.
?!
Not so sure about that
WILL YOU JOIN ME, MIKUNI?
YES.
...!!
Now she can't refuse.

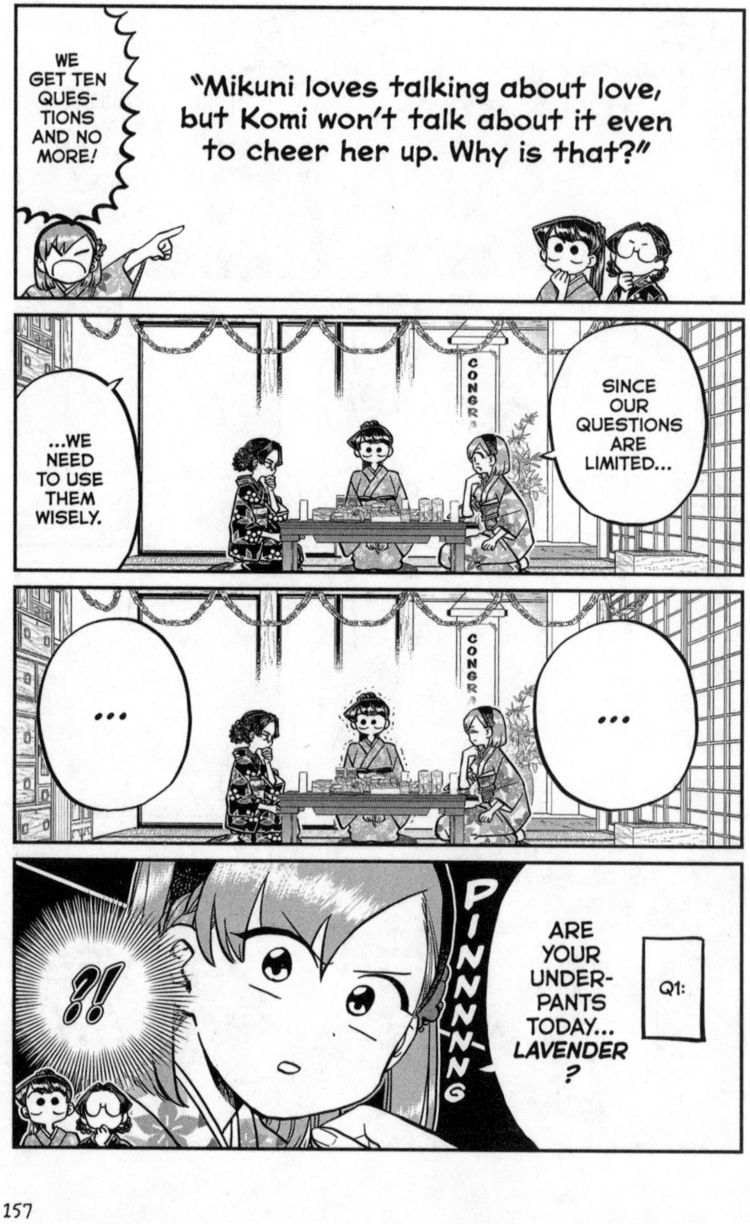
"Mikuni loves talking about love, but Komi won't talk about it even to cheer her up. Why is that?"
WE GET TEN QUES-TIONS AND NO MORE!
CONGRA
SINCE OUR QUESTIONS ARE LIMITED...
...WE NEED TO USE THEM WISELY.
CONGRA
...
...
Q1:
ARE YOUR UNDER-PANTS TODAY... LAVENDER ?
PINNNNNG
?!

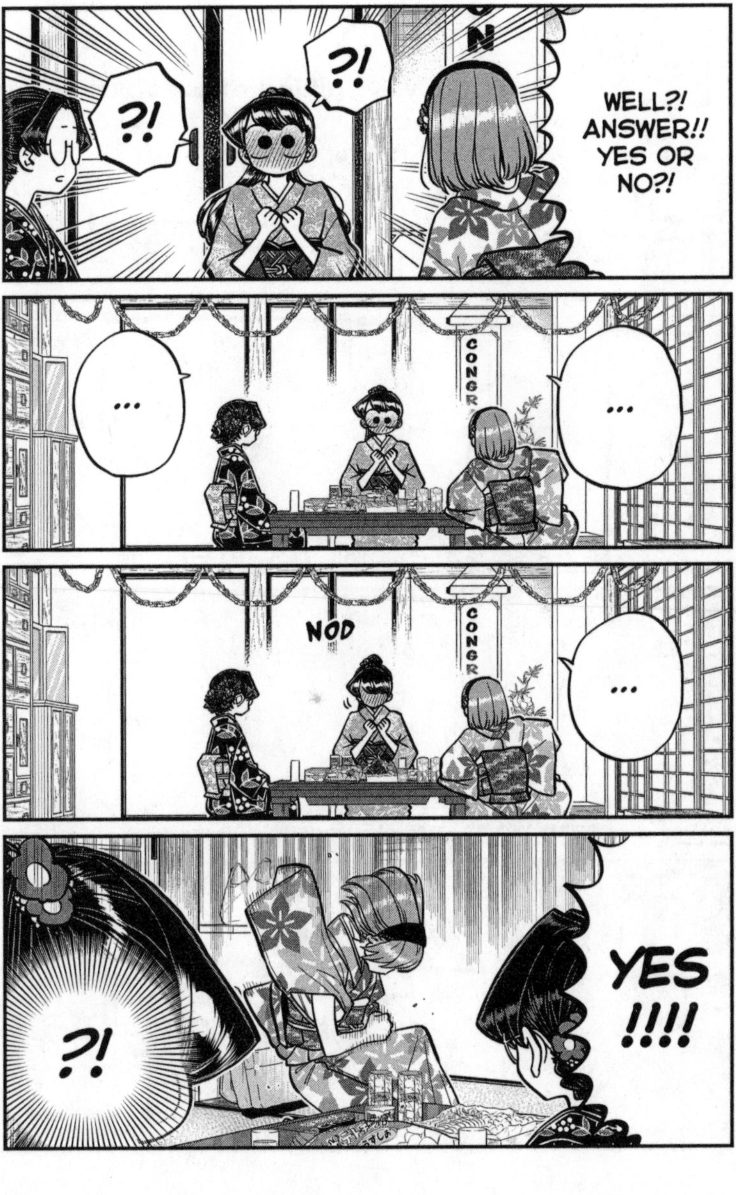
WELL?! ANSWER!! YES OR NO?!
?!
?!
...
...
...
NOD
YES !!!!
?!

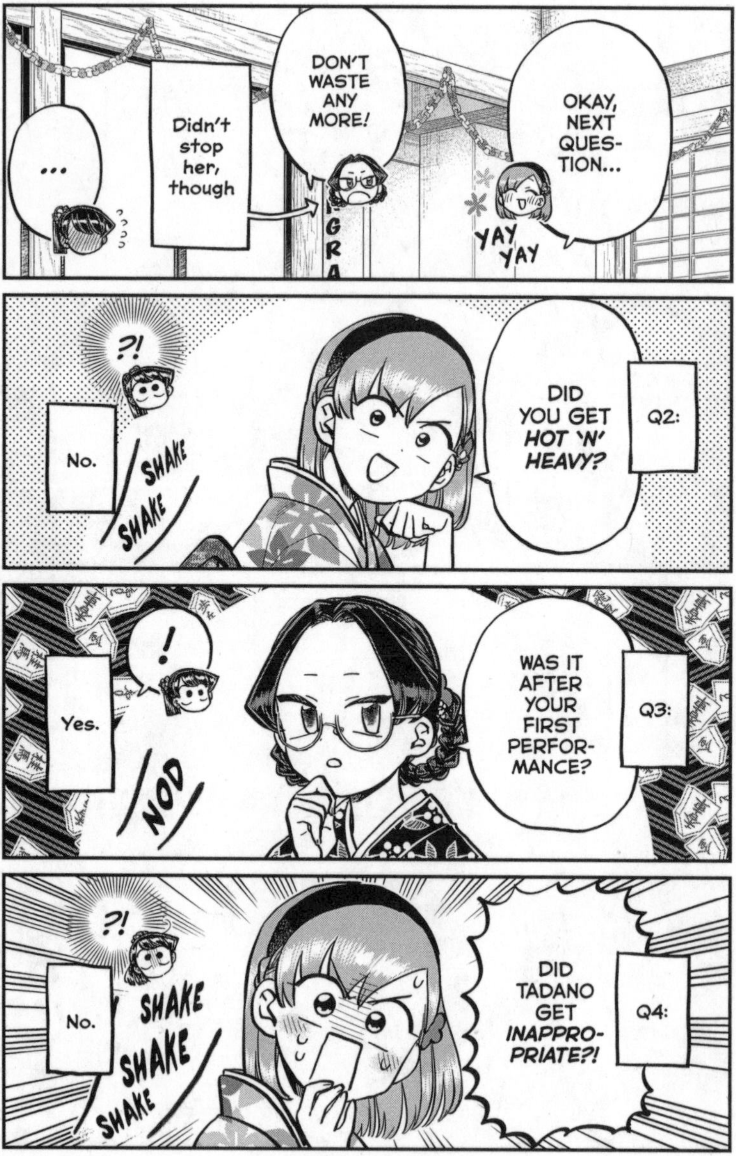
OKAY, NEXT QUES-TION...
YAY YAY
DON'T WASTE ANY MORE!
Didn't stop her, though
...
Q2:
DID YOU GET HOT 'N' HEAVY?
?!
No.
SHAKE SHAKE
Q3:
WAS IT AFTER YOUR FIRST PERFOR-MANCE?
!
Yes.
NOD
Q4:
DID TADANO GET INAPPRO-PRIATE?!
?!
No.
SHAKE SHAKE SHAKE

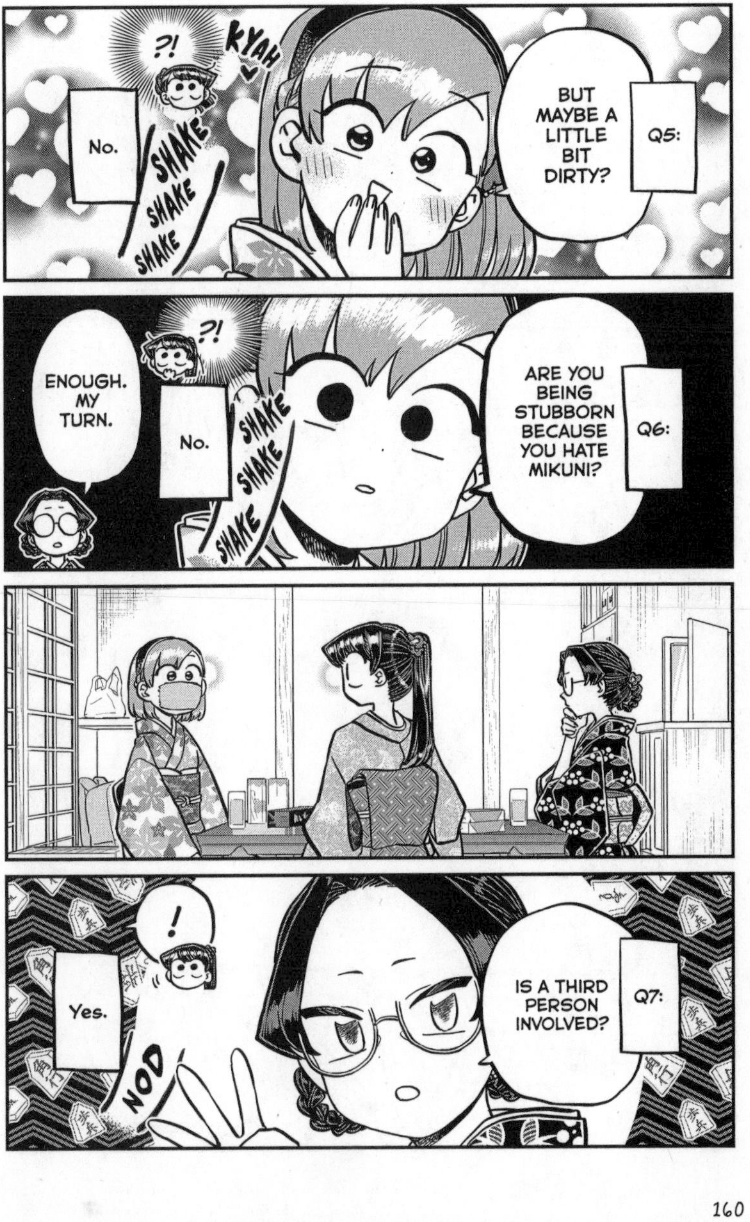
Q5:
BUT MAYBE A LITTLE BIT DIRTY?
KYAH
?!
No.
SHAKE SHAKE SHAKE SHAKE
Q6:
ARE YOU BEING STUBBORN BECAUSE YOU HATE MIKUNI?
?!
SHAKE SHAKE SHAKE
No.
ENOUGH. MY TURN.
Q7:
IS A THIRD PERSON INVOLVED?
!
Yes.
NOD

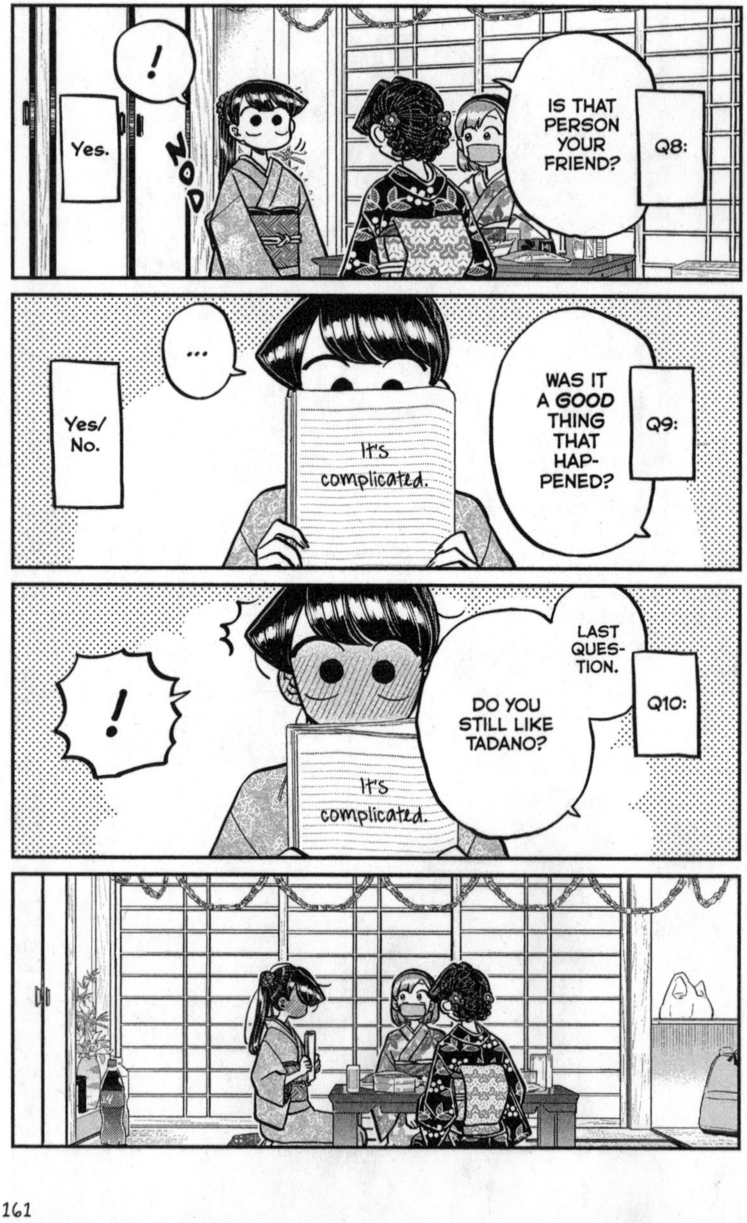
Q8:
IS THAT PERSON YOUR FRIEND?
!
NOD
Yes.
Q9:
WAS IT A *GOOD* THING THAT HAP-PENED?
It's complicated.
...
Yes/ No.
Q10:
LAST QUES-TION.
DO YOU STILL LIKE TADANO?
It's complicated.
!

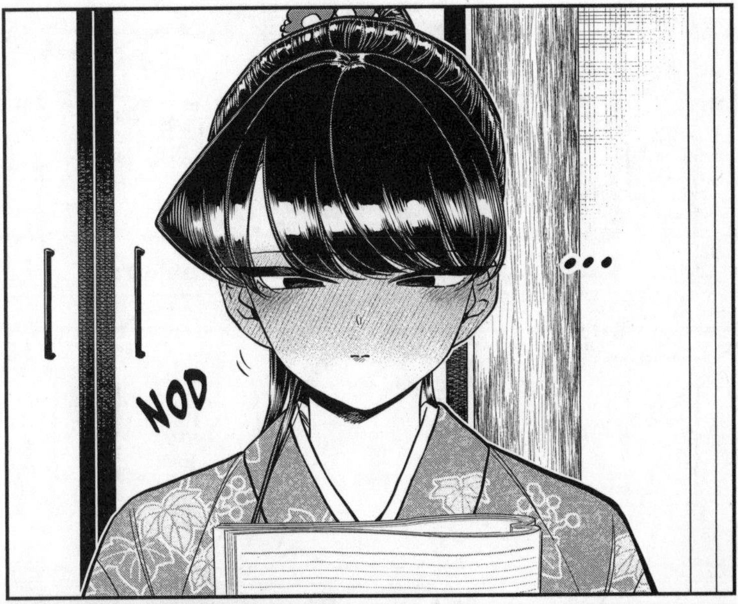
...
NOD

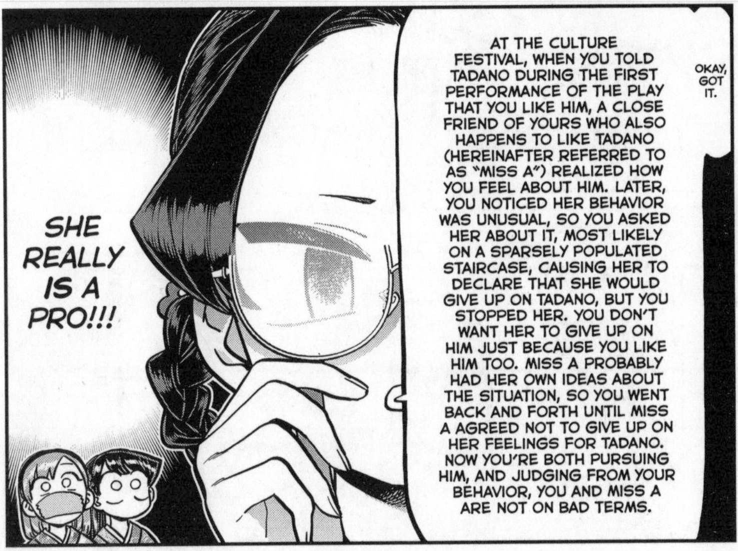
OKAY, GOT IT.
AT THE CULTURE FESTIVAL, WHEN YOU TOLD TADANO DURING THE FIRST PERFORMANCE OF THE PLAY THAT YOU LIKE HIM, A CLOSE FRIEND OF YOURS WHO ALSO HAPPENS TO LIKE TADANO (HEREINAFTER REFERRED TO AS "MISS A") REALIZED HOW YOU FEEL ABOUT HIM. LATER, YOU NOTICED HER BEHAVIOR WAS UNUSUAL, SO YOU ASKED HER ABOUT IT, MOST LIKELY ON A SPARSELY POPULATED STAIRCASE, CAUSING HER TO DECLARE THAT SHE WOULD GIVE UP ON TADANO, BUT YOU STOPPED HER. YOU DON'T WANT HER TO GIVE UP ON HIM JUST BECAUSE YOU LIKE HIM TOO. MISS A PROBABLY HAD HER OWN IDEAS ABOUT THE SITUATION, SO YOU WENT BACK AND FORTH UNTIL MISS A AGREED NOT TO GIVE UP ON HER FEELINGS FOR TADANO. NOW YOU'RE BOTH PURSUING HIM, AND JUDGING FROM YOUR BEHAVIOR, YOU AND MISS A ARE NOT ON BAD TERMS.
SHE REALLY IS A PRO!!!

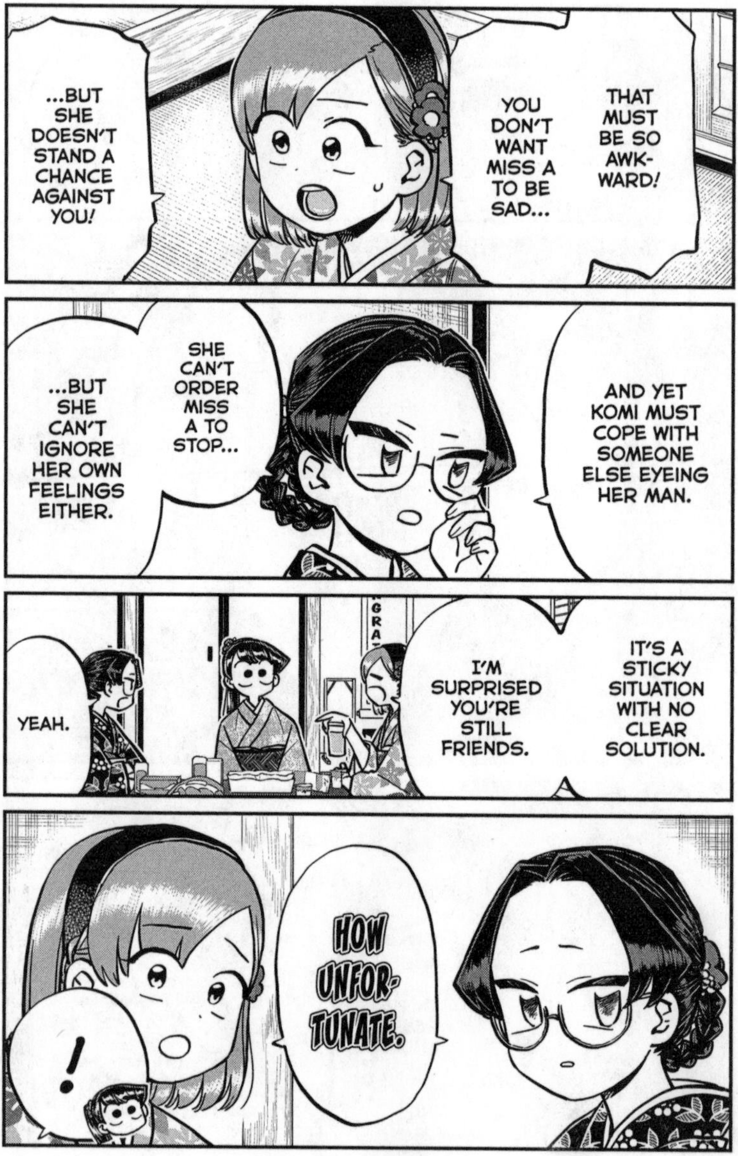
THAT MUST BE SO AWKWARD!
YOU DON'T WANT MISS A TO BE SAD...
...BUT SHE DOESN'T STAND A CHANCE AGAINST YOU!
AND YET KOMI MUST COPE WITH SOMEONE ELSE EYEING HER MAN.
SHE CAN'T ORDER MISS A TO STOP...
...BUT SHE CAN'T IGNORE HER OWN FEELINGS EITHER.
IT'S A STICKY SITUATION WITH NO CLEAR SOLUTION.
I'M SURPRISED YOU'RE STILL FRIENDS.
YEAH.
HOW UNFORTUNATE.
!

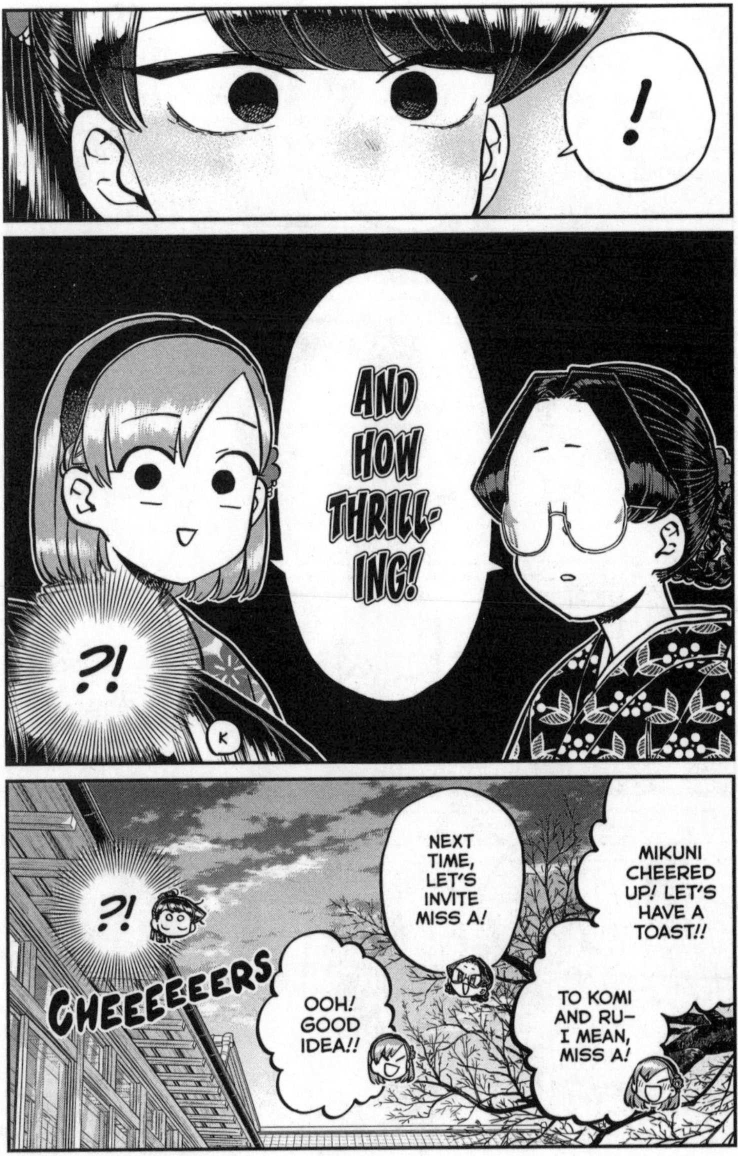
!
AND HOW THRILL-ING!
?!
MIKUNI CHEERED UP! LET'S HAVE A TOAST!!
TO KOMI AND RU— I MEAN, MISS A!
NEXT TIME, LET'S INVITE MISS A!
OOH! GOOD IDEA!!
CHEEEEEERS
?!

Communication 245 — The End

Komi Can't Communicate

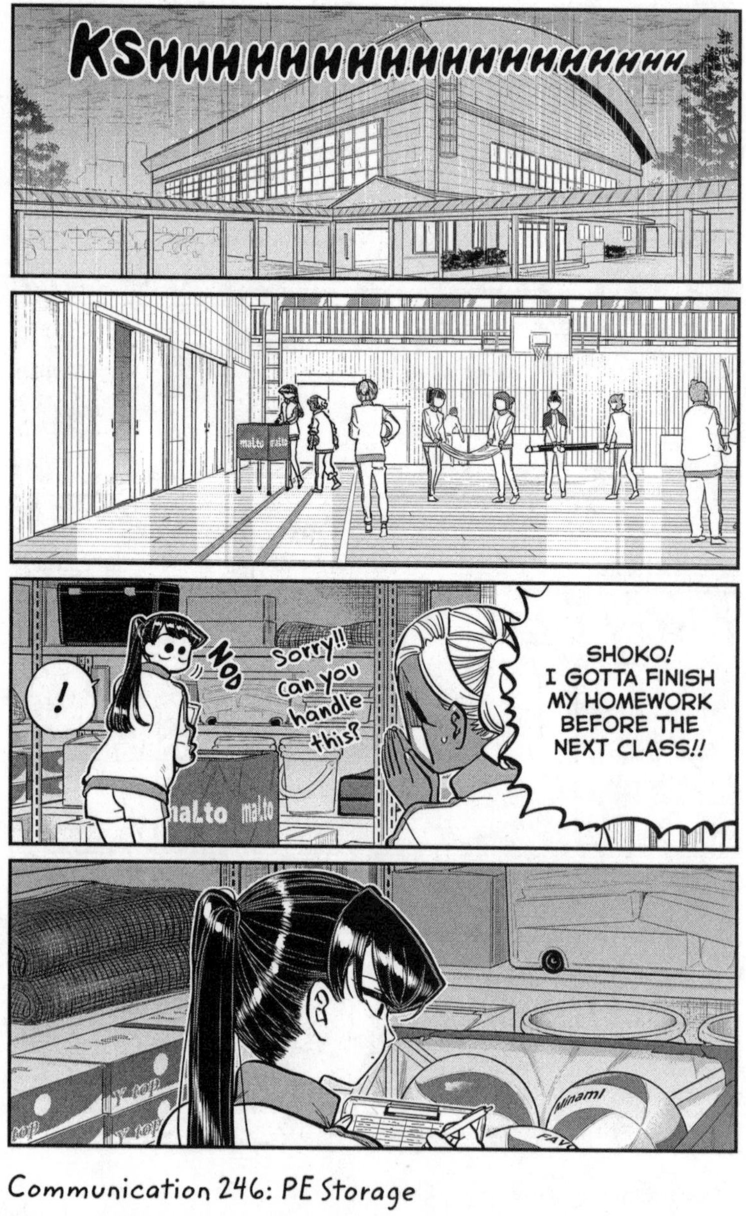
KSHHHHHHHHHHHHHHHHHHH
SHOKO! I GOTTA FINISH MY HOMEWORK BEFORE THE NEXT CLASS!!
Sorry!! can you handle this?
NOD
!
mai.to mai.to
mal.to mai.to
Minami

Communication 246: PE Storage

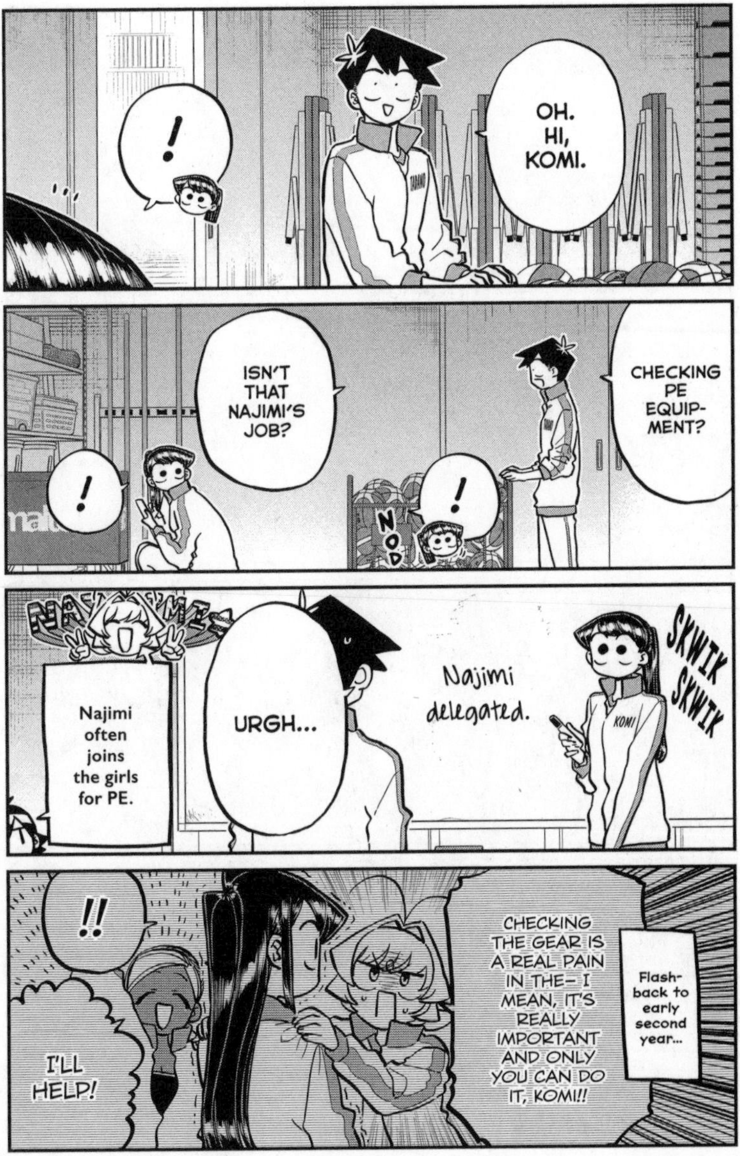
OH. HI, KOMI.
!
...
CHECKING PE EQUIPMENT?
!
NOD
ISN'T THAT NAJIMI'S JOB?
!
SKWIK SKWIK
Najimi delegated.
URGH...
Najimi often joins the girls for PE.
Flashback to early second year...
CHECKING THE GEAR IS A REAL PAIN IN THE– I MEAN, IT'S REALLY IMPORTANT AND ONLY YOU CAN DO IT, KOMI!!
!!
I'LL HELP!

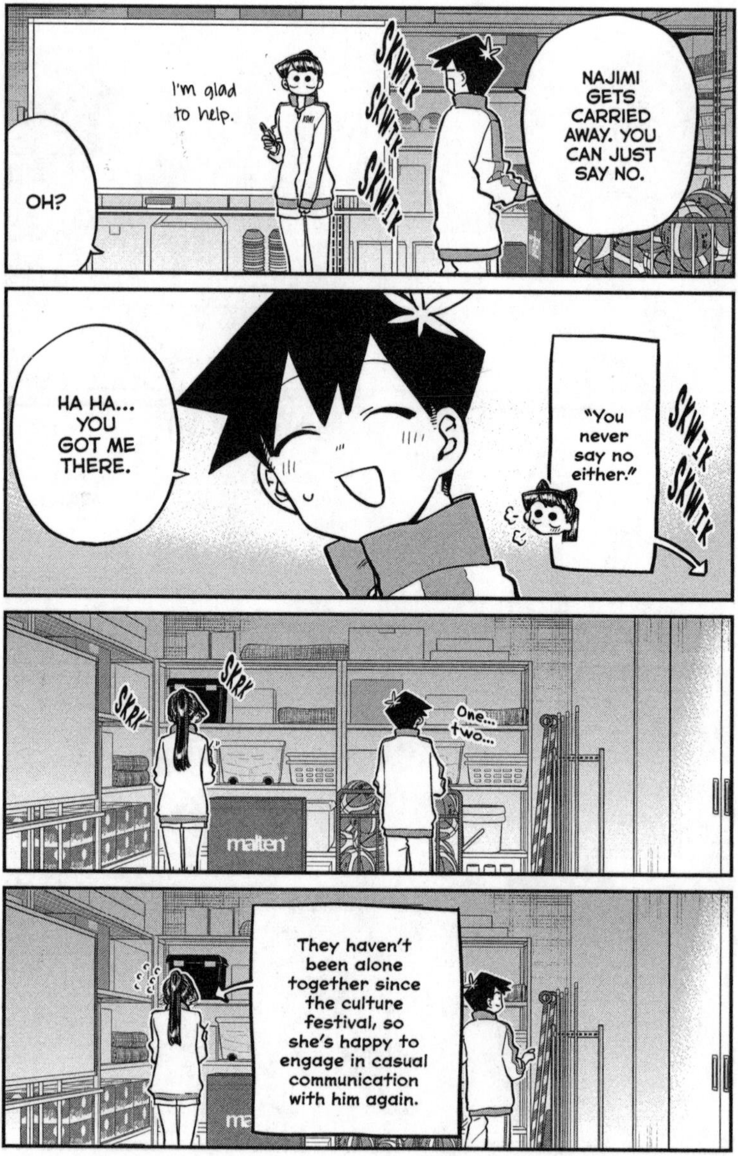
NAJIMI GETS CARRIED AWAY. YOU CAN JUST SAY NO.
SKWIK SKWIK SKWIK
I'm glad to help.
OH?
SKWIK SKWIK
"You never say no either."
HA HA... YOU GOT ME THERE.
One... two...
SKRK
SKRK
They haven't been alone together since the culture festival, so she's happy to engage in casual communication with him again.

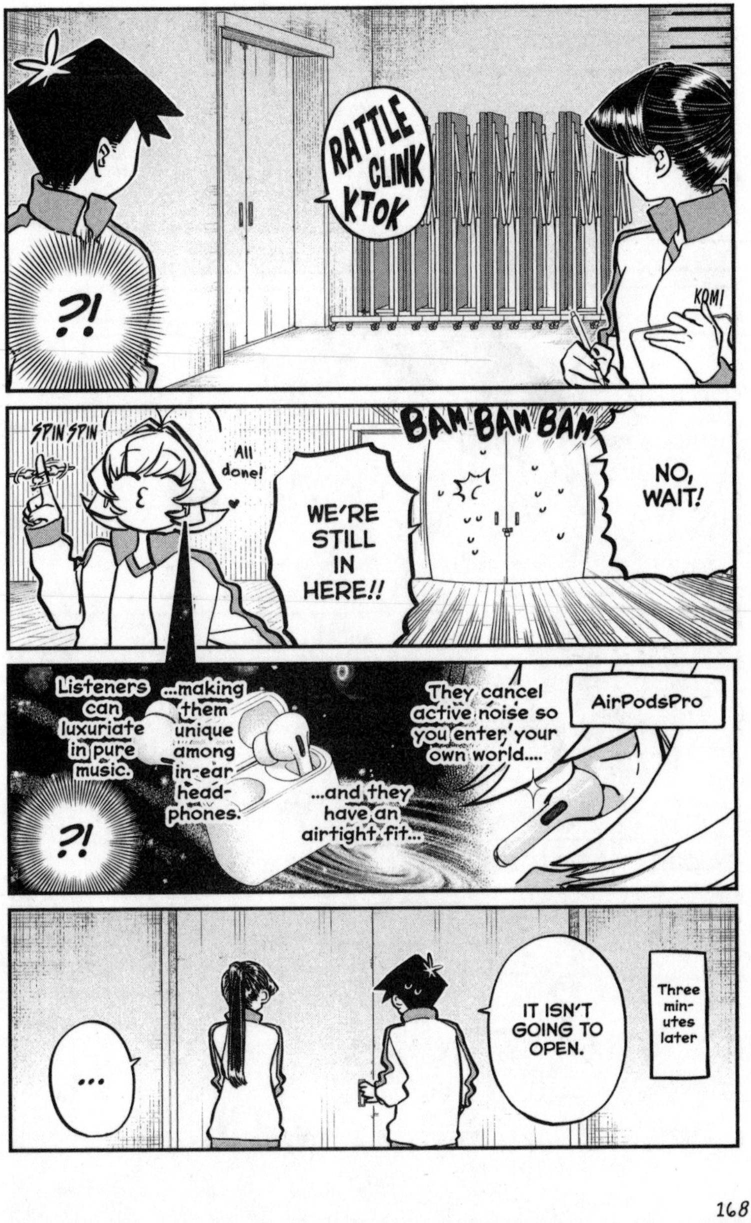
RATTLE CLINK KTOK
KOMI
?!
NO, WAIT!
BAM BAM BAM
WE'RE STILL IN HERE!!
All done!
SPIN SPIN
AirPodsPro
They cancel active noise so you enter your own world....
...and they have an airtight fit...
...making them unique among in-ear head-phones.
Listeners can luxuriate in pure music.
?!
Three min-utes later
IT ISN'T GOING TO OPEN.
...

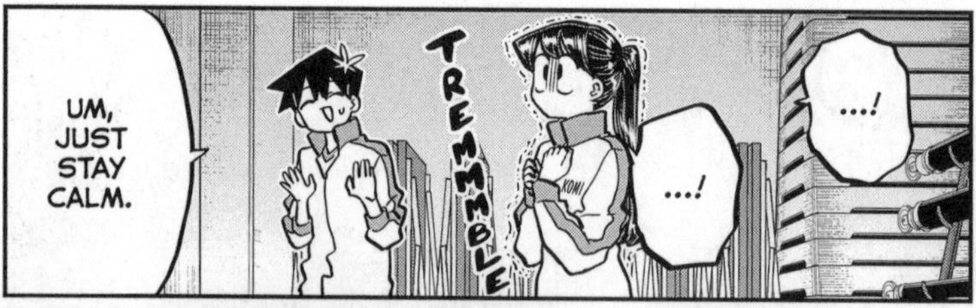
...!
...!
TREMMMBLE
UM, JUST STAY CALM.
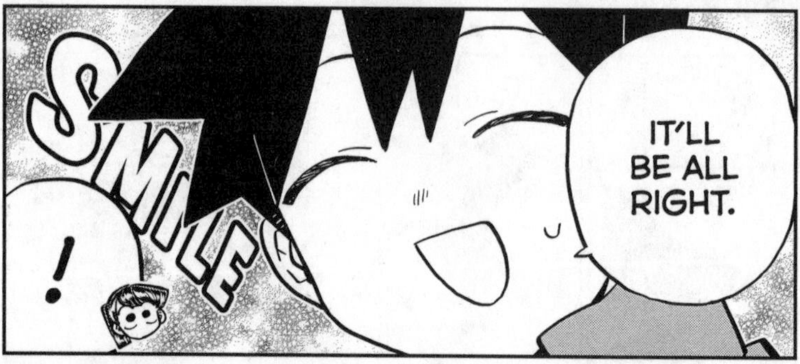
IT'LL BE ALL RIGHT.
SMILE
!
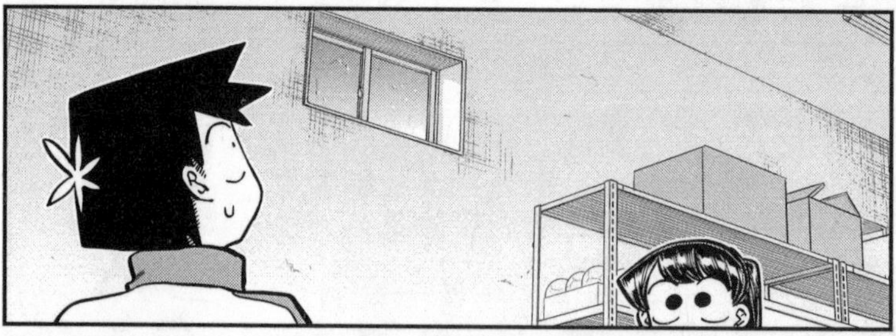
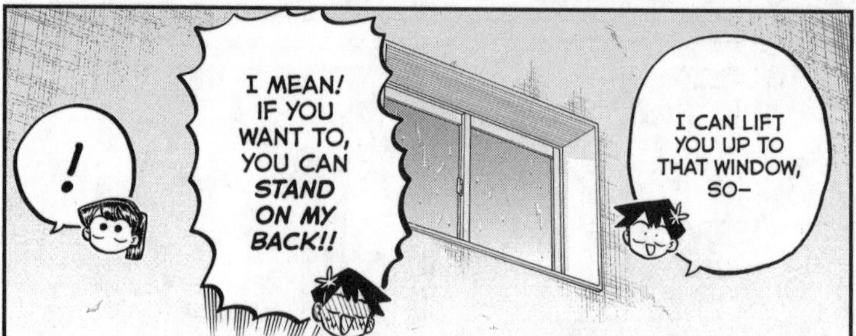
I CAN LIFT YOU UP TO THAT WINDOW, SO–
I MEAN! IF YOU WANT TO, YOU CAN STAND ON MY BACK!!
!

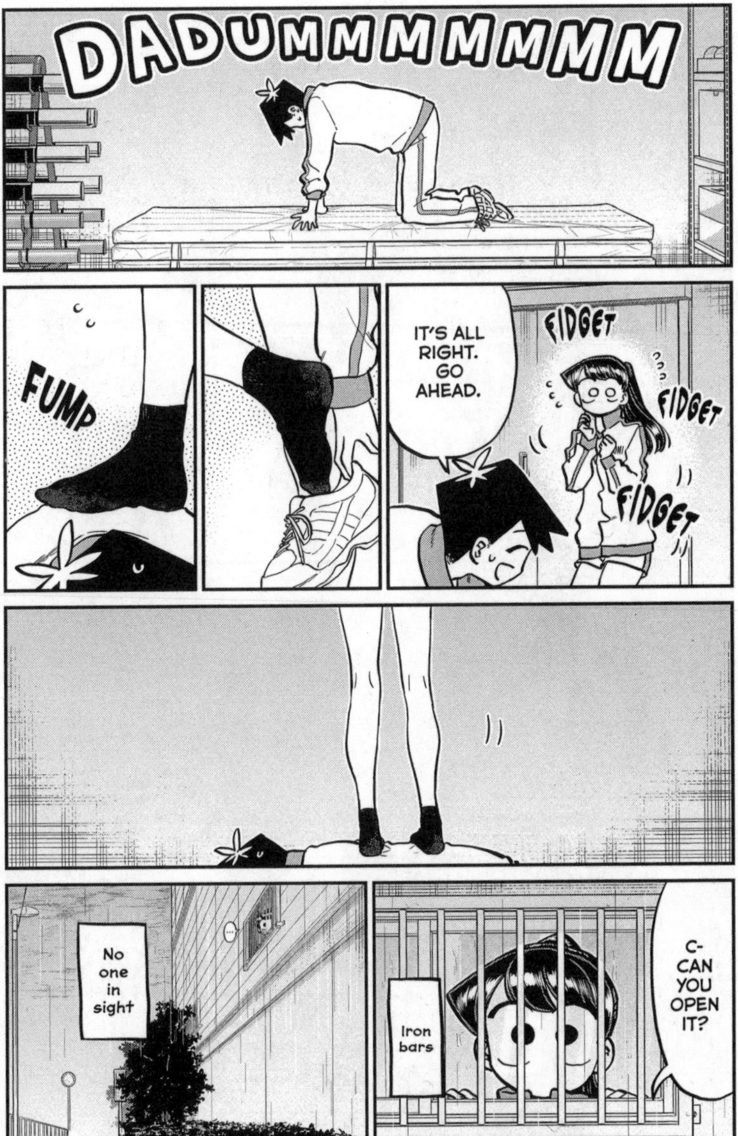
DADUMMMMMMMM
IT'S ALL RIGHT. GO AHEAD.
FIDGET
FIDGET
FIDGET
FUMP
C-CAN YOU OPEN IT?
Iron bars
No one in sight

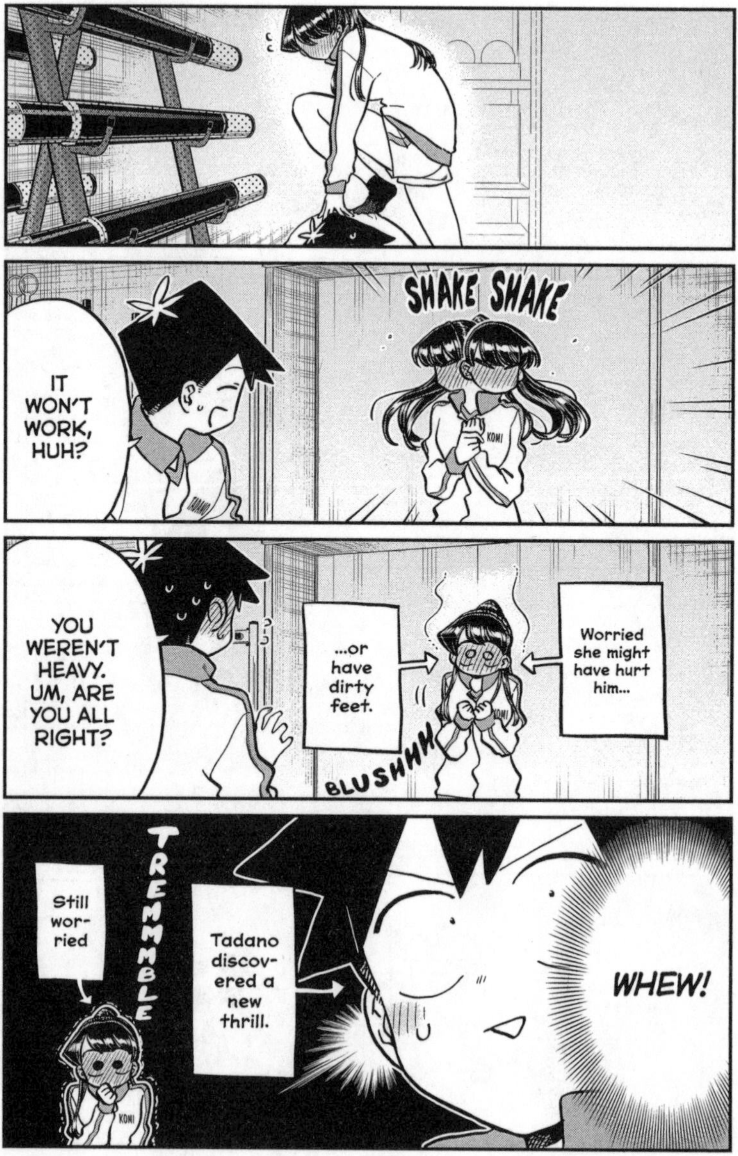
SHAKE SHAKE
IT WON'T WORK, HUH?
Worried she might have hurt him...
...or have dirty feet.
YOU WEREN'T HEAVY. UM, ARE YOU ALL RIGHT?
BLUSHHH
WHEW!
Tadano discov-ered a new thrill.
TREMMMBLE
Still wor-ried

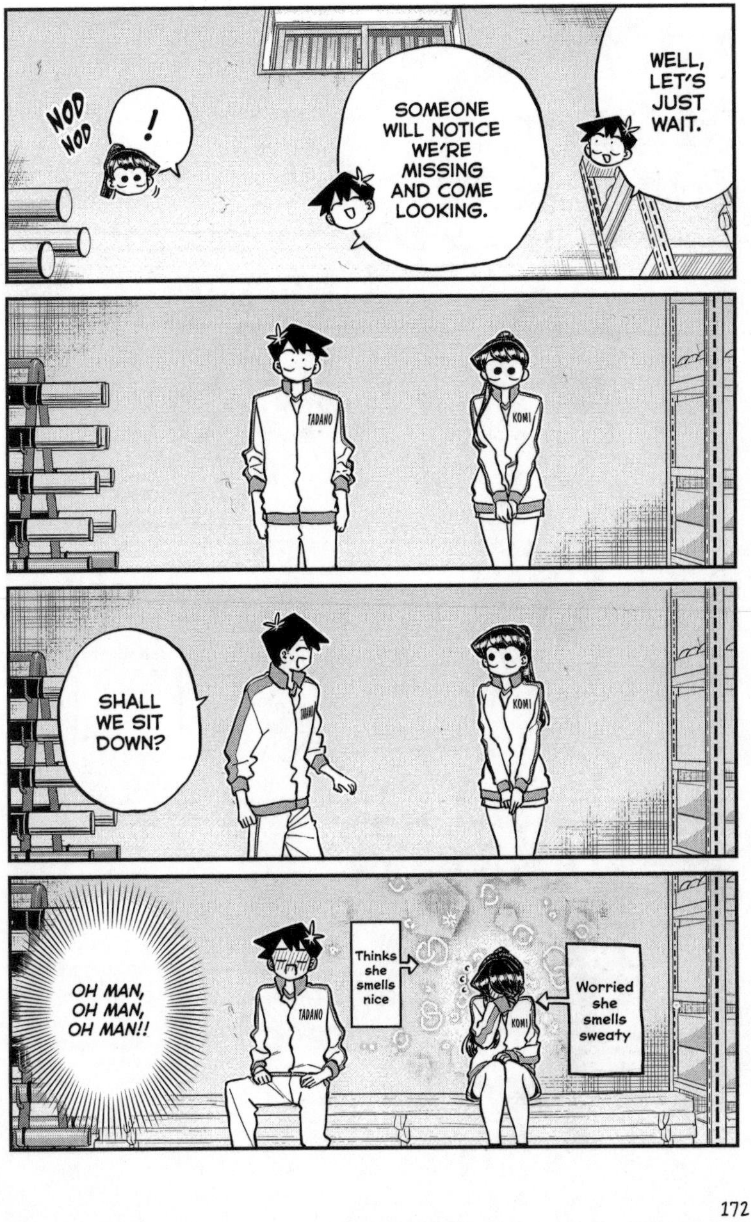
WELL, LET'S JUST WAIT.
SOMEONE WILL NOTICE WE'RE MISSING AND COME LOOKING.
!
NOD NOD
KOMI
TADANO
KOMI
TADANO
SHALL WE SIT DOWN?
Worried she smells sweaty
KOMI
Thinks she smells nice
TADANO
OH MAN, OH MAN, OH MAN!!

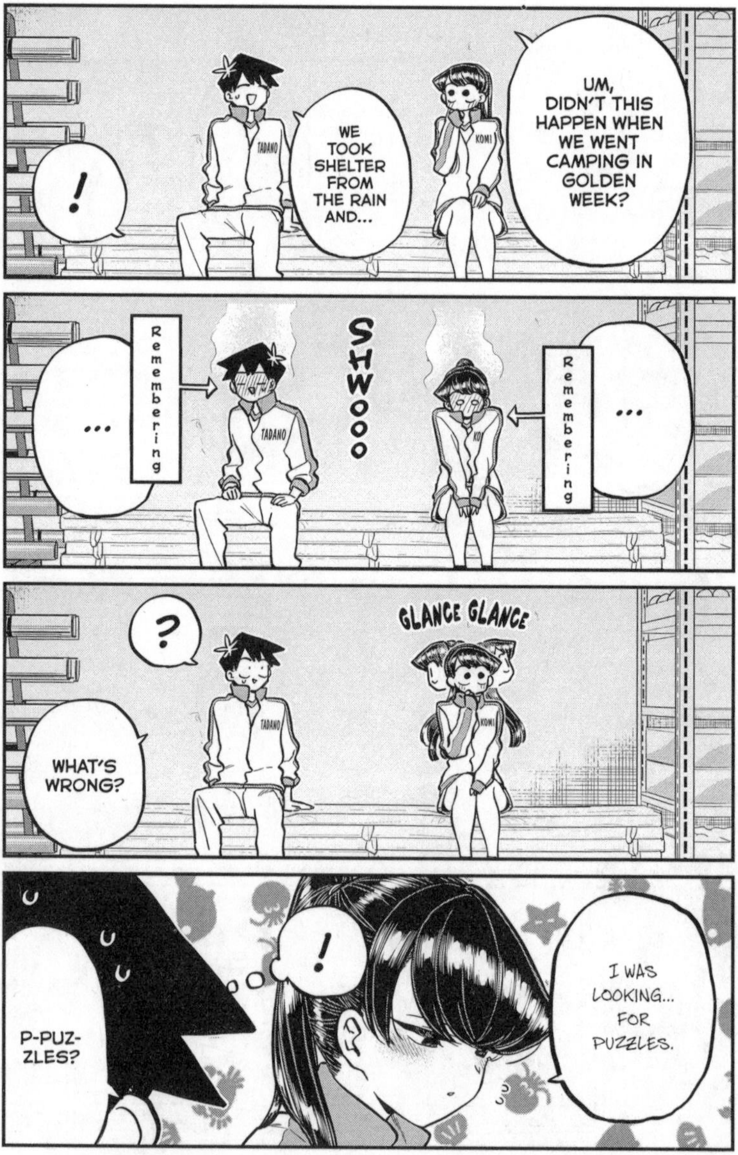
UM, DIDN'T THIS HAPPEN WHEN WE WENT CAMPING IN GOLDEN WEEK?
WE TOOK SHELTER FROM THE RAIN AND...
!
...
Remembering
SHWOOO
Remembering
...
GLANCE GLANCE
?
WHAT'S WRONG?
I WAS LOOKING... FOR PUZZLES.
!
P-PUZ-ZLES?

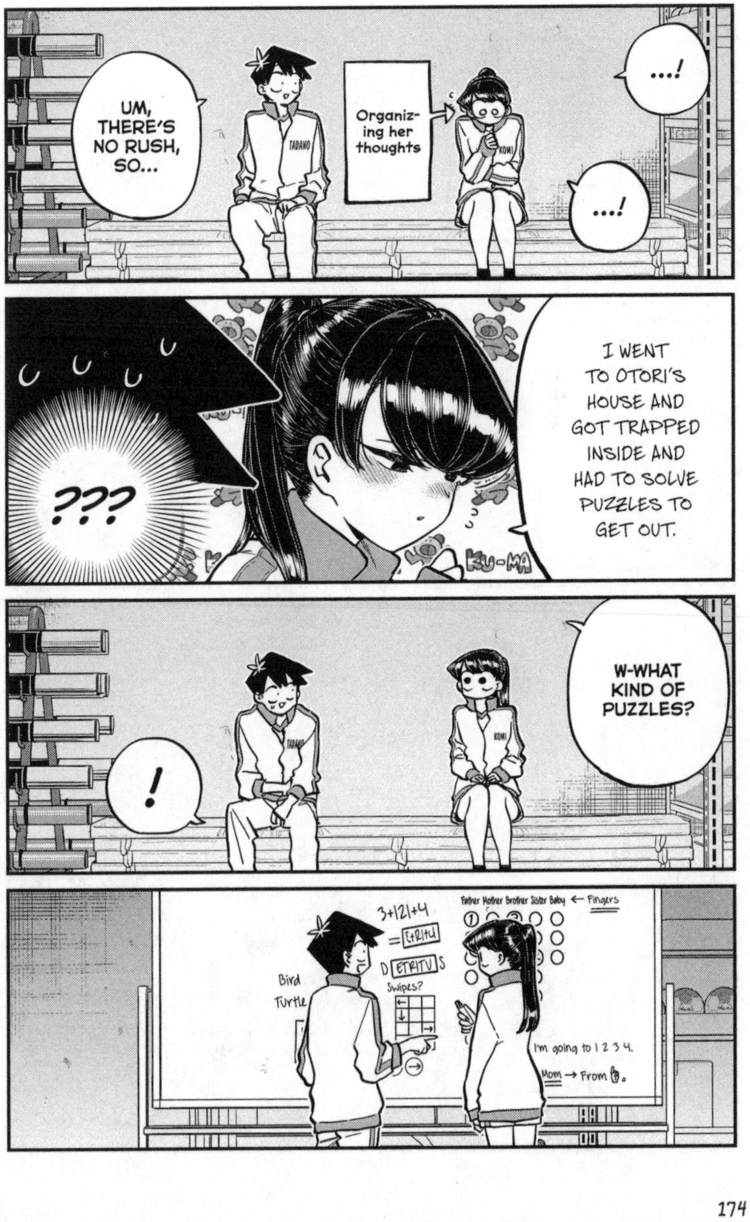
...!
...!
Organiz-ing her thoughts
UM, THERE'S NO RUSH, SO...
I WENT TO OTORI'S HOUSE AND GOT TRAPPED INSIDE AND HAD TO SOLVE PUZZLES TO GET OUT.
???
KU-MA
W-WHAT KIND OF PUZZLES?
!
Father Mother Brother Sister Baby ← Fingers
3+121+4
D ETRITU S
Swipes?
Bird
Turtle
I'm going to 1 2 3 4.
Mom → From

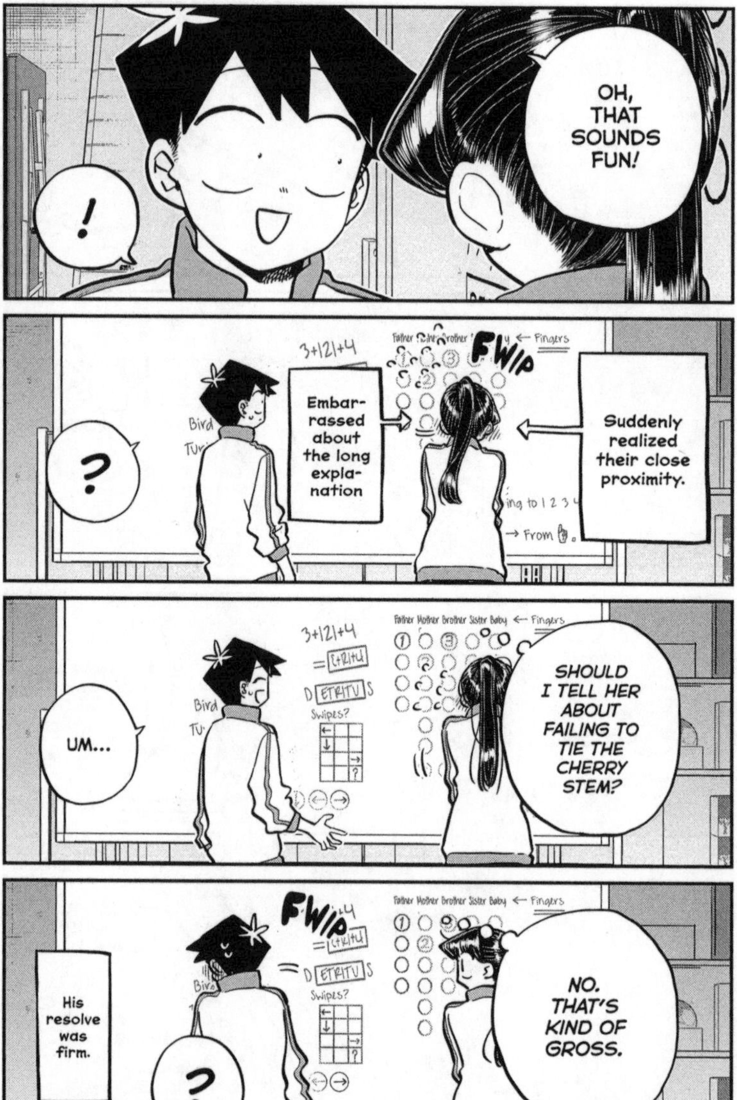
OH, THAT SOUNDS FUN!
!
Suddenly realized their close proximity.
FWIP
Embarrassed about the long explanation
?
Father Mother Brother Sister Baby ← Fingers
SHOULD I TELL HER ABOUT FAILING TO TIE THE CHERRY STEM?
Swipes?
UM...
NO. THAT'S KIND OF GROSS.
FWIP
?
His resolve was firm.

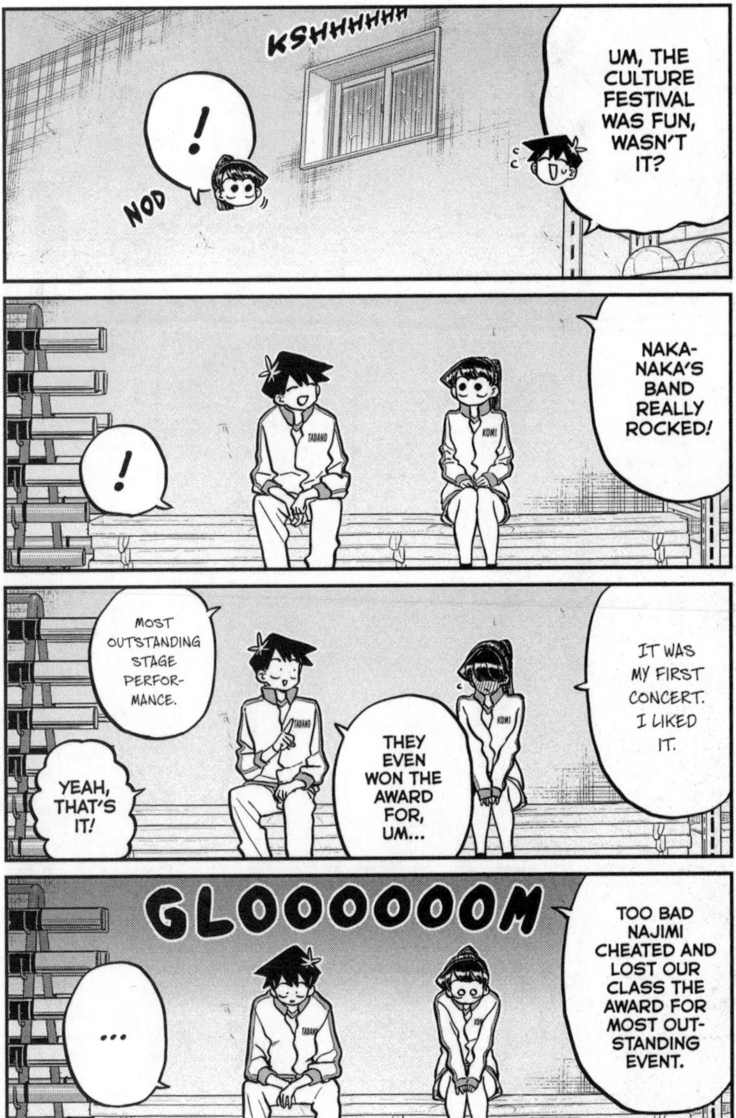
UM, THE CULTURE FESTIVAL WAS FUN, WASN'T IT?
KSHHHHHH
!
NOD
NAKA-NAKA'S BAND REALLY ROCKED!
!
IT WAS MY FIRST CONCERT. I LIKED IT.
THEY EVEN WON THE AWARD FOR, UM...
MOST OUTSTANDING STAGE PERFOR-MANCE.
YEAH, THAT'S IT!
TOO BAD NAJIMI CHEATED AND LOST OUR CLASS THE AWARD FOR MOST OUT-STANDING EVENT.
GLOOOOOOM
...

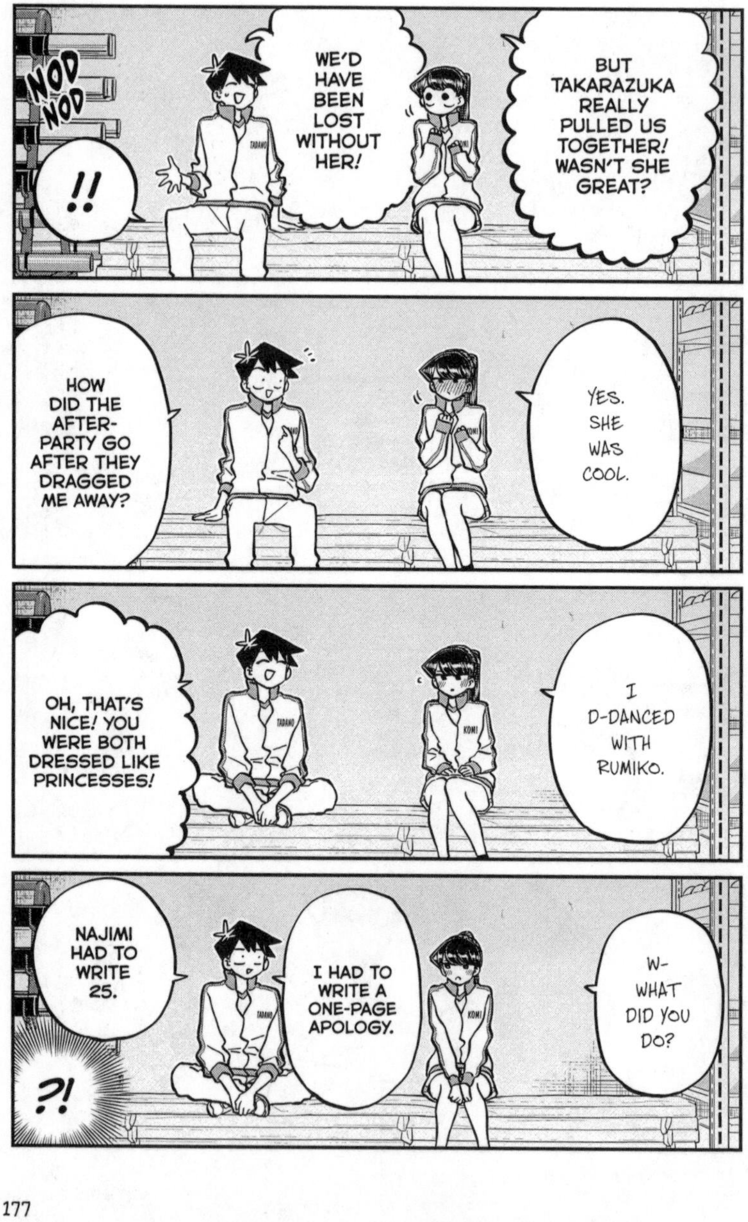
BUT TAKARAZUKA REALLY PULLED US TOGETHER! WASN'T SHE GREAT?
WE'D HAVE BEEN LOST WITHOUT HER!
NOD NOD
!!
YES. SHE WAS COOL.
HOW DID THE AFTER-PARTY GO AFTER THEY DRAGGED ME AWAY?
I D-DANCED WITH RUMIKO.
OH, THAT'S NICE! YOU WERE BOTH DRESSED LIKE PRINCESSES!
W- WHAT DID YOU DO?
I HAD TO WRITE A ONE-PAGE APOLOGY.
NAJIMI HAD TO WRITE 25.
?!

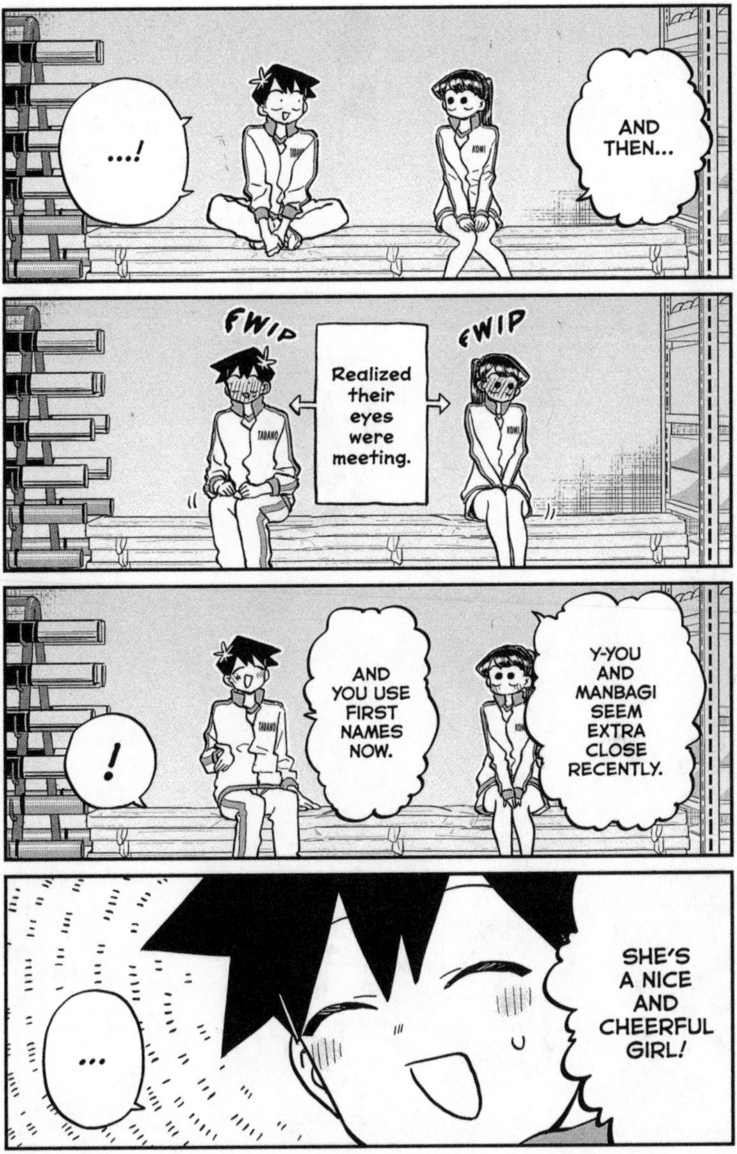
AND THEN...
...!
FWIP
Realized their eyes were meeting.
FWIP
Y-YOU AND MANBAGI SEEM EXTRA CLOSE RECENTLY.
AND YOU USE FIRST NAMES NOW.
!
SHE'S A NICE AND CHEERFUL GIRL!
...

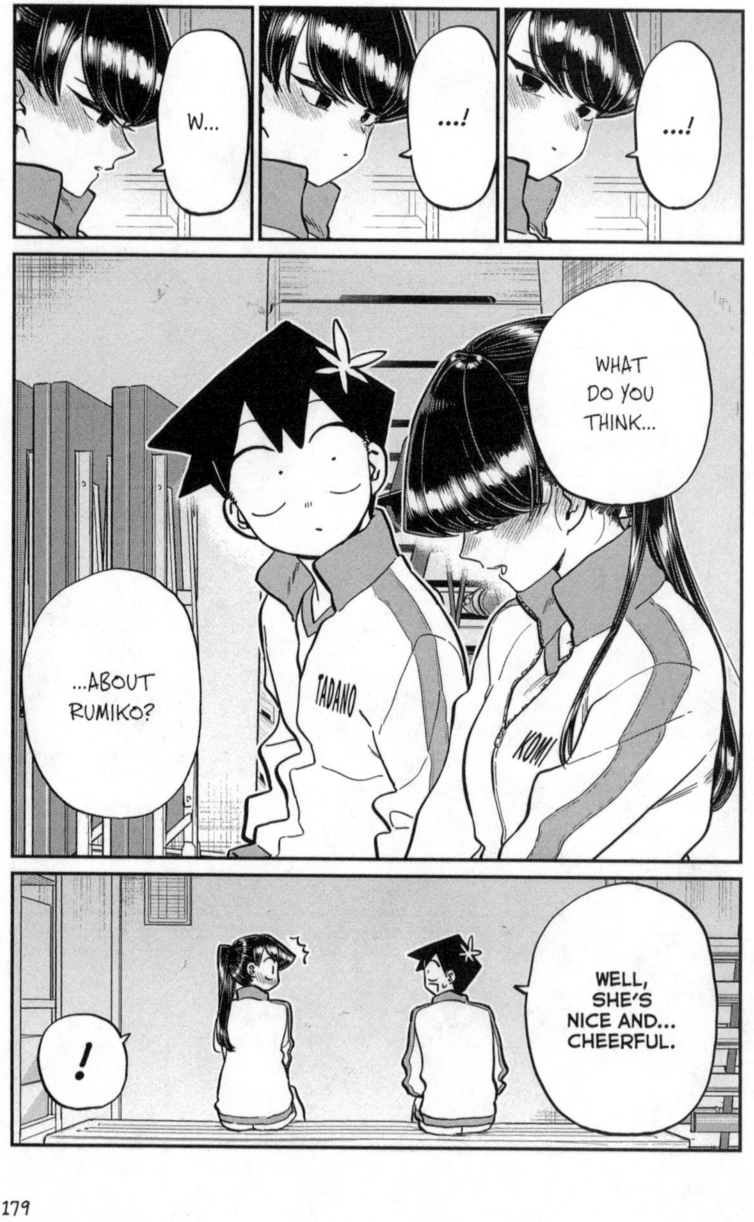
...!
...!
W...
WHAT DO YOU THINK...
...ABOUT RUMIKO?
KOMI
TADANO
WELL, SHE'S NICE AND... CHEERFUL.
!

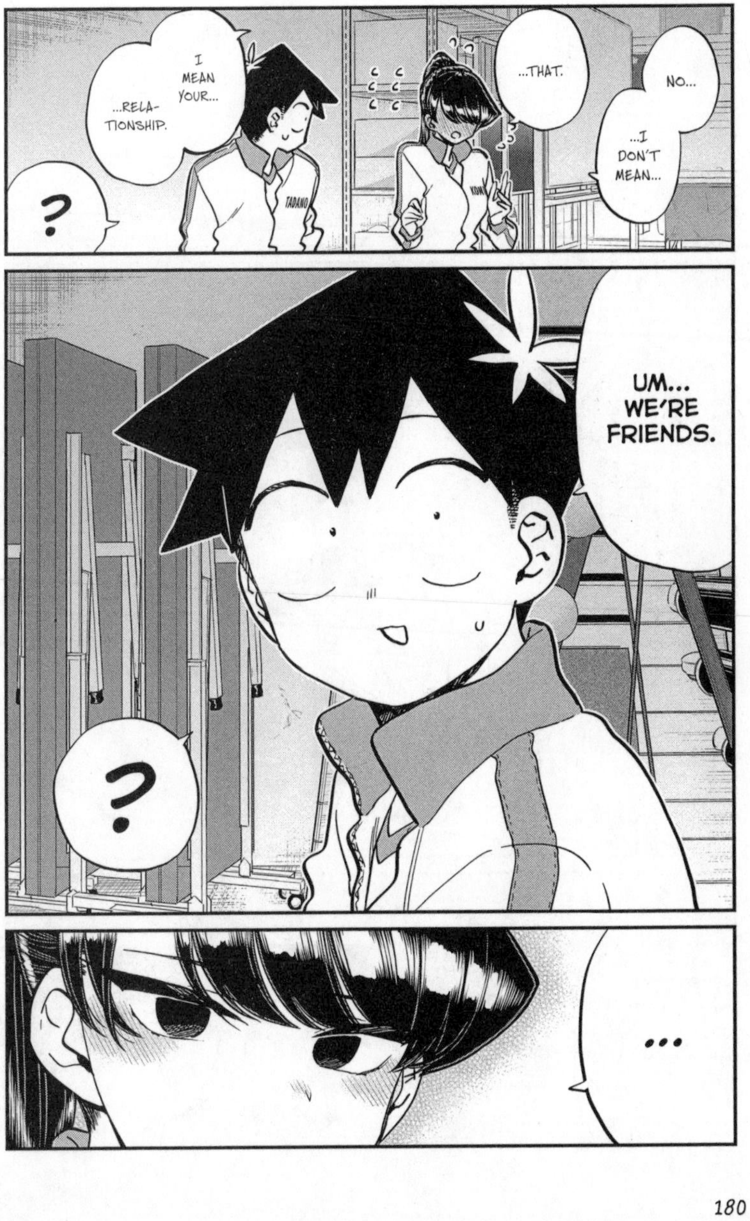
NO... ...I DON'T MEAN...
...THAT.
I MEAN YOUR... ...RELA-TIONSHIP.
?
UM... WE'RE FRIENDS.
?
...

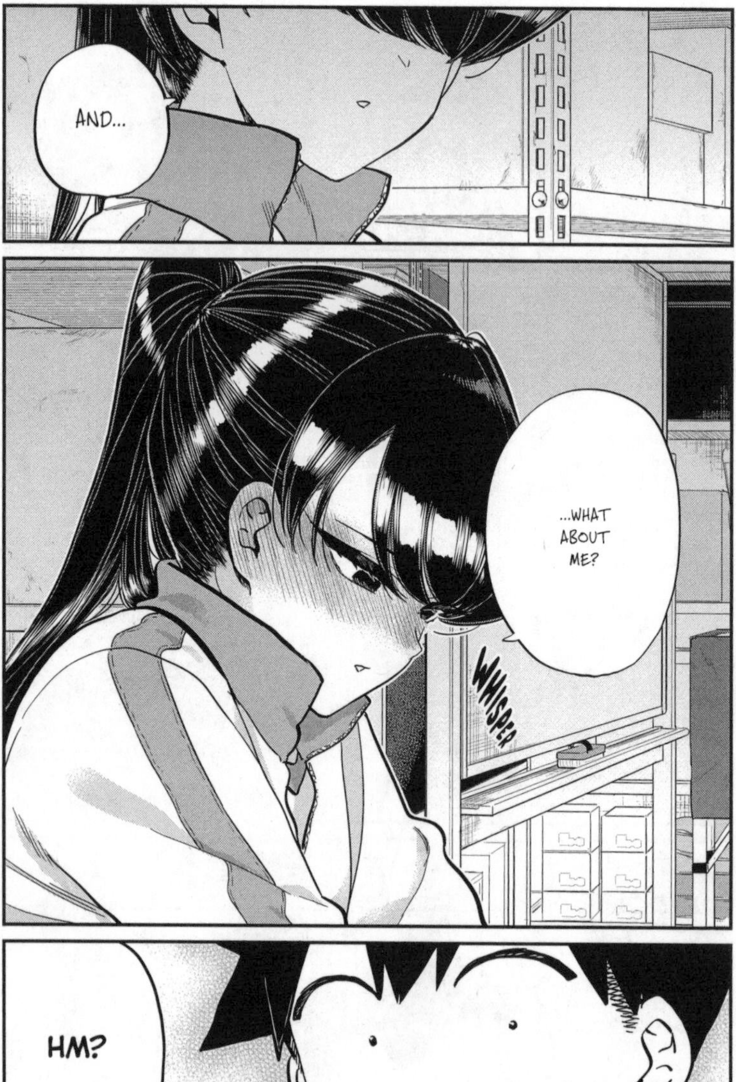
AND...
...WHAT ABOUT ME?
WHISPER
HM?

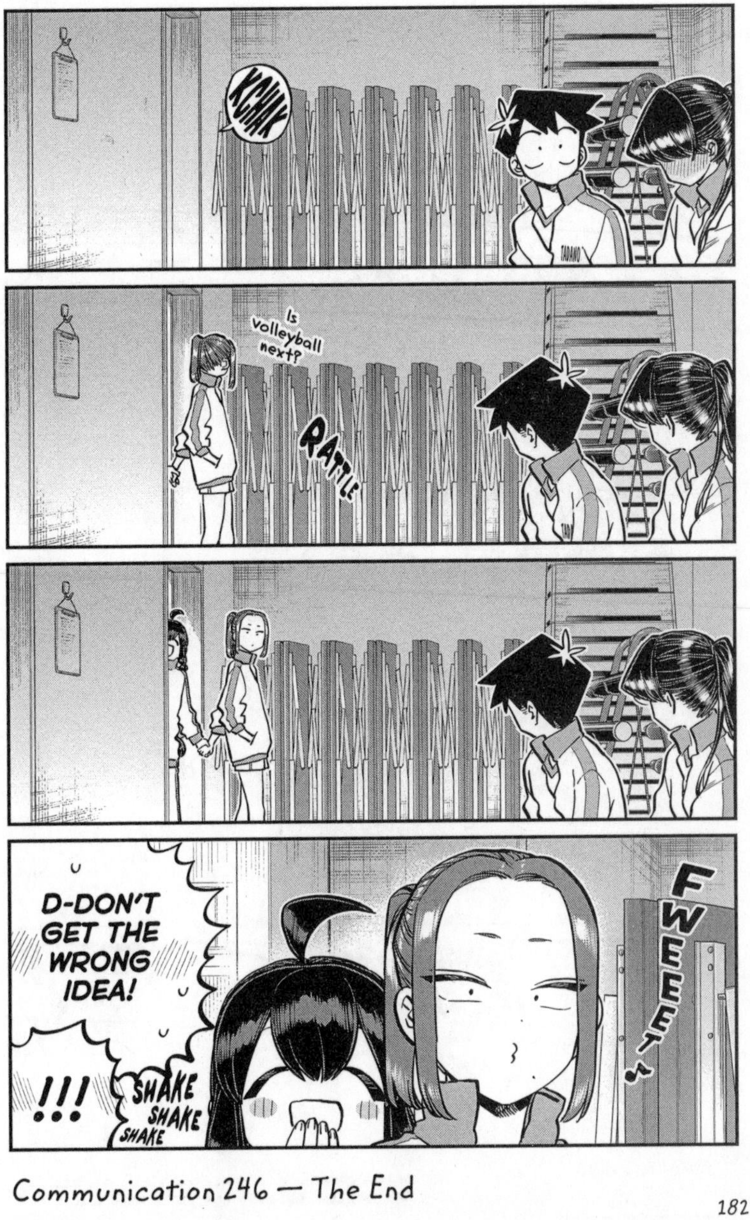
KCHAK
Is volleyball next?
RATTLE
FWEEET♪
D-DON'T GET THE WRONG IDEA!
!!!
SHAKE SHAKE SHAKE

Communication 246 — The End

Komi Can't Communicate

Communication 241: The Puzzle Answers

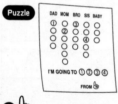

DAD	MOM	BRO	SIS	BABY
①	○	③	○	○
○	②	○	○	○
○	○	○	④	○
○	○	○	○	○
○				

I'M GOING TO ① ② ③ ④

FROM 👆

❶ 👆 **was a hint.**

This letter is from Otori's mother. So [pointing finger] means her mother.

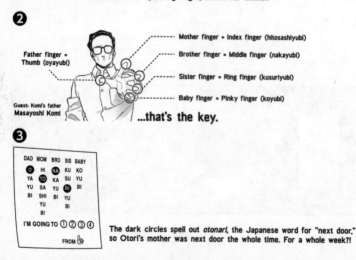

❷

Father finger =
Thumb (oyayubi)

Guest: Komi's father
Masayoshi Komi

Mother finger = Index finger (hitosashiyubi)

Brother finger = Middle finger (nakayubi)

Sister finger = Ring finger (kusuriyubi)

Baby finger = Pinky finger (koyubi)

...that's the key.

❸

DAD	MOM	BRO	SIS	BABY
O	HI	**NA**	KU	KO
YA	**TO**	KA	SU	YU
YU	SA	YU	**RI**	BI
BI	SHI	BI	YU	
	YU		BI	
	BI			

I'M GOING TO ① ② ③ ④

FROM 👆

The dark circles spell out *otonari*, the Japanese word for "next door," so Otori's mother was next door the whole time. For a whole week?!

Komi Can't Communicate Bonus

Can They Tie a Cherry Stem?

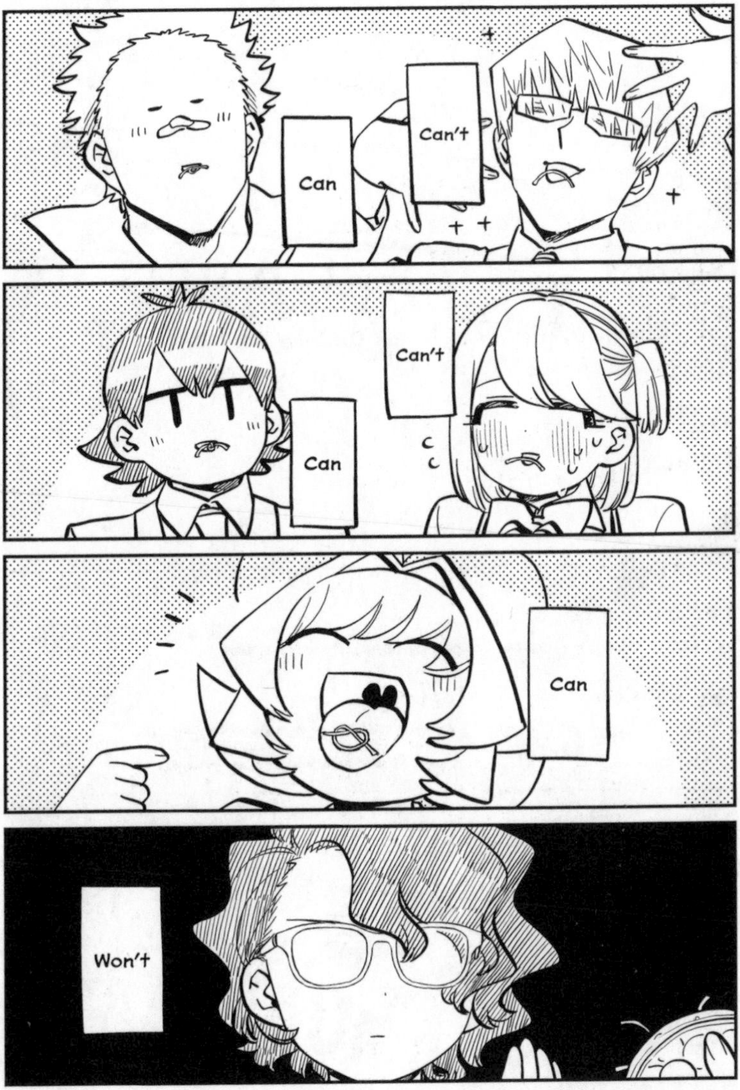

Can't
Can
Can't
Can
Can
Won't

Komi Can't Communicate Bonus

Can Komi Make a Hundred Friends? Toro's Sweet 'n' Gloopy Honey

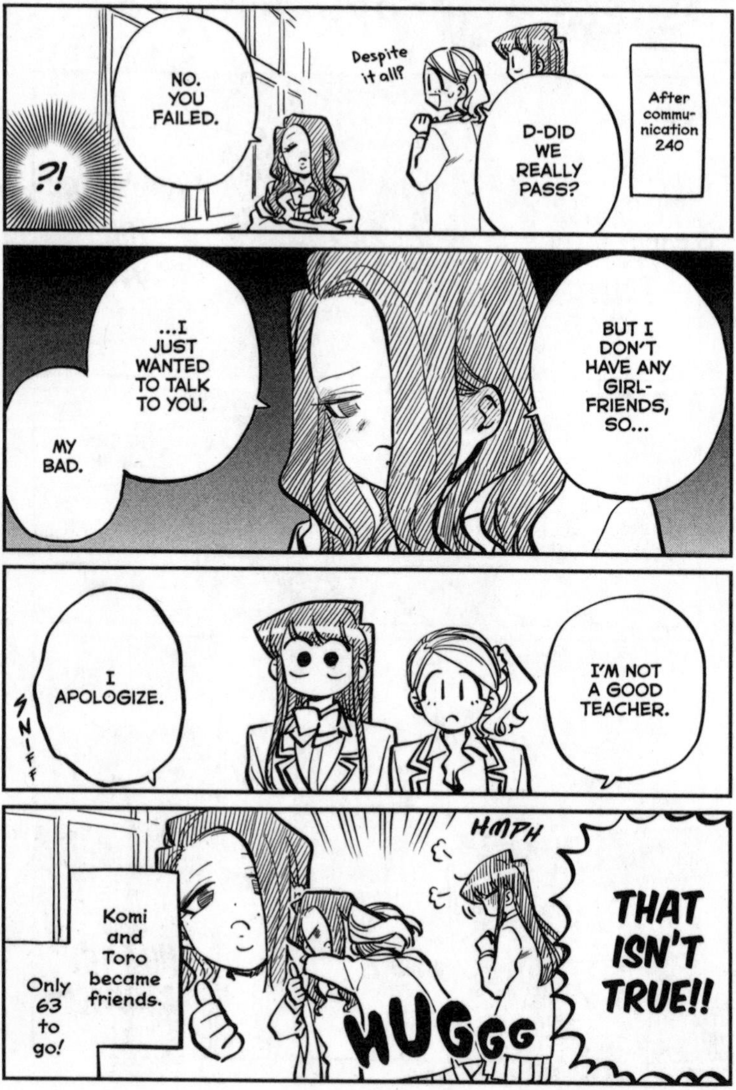
After communication 240
D-DID WE REALLY PASS?
Despite it all?
NO. YOU FAILED.
?!
BUT I DON'T HAVE ANY GIRLFRIENDS, SO...
...I JUST WANTED TO TALK TO YOU.
MY BAD.
I'M NOT A GOOD TEACHER.
I APOLOGIZE.
SNIFF
THAT ISN'T TRUE!!
HMPH
HUGGG
Komi and Toro became friends.
Only 63 to go!

Komi Can't Communicate

Character Popularity Poll!!

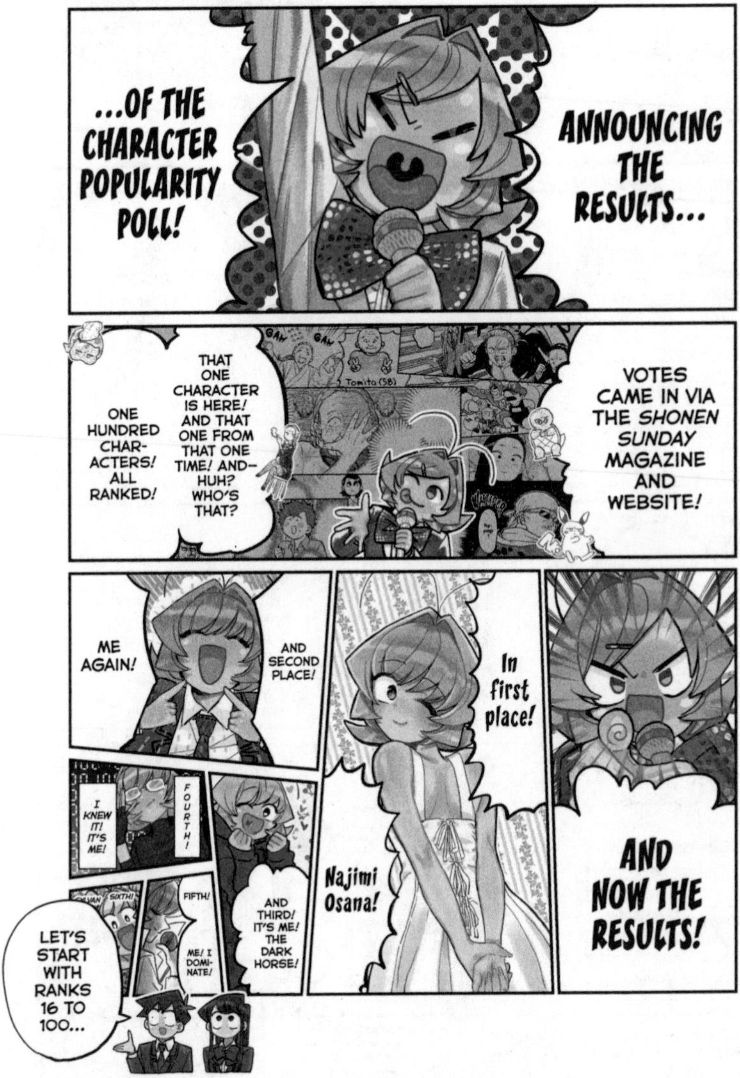
ANNOUNCING THE RESULTS...
...OF THE CHARACTER POPULARITY POLL!
VOTES CAME IN VIA THE *SHONEN SUNDAY* MAGAZINE AND WEBSITE!
Tomita (58)
THAT ONE CHARACTER IS HERE! AND THAT ONE FROM THAT ONE TIME! AND— HUH? WHO'S THAT?
ONE HUNDRED CHAR-ACTERS! ALL RANKED!
AND NOW THE RESULTS!
In first place!
Najimi Osana!
AND SECOND PLACE!
ME AGAIN!
FOURTH!
I KNEW IT! IT'S ME!
AND THIRD! IT'S ME! THE DARK HORSE!
FIFTH!
ME! I DOMI-NATE!
SIXTH!
LET'S START WITH RANKS 16 TO 100...

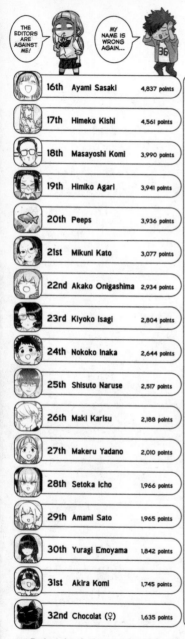

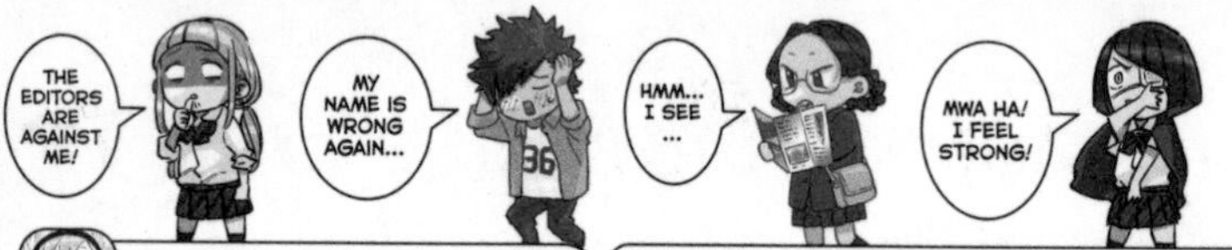
THE EDITORS ARE AGAINST ME!
MY NAME IS WRONG AGAIN...
HMM... I SEE ...
MWA HA! I FEEL STRONG!

16th	Ayami Sasaki	4,837 points
17th	Himeko Kishi	4,561 points
18th	Masayoshi Komi	3,990 points
19th	Himiko Agari	3,941 points
20th	Peeps	3,936 points
21st	Mikuni Kato	3,077 points
22nd	Akako Onigashima	2,934 points
23rd	Kiyoko Isagi	2,804 points
24th	Nokoko Inaka	2,644 points
25th	Shisuto Naruse	2,517 points
26th	Maki Karisu	2,188 points
27th	Makeru Yadano	2,010 points
28th	Setoka Icho	1,966 points
29th	Amami Sato	1,965 points
30th	Yuragi Emoyama	1,842 points
31st	Akira Komi	1,745 points
32nd	Chocolat (♀)	1,635 points
33rd	Shuki Ohai	1,609 points
34th	Sokemon	1,556 points
35th	Owner of Ramen Right?!	1,555 points
36st	Old Woman at Lottery Game	1,463 points
37th	Hoshiko Teshigawara	1,447 points
38th	Miwa Omojiri	1,383 points
39th	Gonzales	1,326 points
40th	Komi's Stuffed Animal	1,286 points
41st	Chika Netsuno	1,035 points
42nd	Ai Katai	953 points
43rd	Shizuka Odoka	934 points
44th	Chii Saiko	923 points
45th	Maya Takarazuka	889 points
46th	Great Combat: Swamp Brothers	847 points
47th	Mono Shinobino	822 points
48th	Shigeo Chiarai	796 points
49th	Lily Sukida	791 points
50th	Gojuro Yamada	745 points
51st	Yuiko Komi	725 points
52nd	Ryoko Tenjoin	707 points
53rd	Son Totoi	639 points
54th	Gorimi	621 points
55th	Yuji Otaku	610 points
56th	Yuji Otaku	606 points
57th	Yakuna Kato	594 points
58th	Kingyo Baba	570 points
59th	Sensei	555 points
60th	Tatsuhito Akido	503 points
61st	Miss Maron	481 points
62nd	Taisei Sonoda	461 points
63rd	Hoshio Jukujosky Maeda	455 points
64th	Strong Boy Students	431 points
65th	Toshio Seikimatsu	373 points
66th	Tabimaru	363 points
67th	Mutan	351 points
68th	Katai's Parents (Ken, Misao)	350 points
69th	Ryoko Komi	333 points
70th	Shiki Gekidan	325 points
71st	Lola Michisato	310 points
72nd	Hajime Gokudo	279 points
73rd	Reika Tsunde	278 points
74th	Maa & Shii	269 points
75th	Elizabeth	236 points
75th	Shota Shiota	236 points
77th	Kamiko Arai	232 points
78th	Matsuri Agari	227 points
79th	Masuko Fuwa	225 points
80th	Vice-Principal	219 points
81st	Saku Fushima	218 points
82nd	Yae Hamaki	201 points
83rd	Kaname Bodo	187 points
84th	Eiko Ushiroda	169 points
85th	Tomita	165 points
86th	Class Thugs	150 points
87th	Onemine's Family (Kazuya, Nana, Nono)	136 points
88th	Momo Natsukido	133 points
89th	Goro Suteno	112 points
90th	Minori Aizawa	111 points
91st	Nita Father and Daughter	107 points
92nd	Natsu Fukusuki	105 points
93rd	Inui and Sarutahiko	94 points
94th	Nareka Ido	82 points
95th	Spiri Urana	73 points
96th	Sam Samurai	72 points
97th	Shinto Priest	68 points
98th	Itsuya Oki	66 points
99th	Men Kicho	48 points
100th	Makina Kusari	19 points

⬅ Ranks 1 though 15 are on the following pages! Ranks 1-7 + ? are new illustrations.

*The magazine and website had different rules for voting. These results reflect the total of the two.

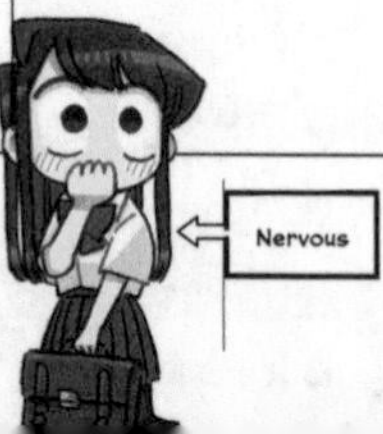
Nervous

Thank you for so many votes!

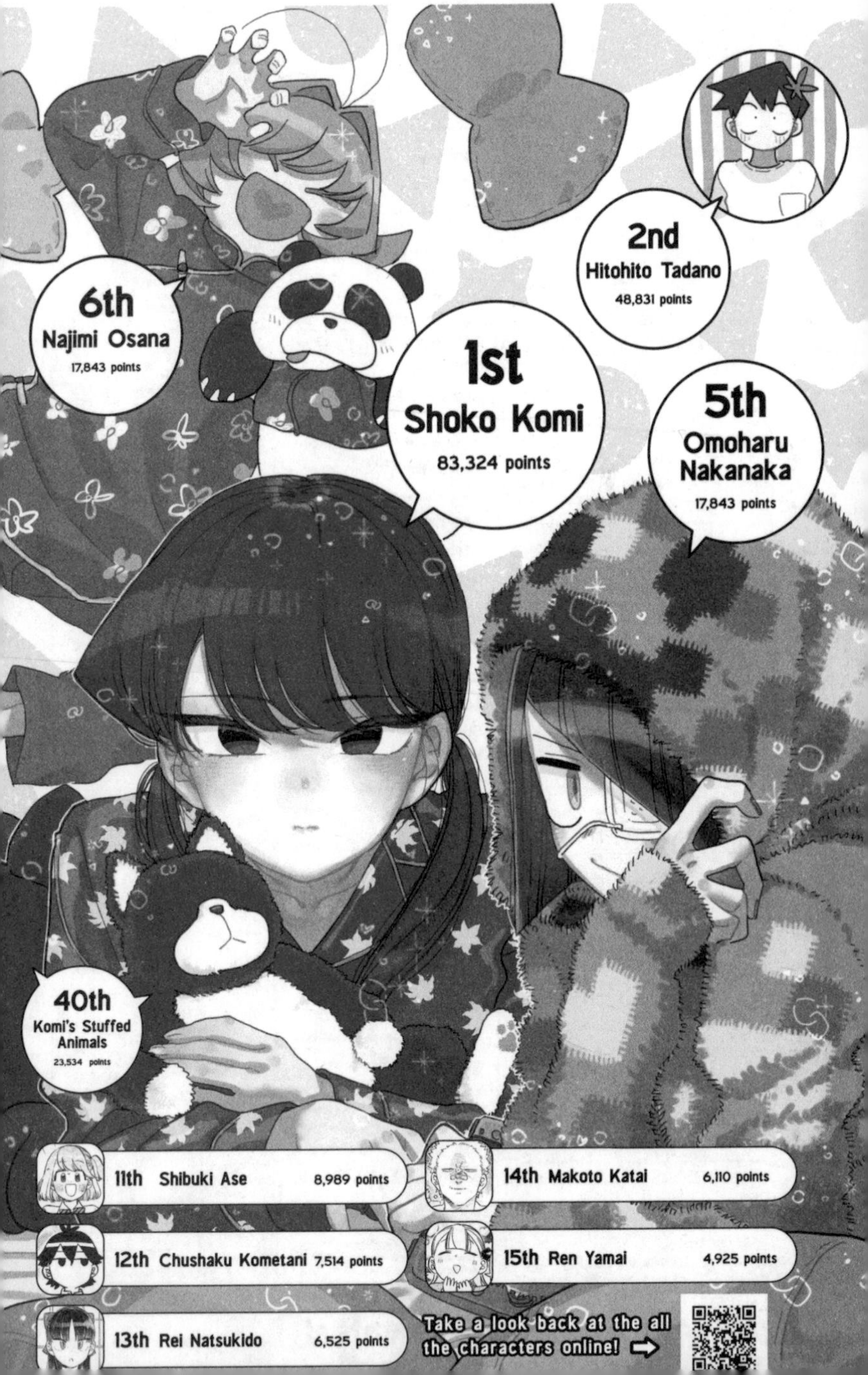
1st
Shoko Komi
83,324 points
2nd
Hitohito Tadano
48,831 points
5th
Omoharu Nakanaka
17,843 points
6th
Najimi Osana
17,843 points
40th
Komi's Stuffed Animals
23,534 points
11th Shibuki Ase 8,989 points
12th Chushaku Kometani 7,514 points
13th Rei Natsukido 6,525 points
14th Makoto Katai 6,110 points
15th Ren Yamai 4,925 points
Take a look back at the all the characters online!

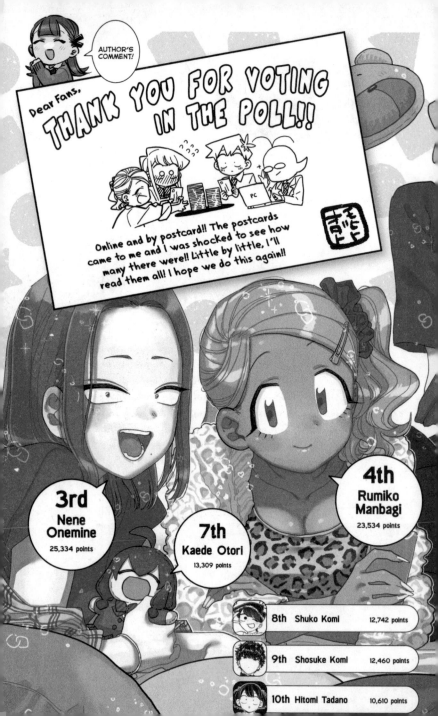

AUTHOR'S COMMENT!

Dear Fans,

THANK YOU FOR VOTING IN THE POLL!!

Online and by postcard!! The postcards came to me and I was shocked to see how many there were!! Little by little, I'll read them all! I hope we do this again!!

3rd
Nene Onemine
25,334 points

4th
Rumiko Manbagi
23,534 points

7th
Kaede Otori
13,309 points

	8th	Shuko Komi	12,742 points
9th	Shosuke Komi	12,460 points
10th	Hitomi Tadano	10,610 points

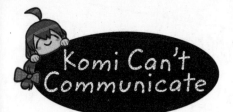

Komi Can't Communicate

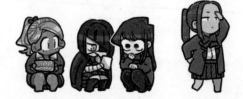

Tomohito Oda won the grand prize for *World Worst One* in the 70th Shogakukan New Comic Artist Awards in 2012. Oda's series *Digicon*, about a tough high school girl who finds herself in control of an alien with plans for world domination, ran from 2014 to 2015. In 2015, *Komi Can't Communicate* debuted as a one-shot in *Weekly Shonen Sunday* and was picked up as a full series by the same magazine in 2016.

Komi Can't Communicate

VOL. 18
Shonen Sunday Edition

Story and Art by Tomohito Oda

English Translation & Adaptation/John Werry
Touch-Up Art & Lettering/Eve Grandt
Design/Julian [JR] Robinson
Editor/Pancha Diaz

COMI-SAN WA, COMYUSHO DESU. Vol. 18
by Tomohito ODA
© 2016 Tomohito ODA
All rights reserved.
Original Japanese edition published by SHOGAKUKAN.
English translation rights in the United States of America, Canada, the United
Kingdom, Ireland, Australia and New Zealand arranged with SHOGAKUKAN.

Original Cover Design/Masato ISHIZAWA + Bay Bridge Studio

Printed in the U.S.A.

Published by VIZ Media, LLC
P.O. Box 77010
San Francisco, CA 94107

10 9 8 7 6 5 4 3 2 1
First printing, April 2022

viz.com

shonensunday.com

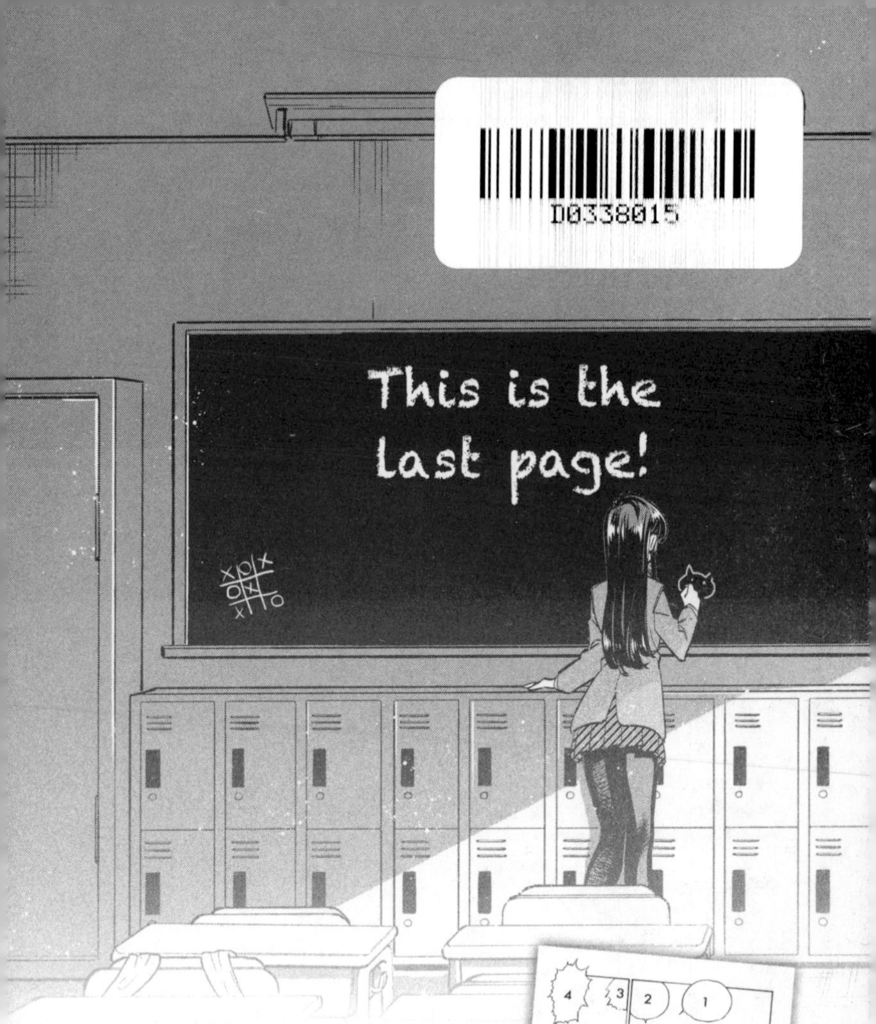
This is the last page!

Komi Can't Communicate has been printed in the original Japanese format to preserve the orientation of the artwork.

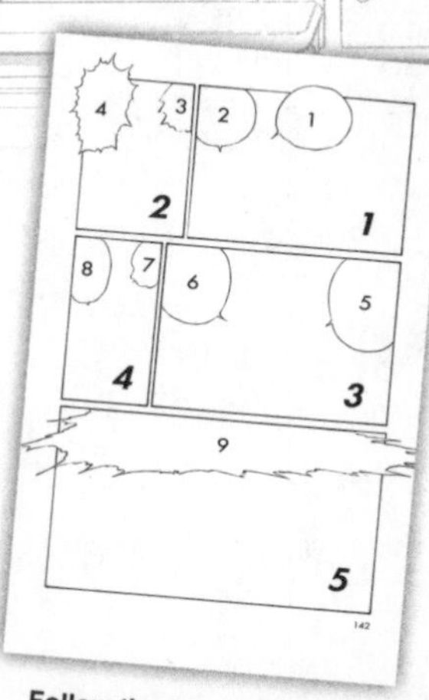

Follow the action this way.